AF180466

Macroeconomics Principles, Applications and Policy Implications

Macroeconomics Principles, Applications and Policy Implications

First Edition

Nurul Samiul Aman

University of Massachusetts - Boston

cognella

SAN DIEGO

Bassim Hamadeh, CEO and Publisher
John Remington, Executive Editor
Gem Rabanera, Senior Project Editor
Abbey Hastings, Associate Production Editor
Jess Estrella, Senior Graphic Designer
Trey Soto, Licensing Coordinator
Natalie Piccotti, Director of Marketing
Kassie Graves, Vice President of Editorial
Jamie Giganti, Director of Academic Publishing

Copyright © 2020 by Cognella, Inc. All rights reserved. No part of this publication may be reprinted, reproduced, transmitted, or utilized in any form or by any electronic, mechanical, or other means, now known or hereafter invented, including photocopying, microfilming, and recording, or in any information retrieval system without the written permission of Cognella, Inc. For inquiries regarding permissions, translations, foreign rights, audio rights, and any other forms of reproduction, please contact the Cognella Licensing Department at rights@cognella.com.

Trademark Notice: Product or corporate names may be trademarks or registered trademarks and are used only for identification and explanation without intent to infringe.

Cover image: Copyright © 2017 Depositphotos/hstiver.
Design Image: Copyright © 2012 Depositphotos/shirophoto.

Printed in the United States of America.

cognella® ACADEMIC PUBLISHING
3970 Sorrento Valley Blvd., Ste. 500, San Diego, CA 92121

To My Wonderful Wife Nilufar Aman and son Samuel Mahmud Aman

Contents

Preface

Back in early 1972, I had just gotten myself out of the transition from the struggle of liberation in the war of independence for Bangladesh as a sovereign country after 25 years of economic and religious suppression by the military rule of Pakistan. As I was about to attend my college freshman year in a newly independent country with no resources for the people or government to move forward, a widespread famine broke out, which caused millions of innocent lives to be lost in the newly independent nation. Witnessing that horrific human tragedy while getting ready for my college education, I motivated myself to concentrate my higher education in an area of discipline that would allow me to understand the sources of the poverty and starvation and thus know the tools to eliminate these ongoing struggles for centuries for so many countries in the world. That motivation pulled me into choosing economics as my major.

I studied economics with a great deal of passion and observation in real-world economics that landed me a job after graduation as a junior economist at the Industrial Bank of Bangladesh. But my eyes and mind were focused on going for higher studies in economics at an institution in Boston, Massachusetts. I eventually made that mission a reality by getting myself admitted to the graduate school at Northeastern University in 1982, from where I landed corporate jobs and a teaching career in Boston. However, I had never thought of writing an economics textbook as an optional endeavor at this late stage in my career. But writing this macroeconomics textbook did not come from my own list of wishes. It was in February 2013 that I received an email from John Remington, the executive editor of Cognella Academic Publishing, inviting me to consider writing an economics textbook. I was not able to accept that invitation right away for two practical reasons: first, my teaching commitment and family responsibilities required plenty of time and, second, the intensity of competition to write a successful textbook in economics required deeper understanding and thought from the point of view concerning resources constraints and existing market conditions. Then a few years passed by, and I heard from John Remington again, in 2016, with an invitation to reconsider. That is when I accepted the daunting task of writing the preliminary edition of this textbook, which was published in December 2018. I must convey my sincere gratitude to John Remington for not giving up on me in his pursuit of completing this project.

After going through a year of extensive peer review from my distinguished colleagues and valuable feedback from my dedicated students, I am so delighted to have written *Macroeconomics Principles, Applications, and Policy Implications*. In this first edition, I have introduced the basic principles of understanding economics and their links to our everyday lives in a constantly changing business and social environment in a world of high technology innovation and digital economy powered by the internet revolution.

The focus of this textbook is to reorganize the basic foundation of economics knowledge, which was already developed and published by so many distinguished philosophers and the greatest thinkers in social science since 1776, when the first economics philosophy book, *The Wealth of Nations*, was written and published by Adam Smith. Since this textbook is specifically written for undergraduate students taking introductory economics courses, I have made the best possible effort not only to simplify the concepts of economics terminologies but also to relate to real-world applications in business and society. With that in mind, I have introduced the application of demand and supply models of economics in the areas of sports, music entertainment, housing market, bond market, stock market, loanable fund market, and other related financial markets. In **Chapters 1 through 5**, students will be exposed to the steps of the learning process from theoretical concepts to applications to bring a great deal of interest in relating the basic theories to our real world of business and economics.

For example, **Chapter 1** starts with the concept of scarcity of economic resources and the rationale for studying economics to use limited resources efficiently and thus maximize our economic and social desires to fulfill unlimited demands. In this context, I explain and discuss the importance of understanding the concept of opportunity cost and its application in making decisions in either accepting a job after high school or going to college for higher education. This chapter also distinguishes the structural differences between the factory-based old economy of the 20th century and the knowledge-based **new economy** of the twenty-first century.

Similarly, I introduce the concept of basic demand and supply model in **Chapter 2**, where I explain its working mechanism with a theoretical foundation. Then I relate the model structure to the economics of the housing market in the city of Boston with its policy implication. I also extend the demand and supply concept further into sports economics and music entertainment with an emphasis on the power of competition in the market behavior to determine the right price and quantity.

Chapter 3 explains the criteria for measuring market efficiency and its applications with real-world examples. I also explain the rationale for government policy intervention in the case of market failure to maximize the economic efficiency and welfare for society as a whole. **Chapter 4** extends the application of the demand and supply model in the health-care industry and its micro- and macroeconomics policy implications in the context of the US economy. This chapter is particularly important to learning issues regarding health-care economics, the fastest-growing industry in the United States and its importance for significant contribution to gross domestic product (GDP) and health-care services to an increasingly aging population. **Chapter 5** is an extension of the demand and supply model, applying the concept to bond, stock, and financial markets. This Wall Street approach to market dynamics is also related to both micro- and macroeconomics, with their important policy implications.

Chapter 6 introduces the key macroeconomic variables and how to measure them conceptually and numerically by using actual data for the US economy, such as GDP growth rate, unemployment rate, and inflation rate, and their effects on our living standard. **Chapter 7** extends the macroeconomics model discussed in **Chapters 4 and 6** and analyzes their application in the context of the US economy.

Chapter 8 introduces the real sector model of Keynesian macroeconomics with numerical data estimation to determine the equilibrium output and employment. Students may notice that this chapter is a bit different than previous chapters in the sense that the model structure is focused on the aggregate expenditure model to determine equilibrium GDP/output without the price level. Therefore, the model structure is presented through a numerical exercise with graphical illustration for a clear understanding of the working mechanism of the economy. This aggregate expenditure model is a simplified version for the determination of equilibrium output and employment. **Chapter 9** explains the working mechanism of the fiscal and monetary policy of the government. This chapter gives an in-depth analysis of policy implications for business-cycle fluctuations, such as recession, inflation, and stagflation. The role of economic policy in fine-tuning the economy toward full employment and price stability is the key focus of this chapter.

Chapter 10 analyzes the basic theories of monetary economics and their applications from the Keynesian perspective. The money demand theory and the measures of money supply aggregates are explained in the context of the US economy. The method of money creation in the banking system and its policy implications are discussed in detail. The analysis of money market equilibrium to determine the interest rate and money supply is the key focus of this chapter. The role of monetary policy actions by the Federal Reserve System (the central bank) in stabilizing the economy is also discussed in detail. **Chapter 11** discusses the state of the current budget deficit and public debt for the US economy and their effect on macroeconomic variables, such as employment, output, inflation, and interest rate. The role of fiscal and monetary policy actions in reducing the budget deficit and its ramifications in the economy are discussed in detail for both the short and long run.

Chapter 12 provides a comparative analysis of monetary theories and policy implications from the viewpoints of Keynesian and classical perspectives. Focus is made regarding the ongoing policy debate in the context of these two alternative approaches of monetary policy actions in the case of the US economic policy institution: the Federal Reserve. **Chapter 13** introduces the theory of inflation and unemployment trade-off (called the Phillips curve) to help students understand macroeconomic fluctuation and its sources. The empirical evidence of the theory is presented based on this theory, originally developed by English economist A. W. Phillips in the 1960s. The policy implications for the Phillips curve are discussed in detail in the context of the US economy and its relevance in the short and long run.

Chapter 14 introduces the open-economy macro model by extending the macroeconomic model to the foreign-trade sector. The contribution of export and import components of the aggregate demand model toward GDP is discussed. The determinants of export and import are discussed with their policy implications in the global economy and finance. The case for international trade under the theory of comparative advantage is discussed with numerical examples of trade between China and the USA. The Keynesian macroeconomic model is reintroduced in this chapter by adding the foreign-trade sector for exports and imports. The working mechanism of balance of trade and balance of payment is introduced with actual data for the US economy. The concept of the fixed exchange rate system under the Bretton Woods Agreement of 1945 and its comparison with the floating exchange rate system is discussed in detail to help students understand the growing trade deficit for the United States with its trading partners, especially China. **Chapter 15**, the last chapter of the book, introduces the economics of the foreign exchange market and its role in the global economy. The working mechanism of the floating exchange rate system to determine the exchange rate equilibrium is analyzed in a comprehensive manner. I also discuss the effect of exchange rate fluctuation on exports and imports for the US economy with actual data of the balance of trade and balance of payment position in recent years. The role of the fiscal and monetary policy actions is also discussed in detail for bringing balance to trade stability.

Suggested Notes to Students

It is my great pleasure to introduce my first textbook to students. To learn the key concepts of economics effectively, I would like to suggest that you read the key objectives at the beginning of each chapter. Reviewing those key learning objectives will guide you through the steps of effectively reading and learning the contents in subsequent sections of each chapter.

As you read the sections in each chapter, there are three important things to keep in mind for effective understanding of the concepts and applications. First, read the concepts and try to relate to the real-world example. Second, connect the concept to the diagram provided in that section. Third, relate the concept and diagram(s) to the data, if given, and analyze for practical use and policy implications. These three important steps are expected to assist you in grasping the concepts and their applications effectively.

Also, read the summary of the chapter to further review key terms and concepts in each of the sections. Reviewing the key areas is expected to help you learn the concepts introduced in each chapter. I have also provided some basic questions at the end of each chapter under "**Application Activities**." These questions are provided as practice and are part of your homework, based on the contents you have read in the chapter. The questions are also directly related to the real-world applications of the theoretical concepts introduced in chapter sections.

Acknowledgments

In the long process of writing this introductory macroeconomics textbook, I am greatly honored to have received valuable ideas and generous support from my dear friends and distinguished colleagues Jennifer Clifford, University of Massachusetts Boston (UMB); Adugna Lemi, UMB; Sid Abdullah, Central Connecticut State University; and from Cognella Academic Publishing, John Remington, Gem Rabanera, Abbey Hastings, Danielle Menard, Jess Estrella, Jess Wright, and Chelsey Schmid. I am very grateful and fortunate to have their tremendous support and encouragement while going through the journey of writing the manuscript of this text.

Gratitude to My Distinguished Reviewers

It has been a great honor and privilege to receive tremendous support from my distinguished colleagues who have generously given their precious time to review my preliminary textbook. Without their valuable inputs and suggestions, it would not have been possible to produce this textbook. I sincerely extend my thanks and gratitude to the following honorable colleagues and friends:

Abu Abdullah, Duke University

Siddiq Abdullah, Central Connecticut State University

Kenneth Ardon, Salem State University

Jennifer Clifford, University of Massachusetts Boston

Ellen Frank, University of Massachusetts Boston

Farida Khan, University of Colorado, Colorado Spring

Ahmed Mushfiq Mobarak, Yale University

Joanne Spitz, University of Massachusetts Boston

My Indebtedness to My Family

My final note of thanks and sincere indebtedness goes to my beloved wife, Nilufar Aman, and our son, Samuel Mahmud Aman, for their continuous support and encouragement during the journey that led to the final production of this text. Their moral support and understanding have been a big contribution to this effort.

Chapter 1

Key Concepts of Economics and Its Application in the Financial Well-Being of Society

Learning Objectives

As they read the chapter, students will learn the following:

- Economics and opportunity cost: concepts and rational choices in the allocation of time, money, and other related resources
- Real-world applications of opportunity cost
- Examples of economics in everyday life and entertainment
- Economics, technology, and society and their interaction in the digital age
- Understand economics with graphs, equations, and data

1.1. The Core Concept of Economics and Opportunity Cost: Making Alternative Decisions in Allocating Time and Resources

The core concept of economics comes from the answer to the question asked in all economics textbooks: "Why study economics?" Although there is no simple answer to this broad question, **economics** is a branch of social science that deals with the unlimited desires/wants of human beings and the limited resources to fulfill those desires. Unlimited wants describe the natural behavior of human beings for good reason—they are thriving forces that keeps everyone moving to accomplish their infinite desires. However, the constraints of limited resources make it a challenge to fulfill unlimited desires. The study of economics addresses this challenge by finding ways to allocate limited resources efficiently and thus maximize the unlimited wants and desires. The best practice of economics is to use alternative models to integrate the limited human and material resources to maximize the material well-being of society. More specifically, economics tries to answer three questions (Q1, Q2, and Q3) related to the efficient allocation of limited resources to satisfy unlimited wants.

Q1. What products to produce (the right selection of products to satisfy the needs and wants of individuals)?

Q2. How to produce (the technology of production)?

Q3. For whom to produce (the distributional tasks)?

To answer these three core questions, numerous theories, models, and paradigms have been developed by economists, philosophers, and historians. The fundamental model developed by those philosophers came from the structure of the theory of demand and supply originally developed by Adam Smith in his famous book *The Wealth of Nations* (1776). The core concept of demand and supply is still the basic tool to answer the aforementioned questions and to guide their applications in every aspect of human society. The next few sections of this chapter will analyze the dimensions of demand and supply in greater detail.

1.2. Concept of Opportunity Cost and Real-World Applications

Opportunity cost relates to the next best or most desired goods and services that are forgone (that were given up) to obtain something else. It means that given the scarcity of resources (e.g., time, money, knowledge, skills, and other related capabilities), every individual is forced to make trade-offs in their daily decisions. In making those decisions, individuals must make rational trade-offs between the available options to achieve the best possible results. For example, every individual has only 24 hours a day and 7 days a week to accomplish any mission or tasks he or she may have. A college student, for example, has to allocate time and other resources between classes and other extracurricular activities every day. The opportunity cost of taking one class could be giving up another class at the same time and day of the week. Choosing a major in college as an alternative to other desirable majors is a common dilemma for many college students. In a broader perspective, the opportunity cost of going to college can vary widely from person to person depending on individual preferences and ambitions. The following example of taking a job with a high school diploma versus going to college is a very common measure of opportunity cost when making a rational choice.

The decision between seeking a job after high school or pursuing a college degree demonstrates the importance of understanding the real-world applications of opportunity cost. Suppose the average wage structure for taking a job with a high school diploma has modestly declined over the years.[1] Given this trend, the question arises as to whether the opportunity cost for pursuing a college degree would decrease (regardless of the rising dollar cost of college tuition during the same time). In this situation, the hidden cost is the opportunity cost of not going to college in favor of declining wages for those with high school diplomas. This part of the opportunity cost could be much greater than current dollar expenses for college tuition. In this case, the dollar cost (explicit cost) for college tuition is not the only opportunity cost—the wages forgone from the job in favor of going to college could be much less than the higher wages and career advancement in a specialized profession with a college degree. If real-world statistics reveal the case for the latter, then the opportunity cost for going to college is definitely lower than the potential benefit from the college degree in the long run.

1.2.1. Opportunity Cost Application in Sports Economics

The opportunity cost concept that we applied to college education in the previous section is also commonly used in the world of sports economics. For example, on December 31, 2017, Penn State running back Saquon Barkley announced his eligibility for the 2018 National Football League (NFL) Draft by giving up his pursuit of a college degree at Penn State. This is a good example of making a rational decision. For Mr. Barkley, there is nothing better left for him at Penn State when compared to the golden opportunity to be drafted for an NFL career. Many other college football athletes have made similar decisions—quarterbacks Andrew Luck of the Indiana Colts and Cam Newton of the Carolina Panthers, for example. Famous entrepreneurs and tech moguls, such as Bill Gates of Microsoft, Steve Jobs of Apple, Mark Zuckerberg of Facebook, and Larry Ellison of Oracle, dropped out of college because they saw a high opportunity cost for staying in college when compared to the greater business venture they envisioned and achieved.

The same logic of opportunity cost applies to international trade between countries (i.e., deciding what to produce domestically and what to import from other countries) and is called the theory of comparative advantage. The topic of comparative advantage will be discussed in detail in Chapter 14.

1.3. Examples of Economics in Everyday Life and Entertainment

Assuming that people in general do in fact behave rationally, they make decisions that allocate their limited time and resources to maximize the benefits they desire to obtain. Given that assumption, it is observed that people as both buyers and sellers in the market respond to incentives. Without incentives, the outcome from market interaction may not be sufficient to maximize the level of fulfillment of individuals' desires. That is where the concept of market behavior comes into play—demand and supply behavior in the marketplace reflects the pattern of incentives for buyers and sellers to respond rationally. The behavior of demand and

---

1 Jillian Berman. "A High-School Diploma Is Pretty Much Useless These Days." Huffington Post, December 7, 2017. https://www.huffpost.com/entry/value-college-degree_n_5399573.

supply interaction then determines the price of all goods and services as a signal to clear the market; this price is usually called the equilibrium price. The details of the demand and supply model structure will be explained in Chapter 2. At this point, it is important to realize the power of market forces to signal the right price for the efficient allocation of resources. This process of market forces is explained next with the analysis of **marginal value**. The actual theory and applications of demand and supply are presented in Chapter 2.

1.3.1. Real-World Examples and Applications of Marginal Value

In measuring the efficiency of allocating limited resources, the rational choice theory operates at the margin for making optimal decisions in everyday activities. Although it may be true that individuals and firms do not necessarily make the best choices in their decision-making processes, it is fair to assume that economic agents put together all available information in the best possible ways to buy and sell goods and services to achieve optimal levels of satisfaction. The benefits of the cost of selling and the expenses for buying must satisfy their desire from each of the transactions. For example, Apple priced its high-end iPhone X at around $1,000 in the US market when it released the device before the fall of 2017. The first release of iPhone X at this price sold out very quickly, and the demand continued to rise, resulting in back orders for weeks and months to follow. Now, it may be that the marketing management of Apple underestimated the demand side of the market and could have raised the price over $1,000 per unit to make more profit for the company. However, the rational choice theory assumes that given the best possible information Apple management had, the decision to make the first release and the price they charged could have been the best decision to reach their target volume of revenue and profit. They might have adjusted the price and quantity with the new information gathered afterward.

Another real-world example can be observed each year in the economics of Super Bowl tickets. In 2018, Super Bowl ticket prices in the secondary market started between $5,000 and $50,000 per ticket depending on the position of the seats in the US Bank Stadium in Minneapolis, Minnesota. Given the fixed number of 73,000 seats in the stadium, these price ranges were driven by the changes in demand for tickets from the buyers' desires to purchase the tickets. A number of factors determine the price ranges (e.g., ability to pay, number of fans willing to buy at certain prices, availability of the limited tickets against the number of fans looking for the tickets). Since the number of fans willing to purchase the tickets is much higher than 73,000, the prices for all the seats will continue to rise until all the tickets are sold out. The highest bids for the tickets, whether sold in the regular secondary market or via scalping, would reflect the true market price. This is clearly a real-world example of the maximum willingness to pay for the ticket as a rational choice made by the fans to watch the biggest game of the year. The value the buyers place on each of the tickets (based on their enjoyment of the game or the location of the seat in the stadium) must be higher than the dollar prices they have paid for those tickets. The same concept of rational choice applies to purchasing decisions for concert tickets to see performances by superstars in pop and rock genres in the music industry.

Another example is the increase in ticket prices for Boston Red Sox games against the New York Yankees. Since the traditional rivalry between these two teams is very popular, the willingness to pay for the tickets during Red Sox versus Yankees matches keeps rising—there is an increasing demand for tickets and a fixed supply of total seats at Fenway Park. The willingness of Red Sox fans to pay much higher prices than the ticketed price can be seen as a reflection of rational choice: the value of watching the game must be higher than the dollar price they pay for the tickets. The same concept of rational choice theory applies to the number of college applicants for freshman year far exceeding the number of admissions by top-rated colleges in the United States. In those cases, the smaller increase in tuition and boarding cost doesn't matter because the potential benefit from higher education tends to outweigh the rising cost of education charged by the universities. In other words, given the limited capacity of freshmen year enrollment, the number of applications may far exceed the capacity. Therefore, the excess demand for admission tends to increase the tuition and boarding fees as the basic principle of market behavior. The actual analysis with the demand and supply model structure is made in Chapter 2.

1.4. Economics, Technology, and Society: A New Perspective on Economics in the Digital Age

Amid the emergence of the internet revolution in the 1990s, the technological advancement for providing goods and services has rapidly expanded in the global economy. The rise in productivity of both labor and capital in this digital era of the twenty-first century has transformed the structure of the US economy (and the world economy) from a factory-based economy to a new information age economy. In this new information-based economy, the integration of economics, technology, and society has transformed new ways of thinking about market behavior. The emergence of e-commerce enterprises, such as the Amazon, Alibaba, eBay, YouTube, Pinterest, Facebook, Snapchat, Twitter, Instagram, Spotify, WhatsApp, Google, Uber, Lyft, and Airbnb is the key driving force in the new economy with innovative online technology leading society onto a different path. The characteristics of these newly emerged digital enterprises are driven by rapid globalization, information science, and faster rates of credit flow. Given the new environment of a knowledge-based economy, the productivity of labor and capital (both human capital and physical capital) has increased significantly in recent years. The high productivity of factors of production thus raised the income levels of workers around the world with an increase in wages and living standards. This technological advancement in a digitally charged work environment has also changed the structure of labor market behavior. Under the new structure, members of the labor force make very different choices at their workplaces as compared to workers in the old economy (the factory-based economy in the 20th century). The labor force under this new economy does not tend to rely on traditional desk jobs with a fixed eight to five work schedule. The speedy growth of specialization in high-technology industries has opened up new opportunities for young workers and structurally displaced aging workers to create their own jobs in the form of self-employment, individual contracting, and freelancing. This new trend of labor-market structure in the so-called gig economy is expected to reshape the rational choice and preference patterns of the skilled labor force in the coming decades.

It is also argued that the productivity for knowledge-based skilled workers and their incomes may have increased at the expense of low-skilled workers of the old economy in the manufacturing sector. This mismatch between the capital-intensive new economy and the labor-intensive old economy might have caused the rise in unemployment in low-skilled workers. This mismatch of factor intensity of the production process might have contributed to the increasing level of income inequality at an alarming rate. The ongoing problem of imbalance between the rapid growth of technology and income inequality and unemployment for low-skilled workers has resulted in a new wave of challenges in making rational choices for the labor and capital combination. Further complicating these new challenges are the issues of global warming and related environmental degradation, which are perceived as attributed to rapid industrialization and massive use of fossil fuel energy. The utopian economic theories of the market system do not seem to have adequately addressed these challenges. The market-based concept of economic efficiency actually ignores the problem of externalities caused by increasing levels of market power and environmental degradation. To address these challenges, the economy requires the increasing role of public policy and regulations that certainly contradict traditional ***laissez-faire*** economics (leave the market alone). This issue of contradiction and conflicting theories of economics and social science seems to call for a new way of thinking to transform the current education system, social structure, and technology to be compatible with a sustainable economic reality. In doing so, innovative public policies are needed to provide educational reform and examine the role of human capital. This book will discuss these issues in greater detail in later chapters.

1.5. Understanding Economics with Graphs, Equations, and Data

In the study of economics principles, it is necessary to use simple mathematical concepts to explain the connections among basic economic theories and evaluating real-world data. For example, graphically illustrating demand and supply equations with real-world data is a basic foundation of economics. Therefore, it is important to review the introductory levels of algebra, calculus, and geometry as basic tools for this course in economics. The following tools are useful for reading the contents of the demand and supply models in the next chapter.

1.5.1. The Slope of an Equation: Linear and Nonlinear Equations

The slope of an equation of two variables is the ratio of changes between the variables. This ratio indicates the behavior or pattern of the relationship between those two variables as the values change. Consider the following equation of two variables, X and Y.

$Y = f(X)$, where Y is a dependent variable and X is an independent variable, meaning that if the value of X changes, it will change the value of Y. The slope of the equation can be expressed by taking the derivative of this general expression as follows:

dY/dX = the slope (the ratio of change between Y and X). More specifically, the earlier general expression of the equation can be stated with real-world values:

$$Y = a + bX \text{ ....Eqn (1.1)}$$

where a is a constant value of Y independent of X or when X = zero, and b is the slope of this equation (1.1), thus explaining the pattern of the relationship between X and Y when the value X increases. The slope would be as shown in Figure 1.1 by taking the derivative of this equation: dY/dX = b, and the derivative of a constant value "a" in the equation is zero. Since the value of b stays the same as the value of X changes, this is a linear equation of Y for X. If the value of b were changing as X changed, it would be a nonlinear function (not shown here). With real-world data to fit this equation, the relevant graph is illustrated in Figure 1.1.

In Figure 1.1, the hypothetical linear curve indicates the specific relationship between independent variable X and dependent variable Y such that the point "a" on the vertical y-axis is called the intercept or the fixed value of variable Y when the value of X is zero. However, as the value of X starts increasing from zero, the value of Y will also increase at the rate of value "b" (dY/dX), which is called the slope of the equation of Y for X. More specifically, the straight-line equation Y = a + bX, shown in Figure 1.1, which indicates that the constant slope "b" is the rate at which the value of variable Y will increase in response to a given increase in value of X.

Figure 1.1 A Graph of a Linear Equation

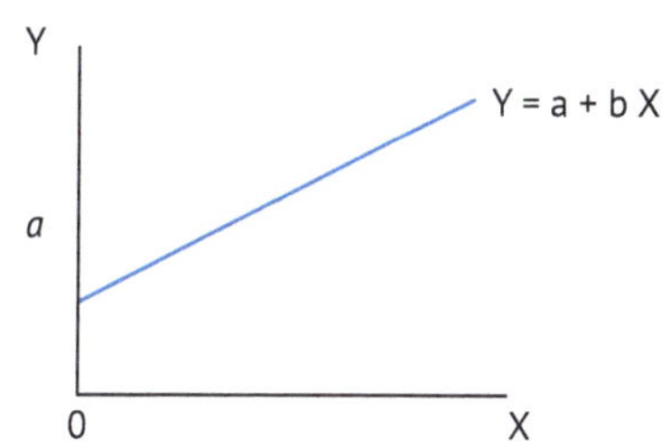

1.5.2. The Data and Equation to Draw the Graph

The previous linear equation can be applied in real-world examples with a set of hypothetical data on a typical consumer's income and spending. Suppose an individual spends his/her after-tax weekly income (economists call it disposable income after taxes are paid) shown in Table 1.1 with different combinations of income and spending, with the assumption of ***ceteris paribus*** (other things staying the same). The ceteris paribus assumption is important to make here because there are other factors than just income that influence the spending behavior of all individuals. In this simple example of a linear equation, only changes in income are considered, keeping other factors unchanged. The other factors could be lifestyle, tax policy of the government, changes in family composition or size, and similar other factors related to the spending of individuals and households.

Table 1.1 represents a hypothetical data set for an individual, indicating the relationship between income (net of taxes paid) and spending behavior, where Y is spending that varies at a constant rate as income (X) increases by the same amount of $100. As we see in the data, when income is zero, there is still some spending of $50 for fulfilling basic necessities, such as food and other daily expenses. However, as income rises at an equal increment of $100 per week, the spending also increases by a constant amount of $80. The slope of this spending

Table 1.1: Data Estimation of a Linear Equation

Income (X) in $s	Spending (Y) in $s	Slope of Income and Spending Equation ΔY/ΔX	Saving (S)	Slope of Income and Saving Equation
0	50	–	−50	–
100	130	80/100 = 0.80	−30	20/100 = 0.20
200	210	80/100 = 0.80	−10	20/100 = 0.20
300	290	80/100 = 0.80	+10	20/100 = 0.20
400	370	80/100 = 0.80	+30	20/100 = 0.20
500	450	80/100 = 0.80	+50	20/100 = 0.20

behavior is calculated in column 3 as $\Delta Y/\Delta X$, shown as a constant rate of 0.80. Since the individual in this example did not spend all of his/her income, the third and fourth columns show the estimation of the corresponding saving equation $S = (X - Y)$ and its slope shown as 0.20 in the last column on the right-hand side. The numerical value of this estimation is plotted in a linear equation (Eqn (1.2)).

$$Y = 50 + 0.8X \text{ ....Eqn (1.2)}$$

where 50 is the intercept and 0.8 is the slope of the equation.

The estimated linear equation (1.2) indicates that an individual spends at an increasing constant rate of 0.8 cents of every dollar increase in income for his/her successive increase in income by the same amount. With the same token, the saving pattern of this individual in column 4 and 5 in the table shows that the corresponding saving rate is also constant at 0.2 as the slope of the saving equation (1.3) as shown below.

$$S = X - Y = X - (a + b X) = X - a - bX = -a + (1 - b) X \text{ ....Eqn (1.3)}$$

where S = saving equation and $1 - b$ is the slope of the saving equation.

Plugging the values of intercept and slope of saving estimated in Table 1.1, the estimated saving equation (1.4) is

$$S = -50 + 0.2 X \text{ ....Eqn (1.4)}$$

The graphical representations of these two linear equations, equation (1.2) and equation (1.4), of spending and saving, respectively, are illustrated in Figure 1.2.

In Figure 1.2, the numerical values of the spending and saving equations are plotted in a single diagram to illustrate how a linear equation demonstrates the constant slope of the changes in two variables. In this example, students may notice that the slope of spending, the Y curve against income (X), is 0.80, and the slope of the saving, the S curve against the same increase in income is 0.20. The spending and saving values are plotted on the vertical axis against corresponding increases in income (X) on the horizontal axis. Students may also practice the same model by using different income and spending combinations and creating a table and graphs by using an Excel spreadsheet. It is also important to note that these two

Figure 1.2

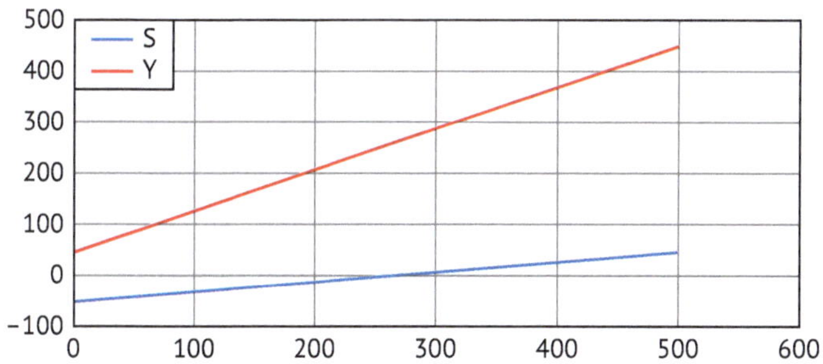

linear curves are based on ceteris paribus assumption. However, if the ceteris paribus assumption is not considered in a situation when changes in other factors, such as tax policy, consumer confidence, or household status, take place, the curves in Figure 1.2 will shift either to the right or to the left, depending on the courses of change that occur. We will come back to this simple technique of measuring many other economic variables in different contexts throughout this textbook. For now, we will end this introductory chapter by highlighting the basic reasoning for studying economics and its importance in our daily activities to maximize our goals for gaining material interests. As students continue to read the subsequent chapters in this textbook, they will use this basic understanding of the opportunity cost concept and its related application by learning many other related models and their relevant applications in the real world. While reading those applications, students are also expected to realize the importance of government policy implications.

Chapter Summary

Section 1.1 of this chapter started with the concept of economics as a study of distinct discipline for understanding the importance of efficiency in allocating our limited resources to maximize economic well-being for everyone. Since the resources are limited, learning the efficiency techniques in allocating our scarce resources is the primary objective of studying economics. In the process of learning the core concept of efficiency in allocating resources, economics study helps answer three core questions:

Q1. What products to produce (the right selection of products to satisfy the needs and wants of individuals)?

Q2. How to produce (the technology of production)?

Q3. For whom to produce (the distributional tasks)?

In answering these core questions, the subsequent chapters of this textbook will demonstrate numerous theories and model structures to go deeper in the process of various aspects of economics and its policy implications for constant improvement of the economic well-being of society.

Section 1.2 introduced the concept of opportunity cost as a trade-off in allocating our limited time and resources for the alternative choice of activities. Opportunity cost relates to the next best or most desired goods and services that are forgone to obtain something else.

This concept is useful for making rational choices in our daily decision-making processes. The real-world examples of the opportunity cost concept include deciding whether to go for a four-year college degree or get a job with a high school diploma. The importance of cost-benefit analysis for making alternative decisions is primarily attributed to the rational choice theory powered by the effective use of opportunity cost. Numerous examples are given in this section in the context of sports economics, college education, and similar choices people have to make every day.

Section 1.3 has introduced the concept of marginal value as an important concept to measure the efficiency in allocating limited resources. The rational choice theory of efficiency in allocation of resources is based on the marginal value from each of our everyday activities. Although individuals do not necessarily make their best choices during their decision-making processes, it is reasonable to say that buyers and sellers are rational on average when gathering the best possible information to maximize their satisfaction from each of the transactions. To fulfill that objective, economic agents must think at the margin, the basic criteria to achieve efficiency. Examples are given in this section in the context of the smartphone market, sports economics, and related market behavior of consumers' and producers' decision-making processes.

Section 1.4 discussed the effect of the digital technology revolution on society, economics, and business in this new century of information economics. The emergence of e-commerce enterprises, such as Amazon, Alibaba, eBay, YouTube, Pinterest, Facebook, Snapchat, Twitter, Instagram, Spotify, WhatsApp, Google, Uber, Lyft, and Airbnb, is the key driving force in the new economy. The newly emerged digital enterprises are driven by rapid globalization, information science, and faster rates of credit flow. The digital economy of the 21st century is knowledge-based, with high productivity of labor and capital (both human capital and physical capital), which thus raised the income level and standard of living for skilled workers globally. The labor-market structure has also changed in the digital economy under which the labor force does not tend to rely on traditional desk jobs with a fixed eight to five work schedule. The speedy growth of specialization in high-technology industries has opened up new opportunities for young workers and structurally displaced aging workers to create their own jobs in the form of self-employment, individual contracting, and freelancing. This new trend of labor-market structure in the so-called gig economy is expected to reshape the rational choice and preference patterns of the skilled labor force in coming decades. The challenge of this new trend in the labor market is coping with growing income inequality and continued massive poverty in the majority of the nations in the world. The study of economics in understanding these challenges is rewarding for students.

Section 1.5 introduced the technical aspects of graphs, equations, and data to integrate the economic variables and their relationship in an effort to measure economic efficiency. The main focus was made on the two-variable case with examples of linear equations to help students understand the numerical values to estimate. Equations (1.1) through (1.4) are useful in understanding the technical concept of measuring the relationship between two variables. Table 1.1 shows the hypothetical data on spending and income to fit equation (1.4). This section also demonstrates the technique used to integrate the theoretical concept to relate to data and graphs as the basic foundations of analyzing the economics model with real-world data. Students are encouraged to practice the examples given in this section and to answer the practice questions in the "Application Activities" section.

Application Activities

Q1. Why is the study of economics an important part of social science? Give an example from the real world.

Q2. If the real wage rate (adjusted for inflation) declines for jobs for high school graduates, would the true opportunity cost of attending college or spending for higher education decline? Give an example.

Q3. How do you measure the efficiency of resource allocation? Give an example from a real-world application of measuring the efficiency of resource allocation.

Q4. Use the following table to measure the opportunity cost of two jobs performed by two different workers in a factory and then answer the questions that follow:

4a. Which of the two workers has the lowest opportunity cost in doing Job 1?

4b. Which of the workers has the comparative advantage in doing Job 1?

Workers	Job 1: Hours to Finish	Job 2: Hours to Finish	Opportunity Cost
Worker 1	3	6	?
Worker 2	4	16	?

Q5. Use the data in Table 1.2 to answer the questions that follow.

Table 1.2: Spending and Income Data

Income (Y)	Consumption (C)	Slope of Consumption	Saving (S)	Slope of Saving
0	100			
100	175			
200	250			
300	325			
400	400			
500	475			

5.1. Fill out the rest of the columns from the information given in columns 1 and 2 for a typical household with income as Y after taxes and consumption as C given in column 2.

5.2. Interpret the slopes for C and S functions in economic terms, as explained in Section 1.5 earlier.

5.3. Graph the data for Y, C, and S on a single diagram to illustrate your answers to 5.1 and 5.2 and explain in your own words.

Chapter 2

Market Systems and Determination of Price

Demand and Supply Interaction with Real-World Examples

Learning Objectives

As they read the chapter, students will learn the following:

- The market system and its scope and limitations in allocating resources efficiently
- Applications of the demand and supply model in sports economics
- Applications of the demand and supply model in the music industry
- Applications of demand and supply in college education

2.1. Market Behavior and Efficient Allocations of Resources: Foundation of Demand and Supply Behavior

The fundamental tool for allocating limited resources is the basic demand and supply model of the market system. In both microeconomics and macroeconomics, the two broad areas of the science of economics are demand and supply, which determine equilibrium and affect price changes, inflation trends, unemployment, full-time employment, government policies on taxes, government regulations, environmental protections, social welfare, universal health care, and national defense. Therefore, the concept of a free market system versus the impact of government intervention in the free market system has been a subject of debate since the **Great Depression** of the 1930s when the market system of free enterprise failed to keep the economy moving with a state of full employment. Although the role of government has significantly improved the fine-tuning of the economy and maximizes the economic well-being of the society in general, the power of demand and supply under a free market system still prevails as a major tool for efficient allocation of resources. Analysis of this ongoing debate will be discussed in Chapter 3. The key focus of this chapter is to understand the basic concepts of demand and supply and how they interact to determine the price and quantity of goods and services under the assumption of both the free market condition and government intervention.

The analysis of free market systems dates back to 1776 when Adam Smith described the concept of an invisible hand through the free flow of demand and supply behavior. Smith's (1776) support for laissez-faire policy was attributed to his explanations for the efficient allocation of resources for both producers (to maximize their profits) and consumers (to maximize their satisfaction). His support for laissez-faire policy is still valid in today's market behavior in regard to housing scarcity in urban areas, interest rates in capital markets, and regulated markets for health insurance, utilities, medicines, sports, and transportation. However, legislative action via price control or quantity control with taxes and subsidies has also been a common practice in those industries. Despite the good intentions of the government to distribute the economic pie more fairly, the effects of these legislative actions may not necessarily make the resource allocations efficient in most of the cases. The detailed analysis of demand and supply models in the next section will help us to better understand the real economics behind this debate by observing the pros and cons of the free market system versus the rationale for government intervention.

2.1.1. Law of Demand

The law of demand states that if the price of any good (commodity) or service rises (e.g., rents for college students in a college town like Boston), then the quantity demanded for that good or service will decline and vice versa, ceteris paribus. The ceteris paribus assumption means that all other possible factors affecting the same demand behavior stay the same for the time being. In our housing example, other factors could be income, location in terms of proximity to public transportation or college campus, rents in alternative areas, and number of rooms and other related facilities. The possible general equation for this demand behavior is expressed next.

D for rent = f (rent, income, college tuition, alternative to rent, distance from public transportation or campus, on-campus housing)

In the general equation above, **f** is the symbol for "function of" the variables mentioned in the parentheses. All variables in the parentheses are independent variables that determine or affect the values of quantity demanded on the left-hand side of the equation, D for rent. In other words, D for rent on the left-hand side is a dependent variable, and the variables on the right-hand side are all independent variables.

The ceteris paribus assumption made earlier implies that for any given short period of time, we will change a key variable of the D function (rent only) and see how the change of rent (the price of housing) affects the demand (demand for housing in the college town of Boston). After detailed analysis of the changes in rent and the quantity of housing, we extend the topic to a situation in which the assumption of ceteris paribus is no longer valid. Given the law of demand stated from the general equation, it will be easier to use a demand schedule with different hypothetical values of rents and quantity demanded, as shown in Table 2.1.

Table 2.1: The Demand Schedule with Ceteris Paribus Assumption

Rents of Housing (in thousands of $)	Quantity Demanded for Housing (in thousands)
0	900
1	700
2	500
3	300
4	100
5	0

The above demand schedule indicates the consistency of the law of demand as an inverse relationship between quantity demanded and the rent for housing, assuming other things (factors) stay the same. Figure 2.1 is a graphical representation of the demand curve based on data from the demand schedule in Table 2.1.

Figure 2.1 The Demand Curve

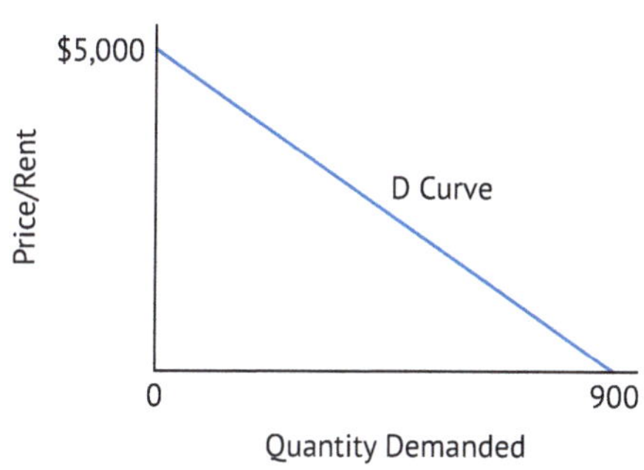

The downward-sloping demand curve in Figure 2.1 illustrates the price/rent and quantity combinations in Table 2.1, with the quantity as 900,000 housing units (apartments, for example) on the horizontal axis against a rental price of $0 and zero demand for apartment rentals against a $5,000 rental price per unit of housing. The other combinations of rent and number of apartments will sit in between the two extreme points to reflect the entire schedule along the demand curve. Given this demand curve, we have accomplished three basic elements of understanding the concept of demand behavior for any goods and services, including this market for housing in Boston. First, we stated the law of demand as a theoretical concept. Second, we have made a hypothetical table of data on quantity demanded against different prices/rents of housing. Third, we have combined the first and second part of the demand theory to illustrate, in the downward-sloping demand curve in Figure 2.1, the whole structure of the demand curve under the ceteris paribus assumption. These three steps are a common process of understanding and analyzing economic models to determine the efficiency for the allocation of limited resources. The next step in this demand theory is to find out what happens when the ceteris paribus assumption is not valid—a situation we call *changes in demand curve* instead of *changes in quantity demanded.* In other words, when changes in quantity demanded happen because of changes in price per unit, the price and quantity combinations move along the same demand curve. On the other hand, when changes in demand happen because of changes in other factors besides price, the whole demand function changes or the whole demand curve shifts either to the right or to the left depending on the kind of effect on the demand function. The explanation of changes in demand with graphical illustration is provided next.

2.1.2. Changes in the Demand Curve (the Shifts of the Demand Curve)

The restrictive assumption of ceteris paribus previously made in the context of the downward-sloping demand curve implies that the changes in its own price/rent of housing will move all combinations of price and quantity along the same demand curve. However, when the assumption of ceteris paribus is not the case, meaning that other factors (determinants) of demand do change, then the entire demand curve will shift inward to the left or outward to the right. This situation is called changes in demand. For example, suppose the enrollment for college students admitted to all Boston area colleges has significantly increased in comparison to the demand schedule and demand curve illustrated in Table 2.1 and Figure 2.1, respectively. This new increase in the enrollment of students will shift the demand curve for housing. Suppose the overall rental demand has increased by 50% with the current rental structure given by the supply of housing (availability). This 50% increase in demand for rents is shown in Table 2.2 below.

Table 2.2: The Demand Schedule without Ceteris Paribus Assumption

Rents of Housing (in thousands of $)	Quantity Demanded for Housing (in thousands)
0	1,350
1	1,050
2	750
3	450
4	150
5	0

With the new demand schedule attributed to the increase in college enrollment shown in Table 2.2, the corresponding shift in the demand curve from Figure 2.1 is illustrated in Figure 2.2.

As indicated by the arrow in Figure 2.2, the D curve has shifted outward to the right because of an increase in enrollment. Using the same concept, suppose that education funding by the State of Massachusetts and the US Department of Education has been significantly reduced because of a new policy tightening government expenses. The new changes in policy will definitely have a negative effect on the enrollment of college students in Boston and elsewhere in the country. In

Figure 2.2 The Shift of the Demand Curve

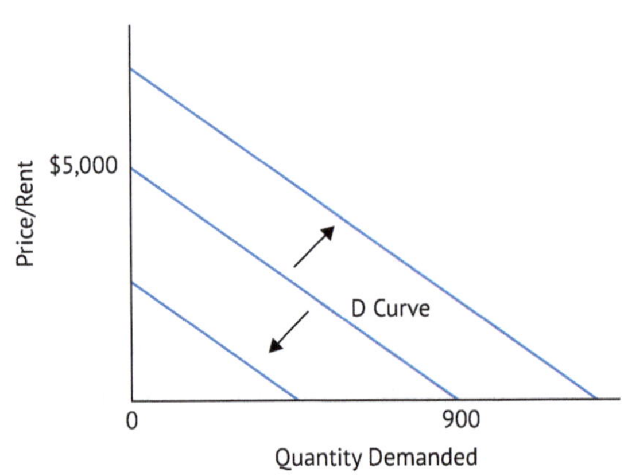

other words, the reduction of the government's education funding at both the state and federal levels will have a negative effect on demand for college admission and thus will reduce the demand for housing in the city. This effect is illustrated in Figure 2.2 by shifting the demand curve inward to the left. It is important to note here that the positive effect of such changes in the determinants will usually shift the demand curve outward to the right and the negative effect of changes of the same will usually shift the demand curve inward to the left. The most common determinants of the demand curve that shift the demand are summarized in Table 2.3.

Table 2.3: Common Determinants (Factors) Shifting the Demand Curve

Determinants of Demand	Explanation of Effects on Demand Shifts
Consumer taste and preference	Changes in taste and preference of consumers, regardless of price per unit of goods and services, will shift the demand rightward or leftward depending on the positive or negative preference pattern of individual consumers. In the previous example of college enrollments, changes in the preference pattern of admitting students will shift the demand for housing because college attendance and demand for housing go together.
Changes in ability to pay (income)	The ability to pay is an important factor in changes in the demand curve. Changes in income may sometimes affect changes in taste or preference as well.
Market size of consumers	The market size of the consumers is an important factor that affects the demand curve. As the number of consumers increases, the demand curve shifts to the right; the curve shifts to the left when the number of consumers decreases.
Expectations of consumers	The change in expectations is a powerful factor in the demand behavior of consumers. Future expectations regarding variables related to the demand curve of any good or service do directly affect the demand curve.
Substitution and complementary goods and services	Changes in price of substitutes and complementary goods and services will alter the demand. For example, college campus housing facilities provided by universities do effect changes in demand for off-campus housing.
Government policies	Changes in government policies, such as tax policy or environmental regulations, on certain goods and services will have an effect on the demand for those goods or services.

2.1.3. Law of Supply

The law of supply dictates that if the price of any good or service increases (e.g., rents for college students in a college town like Boston), then the quantity supplied for that good or service will also increase and vice versa, ceteris paribus. The ceteris paribus assumption means that all other factors affecting the same supply behavior stay the same for the time being. In the housing market example, other possible factors could be location, in terms of proximity to public transportation or college campus; rents offered by other apartment owners; the size and number of rooms and other related facilities; on-campus housing offered by universities; city government policy in giving permits for building new apartments; city zoning policy and environmental policy in housing construction; rent control policy of the state; or federal housing subsidies. The general equation for this supply behavior is given below.

Supply of rent = g (rents of similar apartments, alternative transportation to college, alternatives to rent, rents of other types of apartments, government policy on housing construction, on-campus housing availability for enrolled students, cost of construction of new housing, compliance with environmental requirements)

In the equation above, **"g"** is the symbol for "function of" the variables mentioned in parentheses. All variables in the parentheses are independent variables that determine or affect the quantity supplied on the left-hand side of the equation, S of rent. In other words, the variable S of rent on the left-hand side is a dependent variable, and the variables on the right-hand side are all independent variables.

The ceteris paribus assumption made earlier implies that for any given short period of time, we will change a key variable of the S function (rent only) and see how that change (the price of housing) affects the supply (quantity of available housing in Boston). After detailed analysis of the changes in rent and the quantity of housing supplied, we extend the topic to a situation in which the assumption of ceteris paribus is no longer valid. Given the law of supply stated from the general equation, like the demand analysis, it will be easier to use a supply schedule with different hypothetical values of rents and quantities of housing (Table 2.4).

Table 2.4: The Supply Schedule

Rents of Housing (in thousands of $)	Quantity Supplied for Housing (in thousands)
0	0
1	100
2	200
3	300
4	400
5	500

The supply schedule indicates the consistency of the law of supply as a direct relationship between quantity supplied and the rent for housing, assuming other factors remain the same. The graphical representation of the supply schedule is drawn as a supply curve in Figure 2.3 for a visual presentation and for use in more graphs in subsequent sections and chapters.

The upward-sloping supply curve in Figure 2.3 illustrates the price/rent and quantity-supplied combinations in Table 2.4, with quantity as 500,000 housing units on the horizontal axis against a $5,000 rental price and zero supply for apartment rentals against a price of $0 per unit of housing. The other combinations of rent and the number of available apartments are plotted in between the two extremes to reflect the entire schedule along the supply curve. Given this supply curve, we have accomplished three basic elements of understanding the

Figure 2.3 The Supply Curve

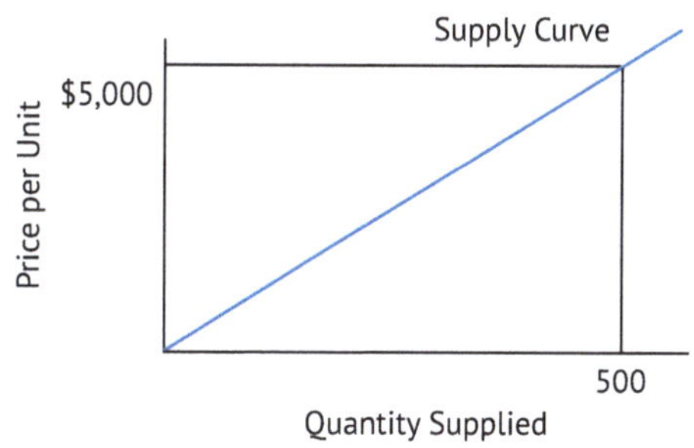

concept of supply behavior (just like the demand curve in Section 2.1.2) for any goods and services, including this market for housing in the city. First, we stated the law of supply as a theoretical concept. Second, we have made a hypothetical table of data delineating the quantity of housing supplied against different prices/rents of housing. Third, we have combined the first and second parts of the supply theory to illustrate, in the upward-sloping supply curve in the previous graph, the entire supply model structure under the ceteris paribus assumption.

The next step in this supply theory is to examine what happens when the ceteris paribus assumption is not valid—a situation we call changes in the supply curve rather than changes in quantity supplied. In other words, when changes in quantity supplied are due to changes in price/rent per unit, the price and quantity combinations move along the same supply curve. On the other hand, when changes in supply are due to changes in other factors besides price, the whole supply function changes or the whole supply curve shifts either to the right or to the left depending on the kind of effect on the supply function.

2.1.4. Changes in Supply Curve (the Shifts of the Supply Curve)

Again, the restrictive assumption of ceteris paribus implies that the changes in price/rent of housing will move all combinations of price/rent and quantity supplied along the same supply curve. However, when the assumption of ceteris paribus is not applicable, meaning that other determinants of supply change as well, then the entire supply curve may change by shifting inward to the left or outward to the right. This situation is called changes in supply. For example, suppose the city authority of Boston has significantly increased the number of permits given to developers for the construction of new apartments in the vacant areas near college campuses. This change in housing policy by the City of Boston will increase the availability of apartments under the same rental fees given in Table 2.4 and Figure 2.3. Suppose the overall supply of new apartments has increased by 20%. This 20% increase in the supply of rental apartments is shown in Table 2.5.

Table 2.5: The Supply Schedule

Rents of Housing (in thousands of $)	Quantity Supplied of Housing (in thousands)
0	0
1	120
2	240
3	360
4	480
5	600

With an increase in newly constructed apartments, as shown in Table 2.5, there is a corresponding shift in the supply curve illustrated in Figure 2.4.

Figure 2.4 The Shift of the Supply Curve

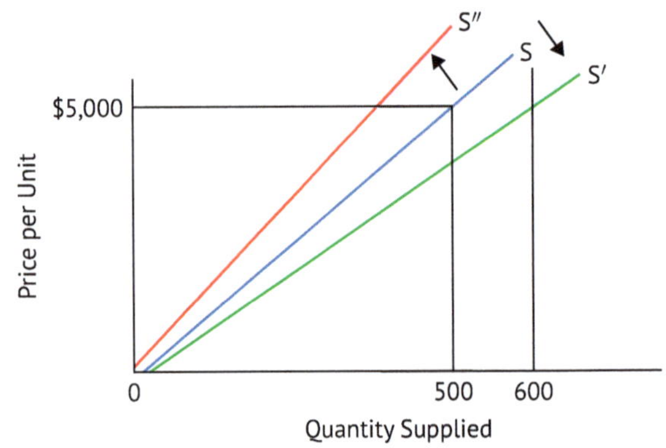

As illustrated by S′ in Figure 2.4, the S curve has shifted outward to the right because of an increase in the availability of new apartments. Suppose that instead of allowing the city authority to provide new permits for housing construction, the conservation department of Boston and the Environmental Protection Agency of the federal government have imposed strict regulations on building new houses in the same area. The new environmental restrictions would probably increase the cost of regulatory compliance for new houses or apartments. As a consequence, the supply of available apartments may reduce. In other words, the legislative restrictions would have a negative effect on the supply of housing and would shift the entire supply curve inward to the left. This possible effect is illustrated in Figure 2.4 by shifting the supply curve inward to the left. As mentioned earlier in the demand curve model, it is important to note that a positive effect on the determinants will usually shift the supply curve outward to the right and a negative effect will usually shift the supply curve inward to the left. In general, the most common determinants of supply curve that shift the supply are summarized in Table 2.6.

Table 2.6: Common Determinants (Factors) Shifting the Supply Curve

Determinants of Supply	Explanation of Effects on Supply Shifts
Legislative policy	Increase in government restrictions on housing construction reduces the supply of housing and vice versa.
Changes in policy on tax and subsidy	Increase in taxes on gasoline consumption reduces the supply of goods and services, which are produced by using the gasoline as inputs.
Change in technology of production	Technological improvement in production reduces the cost of production, increases the productivity of labor, and, thus, shifts the supply curve rightward.
Change in labor cost and labor productivity	The increase in wages bargained by labor unions and hiring unskilled workers increases the cost of production in factories and service industries and thus shifts the supply to the left and vice versa.
Change in cost of other inputs and capital	The decrease in costs of capital (e.g., interest rates, raw materials) will lower the cost of making durable goods (e.g., cars, household appliances) and thus shift the supply curve rightward.

Determinants of Supply	Explanation of Effects on Supply Shifts
Change in expected profit or state of the economy or government policy	The increase in expected profit for goods and services will increase supply. If the economy is expected to do better and government policy is favorable for the company's growth and profit, the supply will shift rightward. The opposite will happen with negative expectations.
Change in number of competitive suppliers	The increase in the number of suppliers of the same products will shift the market supply curve rightward. For example, the rise in e-commerce companies has increased the supply of products available to purchase online.
Change in prices of substitute goods and services	If the price of substitutes increases, say the price of Starbucks coffee and drinks, the price of Dunkin' Donuts coffee and drinks may increase because of the increase in demand for relatively lower-priced Dunkin' Donuts coffee and drinks.

2.1.5. Demand and Supply Interaction and Determination of Market Equilibrium

To analyze the efficiency of allocating the limited resources in the market, it is necessary to bring the market demand (the consumers or buyers) and market supply (the producers or suppliers) together to clear the market. Since desires for consumers/buyers and producers/sellers are opposite in their act of exchanging goods and services, under normal circumstances, the demand curve is downward sloping and the supply curve is upward sloping. In the free market environment, the demand and supply curves moving in opposite directions must interact at the point of intersection to determine the equilibrium—the point at which buyers and sellers meet called the market clearing point. To explain the process of this equilibrium point, Table 2.7 combines the data from Table 2.1 (demand schedule) and Table 2.4 (supply schedule).

Table 2.7: Equilibrium Rent and Quantity of Housing in the Free Market Environment

Rents ($ in 000)	Quantity Demanded (in thousands)	Quantity Supplied (in thousands)	Shortage/ Surplus	Change in Price (increase/ decrease)
0	900	0	Shortage	Increase
1	700	100	Shortage	Increase
2	500	200	Shortage	Increase
3	300	300	Equilibrium	Equilibrium
4	100	400	Surplus	Decrease
5	0	500	Surplus	Decrease

Table 2.7 indicates the process of demand and supply interaction in a rental housing market with six combinations of price (rents) and quantities of apartments, displaying the responses from both demand (tenants) and supply (owners). The quantity demanded and quantity supplied intersect at 300,000 units; therefore, the equilibrium price is $3,000 per unit. This is

the only price and quantity combination to clear the market (the handshake points of intersection). The data in the table 2.7 is illustrated in Figure 2.5 below.

Figure 2.5 Market Equilibrium

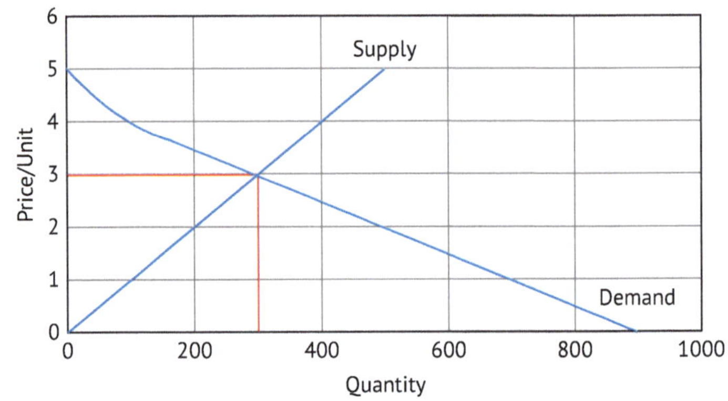

Figure 2.5 illustrates the equilibrium position at the intersection between the demand and supply curves of $3,000 per unit with the quantity demanded equal to the quantity supplied of 300,000 units. It is also clear that for any other rental prices above this equilibrium price of $3,000 per unit, quantity demanded would be less than quantity supplied, creating a surplus (see in Table 2.7 and Figure 2.5). Assuming that all other things besides rental price stay the same (ceteris paribus), the surplus at prices above the equilibrium price will pull the prices down to $3,000 per unit to clear the market. Conversely, with the same ceteris paribus assumption, any rental prices below $3,000 per unit will push the prices up until they reach an equilibrium price at $3,000 per unit, which clears the market. This process of equilibrium price and quantity combination is the point where buyers and sellers handshake to clear the market. In other words, the equilibrium price is a signal that clears the market without any misallocation or distortion of limited resources in the form of surplus (inventory accumulation) or shortages (inventory diminution). However, this mechanism of market equilibrium price and quantity demanded equal to quantity supplied is not static; the ceteris paribus assumption is a restrictive assumption for a short period of transactions. There are several factors mentioned previously that do change the direction of demand and supply behavior in the free market. Those factors constantly change over time as does the ceteris paribus assumption. This phenomenon—the process of shifting demand and supply functions and their curves—is due to changes in factors other than price. These changes in demand and supply do eventually alter the equilibrium point of market interaction. Such changes in equilibrium price and quantity are explained in Section 2.1.6.

2.1.6. Changes in Equilibrium Price and Quantity Owing to the Shift in Demand and Supply

As previously explained, some outside factors may shift the demand and supply curves to the right or to the left. In that case, the equilibrium price and quantity demanded and supplied would end up with a new equilibrium position to clear the market. For example, the new data on demand for housing depicted in Table 2.2 and the same for the supply of housing shown in Table 2.5 were attributed to changes in two outside factors. The increase in college enrollment of students shifted the demand for housing to the right by 50% given the same list of rental prices. At the same time, the supply of newly constructed apartments has also increased by 20% with the increased building permits initiative by the city authority. Given those new demand and supply increases with the same set of rental prices, the new equilibrium of the housing market is illustrated in Figure 2.6. The new equilibrium price is close to $3,500, and the quantity demanded and supplied is about 400,000 units. This is consistent with the concept of demand and supply analyzed so far.

Figure 2.6 New Equilibrium of Housing Market

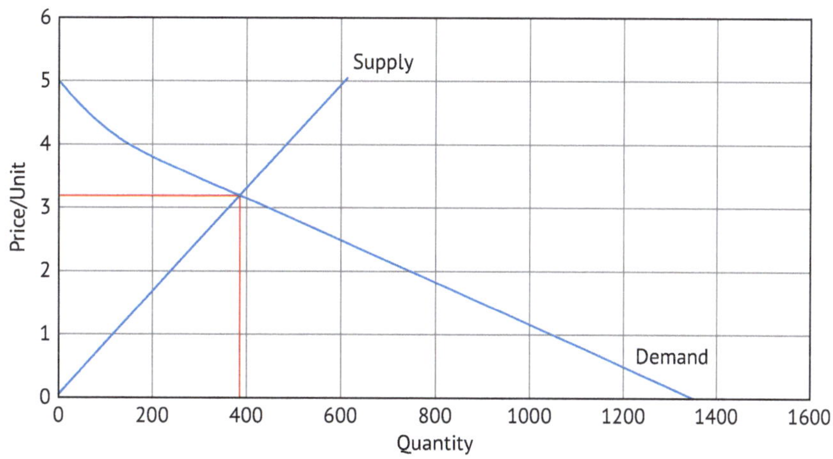

2.1.7. The Scope and Limitations of Demand and Supply Models under Imperfect Competition

In Section 2.1.6, the determination of market equilibrium price and quantity was based on the assumption of perfect competition without any outside forces that may disrupt the process of the free market system. Those forces are very common in the economics of the real world when a laissez-faire market system is disrupted by outside factors, such as natural calamities, war, geopolitical trade wars, government legislations, price support, tariffs, subsidies, rent control, minimum wage laws, and taxes. These factors are so common in business and economics that the free market assumption does not hold true most of the time. As a consequence, the demand and supply behavior constantly change (by shifting) in response to those outside factors that obviously influence the outcome of market equilibrium.

As an example, the legislative agencies of the government take action to protect consumers' health and safety by imposing restrictions on food, medicine, transportation, construction, automobiles, cigarettes, and other health-related products. In compliance with those legislative laws, the cost of production will increase. As a result, the effect of increasing costs of production in those goods and services will shift the supply curve to the left. Given that the demand curve is unchanged, the new equilibrium price will increase, and quantity demanded and supplied at the new equilibrium will be lower. In general, the increase in the cost of production is a negative shock on the supply side and thus shifts the supply curve to the left. Conversely, technological advancement with an increase in efficiency of production and labor productivity will have a positive shock on the supply side and thus will shift the supply curve to the right. For example, the increased tariffs proposed by Donald Trump in January 2017 on fruits and vegetables imported from Mexico to pay for the border wall will definitely shift the supply curve to the left, and American consumers will end up paying for the wall at a higher equilibrium price and lower quantity of imported goods from Mexico. Similarly, the price support and subsidy by the government to dairy products and fruit/vegetable industries will induce the supply curve to shift rightward for those affected products in response to the support program. As a result, the price will decrease and quantity in equilibrium will increase.

The demand side of the market is also influenced by several outside factors. In general, a negative shock on the demand side because of changes in outside factors will shift the demand curve to the left. And given that the supply curve is unchanged, the new equilibrium price and quantity will decline. For example, a decrease in government subsidies on higher education will decrease the demand for college admission and thus shift the demand curve inward to the left. Given the supply curve for college admission capacity, the tuition will decrease with an overall decrease in enrollment. On the other hand, a positive shock because of changes in outside factors, such as an increase in subsidies for higher education, will increase the demand for admission and, therefore, increase the equilibrium quantity of enrollment and tuition. Based on this general concept of D and S changes, students may think about many other real-world examples of economic goods and services and their constant changes in price and quantity with their implications for the welfare of both consumers and suppliers. The effects of government policies on the welfare of both buyers and sellers come from minimum wage law (price floor legislation); rent control (price ceiling legislation); agriculture and manufacturing subsidies; tariffs on imported goods, such as aluminum and steel; and taxes on cigarettes, alcohol, and petroleum. In the next three sections of this chapter, applications and policy implications for changes in demand and supply behavior are discussed in the context of the economics of sports, music, and higher education.

2.2. Applications of Demand and Supply in Sports Economics

Figure 2.7 illustrates that changes in ticket price will not affect the quantity of seats, which are fixed in supply and drawn as a vertical supply curve. Given the downward-sloping demand curve, the equilibrium price and quantity for each category of seats will be determined at the point of intersection between the vertical supply curve and the downward-sloping demand curve. The process of this market interaction has nothing to do with the price on actual tickets the baseball fans purchase. This is because those ticketed prices are regulated, which are already

Figure 2.7 The Market Equilibrium for a Baseball Game

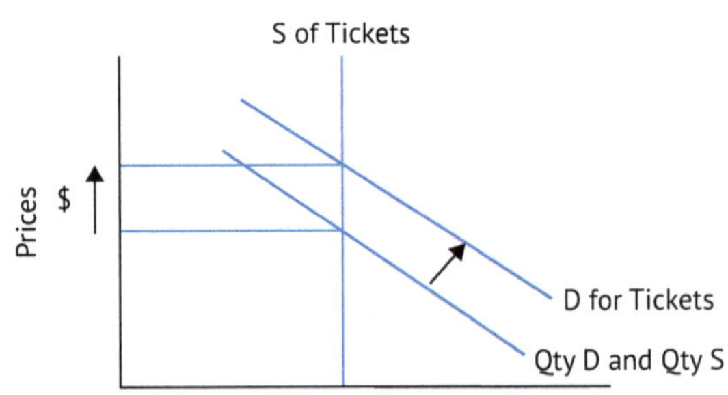

determined long before the season starts every year. When the number of fans willing to purchase more tickets far exceeds the total tickets available for each category of seats (with different pricing schemes on the tickets), the demand curve will shift rightward. As a result, the equilibrium price will increase with no change in quantity of seats bought and sold. In other words, it is fair to conclude that the ticketed price of the baseball tickets may not necessarily reflect the true market price because it is a predetermined regulated price. That is why the actual market price is the scalping price or the price paid for tickets purchased in secondary markets. The shifting of demand to the right goes up even at a higher rate during the playoff matches—not only for baseball games but also for football, basketball, hockey, and soccer games. A real-world example of a rightward shift of the demand curve for the Super Bowl in 2018 is illustrated in the article published by CBS Sports on February 4, 2018.

On February 4, 2018, various sports journals reported that the Super Bowl LII ticket price for the February 6 NFL championship game was increasing at a much faster rate than it did a year before for Super Bowl LI. The following news article is the report by CBS Sports about the price increase for 2018 Super Bowl tickets.

Please click on the link below or use your cell phone to scan the QR code to access the article.

https://www.cbssports.com/nfl/news/super-bowl-52-ticket-prices-minnesota-flooded-with-eagles-fans-as-demand-soars/

Based on the price information noted earlier and its relevance to the application of theories of demand and supply behavior in sports economics, the following three conclusions can be drawn:

a. The rise of the market price was caused by the limited supply of tickets for sale.
b. The increase of the market price across the board was due to the Eagles winning the National Football Conference Championship versus the Minnesota Vikings.
c. The increase of the market price caused by the rise in demand for tickets in the secondary market was also due to the covered dome of the US Bank Stadium in Minneapolis, Minnesota, during the bitter cold of February.

With similar concepts of market behavior in the entertainment industry, the next section will analyze the demand and supply model in the music industry.

2.3. Demand and Supply Model in the Music Industry

Like the market interaction for sports events, music entertainment events, such as concerts and Broadway shows, have a limited number of seats for each event. Depending on the popularity of a particular event, the demand curve will keep shifting to the right until the prices arrive at the highest bidding equilibrium point at the intersection between the vertical supply curve and the downward-sloping demand curve—the same model structure illustrated in the case of NFL games in Section 2.2. The example in Figure 2.8 is of market data for music concerts in 2008 in the United States published by *Pollstar* magazine.

Figure 2.8 Market Trend in the Music Industry

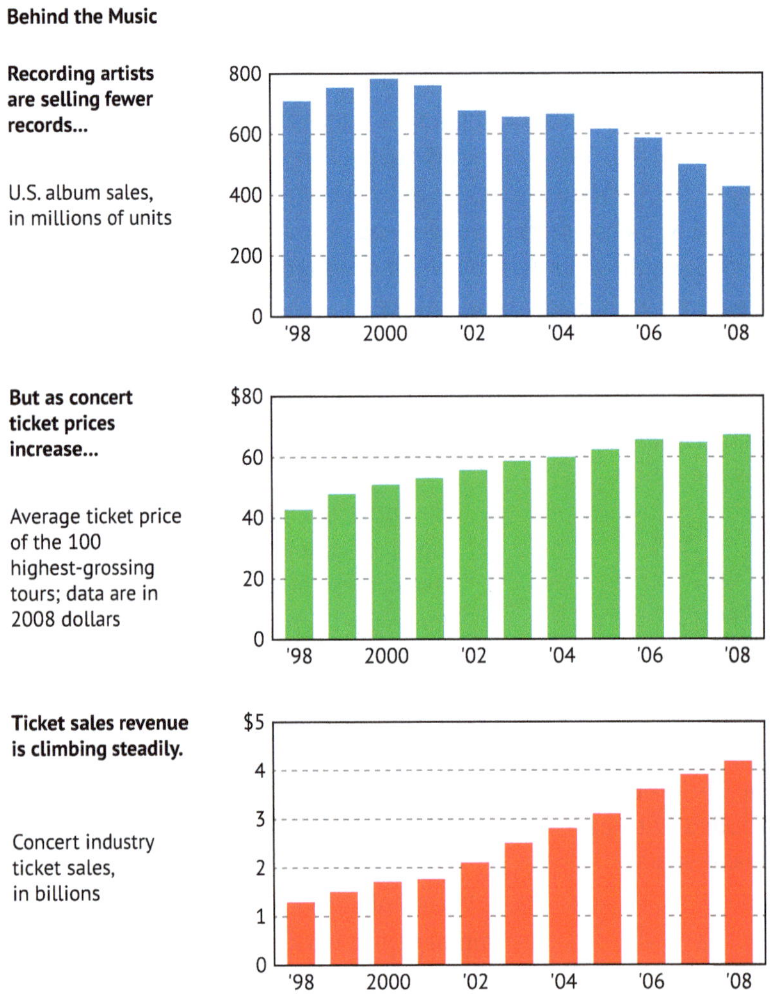

Source: Ethan Smith, "Can He Save Rock 'n' Roll? Irving Azoff Wants to Concentrate Power in the Music World Like Never Before; Bruce Springsteen Objects," *The Wall Street Journal* (2009).

From Figure 2.8, it can be observed that between 1998 and 2008, sales of recording albums in the United States were down almost 50% from their 2000 peak. But over that same period, concert ticket sales revenue more than doubled to 4.2 billion, despite significant increases in average concert ticket prices. The data in the chart clearly indicates the rise in ticket prices has been over 50% in response to an almost 100% increase in ticket sales, resulting in a continuous shift of the demand curve to the right with a very limited increase in the number of seats (except that the number of concerts has been increased). The simultaneous increase in price and tickets sold is mainly attributed to a faster increase in demand for concertgoing fans. On the other hand, the decline in sales revenue for rock albums may be attributed to two factors. First, the increasing number of concert goers might have reduced the purchase of rock albums in those years. Second, the advancement of digital technology and the ability to download music and music videos via YouTube, iTunes, Amazon Music, Spotify, and other competitors lowered the price of rock albums. However, it does not necessarily mean that the demand to purchase digital music has declined at the same time. It might be that the per-unit cost of digital music sales has declined significantly to reflect the decline in sales revenue for rock albums. The next section of this chapter will explain the demand and supply behavior of higher education and its effects on the costs and benefits of higher education.

2.4. Demand and Supply Model for College Education

In Section 1.2 of Chapter 1, an explanation was given about the concept of opportunity cost in the context of deciding to go to college. In that discussion, the long-term benefits of going to college apparently outweighed the short-term opportunity cost for college. As an extension of that discussion, recent statistics show that college enrollment has significantly increased in recent years not only in the United States but also globally. According to a 2017 report published by the National Center for Education Statistics, college enrollment increased by 30% in the United States between the years 2000 and 2015 (from 13.2 million to 17 million). The same report projected that increases in enrollment would reach 19.3 million by 2026 (an increase of 13.5%). Another report published by Inside Higher Ed in September 2017 projected the increase in college enrollment to reach 15% by 2025. These statistics clearly indicate that the demand curve for college admission will continue to shift rightward given the very limited growth in admissions and the rising trend of students seeking higher education. The result of these demand and supply forces in college education allows students of economics to recognize that a steady rise in college tuition can be expected in the years to come. The rising trend of international students seeking admission in both undergraduate and graduate schools in the United States leads to an expected rightward shift of the demand curve at a much faster rate than the statistics based solely on US students seeking college admission. To learn more details about the statistics of demand for higher education, students may visit the US Department of Education website at www.ed.gov.

In Chapter 3, the demand and supply model will explain the context of efficiency and equity under perfect competition. The rationale for government intervention when the free market fails to allocate resources efficiently will be discussed as well.

Chapter Summary

Section 2.1 introduced the basic theoretical foundation of the market system in terms of market demand and supply models with their scope and limitations in allocating resources efficiently. After introducing the concept of the demand and supply paradigm, the power of demand and supply was explained with special reference to Adam Smith's theory of laissez-faire noted in *The Wealth of Nations* (1776) in achieving efficiency in production and distribution. The law of demand and its application in real-world economics were discussed by the integration of hypothetical data and related graphs with the theory of the demand for housing in the city of Boston. Similarly, the law of supply was discussed with the hypothetical data on the supply side of the housing market in Boston. The equilibrium condition for demand and supply interaction was also explained in detail with ceteris paribus assumption by changing the price per unit of housing. The changes in the equilibrium condition were further explained by relaxing the assumption of ceteris paribus. The other factors, such as income, taste, and government policy on the housing market, are allowed to change with the absence of ceteris paribus assumption. The changes in those variables do affect the changes in equilibrium by shifting demand and/or supply curves to arrive at a new equilibrium. The policy implications for changes in market equilibrium price and quantity are also discussed at the end of this section.

Section 2.2 discussed the application of demand and supply models in sports economics. Specific examples were provided, such as the price and seat allocation in stadiums for baseball and football games. Students are encouraged to read the theories of demand and supply first and then to relate to the real-world application of sports economics in major games, such as football, hockey, baseball, basketball, and soccer.

Section 2.3 examined the application of demand and supply models in the music industry. This section explained how the cost and pricing for live music concerts versus digital downloads have significantly changed with the emergence of the digital economy and thus have brought about a major change in the market behavior of the music industry. The digital download system of music has revolutionized the cost and price structure of music CDs and application-based music marketing and sales. Examples of live rock concerts and their sharp contrast to digital music downloads were discussed at the end of this section.

Section 2.4 discussed the application of demand and supply models in college education. The concepts of demand and supply were applied to determine the market efficiency in cost and benefit for going to college. Students are also encouraged to extend these three applications of demand and supply to other industries.

Application Activities

Q1. Define and describe the concept of opportunity cost with an example. What would be your opportunity cost for taking online classes to get a degree at the University of Massachusetts Boston (UMB) compared to taking traditional face-to-face classes at UMB or elsewhere? Provide examples in your answers.

Q2. Draw a supply-demand diagram of the market for rental apartments in Boston in the neighborhoods surrounding UMB. Illustrate the effect on monthly rents because of increased public funding from the State of Massachusetts and a simultaneous increase in enrollment capacity for freshman year admission by the university with no increase in tuition and fees. Explain your hypothetically drawn diagram in your own words.

Q3. Suppose the geopolitical tension in the Arab states in the Middle East and Persian Gulf region has severely disrupted oil exports to the United States. Illustrate and explain in your own words the effect on the price of natural gas and the quantity demanded equal to the quantity supplied in the US market because of this decline in the supply of petroleum (fossil fuel) from the Middle East and the Persian Gulf. Hint: please assume that petroleum and natural gas are substitutes.

Q4. Suppose the state government decided to impose a tax on cigarette purchases to discourage smoking and thus prevent health-related issues for the general public. Draw a graph of demand and supply curves to illustrate and explain briefly the effect that a $2 per pack cigarette tax will have on the equilibrium price and the quantity of cigarettes in the market. In other words, illustrate the increase or decrease of equilibrium price and quantities after the imposition of $2 tax per pack. Briefly explain whether the price change of cigarettes would rise by more than, less than, or exactly $2. Hint: you start with an initial equilibrium price and quantity with D and S of the cigarette market followed by changing the D or S curves in response to tax imposition by the government.

Q5. Suppose the government passed a new legislation for stricter safety and fuel efficiency conditions on the manufacture of new automobiles. Draw a demand and supply diagram and then illustrate and briefly explain the effect of such legislation on the equilibrium price and the quantity of newly manufactured vehicles vis-à-vis the market for used vehicles (draw two different diagrams for new and used vehicles).

Q6. Suppose the ticket prices for next year's Super Bowl were announced a year ahead at a range from $1,000 to $25,000, with rates in between for all categories of seats for the stadium. Without any prior information regarding what teams will play, briefly explain why these price ranges do not reflect the true market price of Super Bowl tickets. Do you expect to see the actual market prices much higher, lower, or exactly the same? Why?

Q7. Ed Sheeran, a British pop and rock singer, was scheduled to perform a concert on September 14, 2018, at 7 p.m. at Gillette Stadium in Foxboro, Massachusetts. The ticket price ranges are from $62 to $8,668. Based on your knowledge of the D and S model for the music entertainment market, briefly explain whether these price ranges truly reflect the market prices. Why or why not?

Chapter 3

Measures of Market Efficiency Versus Economics of Government Intervention in the Free Market Mechanism

Learning Objectives

As they read the chapter, students will learn the following:

- Criteria for measuring market efficiency versus equity
- Foundation of the free market system: the case for laissez-faire (leave the market alone)
- The sources of free-market failure and its effects on society
- The case for government intervention in the free market system and its effects on society
- Pros and cons of government intervention, with examples

3.1. Criteria of Measuring Efficiency and Equity

As mentioned in Chapter 1, the key purpose of studying economics is to learn how to allocate limited resources efficiently. It is also important to extend basic understanding of the distributional pattern of the economic pie so that the disparity between rich and poor can be fairly minimized. This section focuses on economic principles and applications for measuring efficiency and equity to improve the use of resources in both production processes and distribution of goods and services.

3.1.1. What Is Economic Efficiency?

In general, economic efficiency comes from two sides of the original model of demand and supply in the market for goods and services. Demand-side efficiency, also referred to as distributional efficiency, represents the welfare of consumers. Supply-side efficiency represents the welfare of producers. In other words, efficiency in economics looks at two types of efficiency:

Efficiency in distribution for consumers

Efficiency in production for producers

Italian economist Vilfredo Pareto developed the original theory of the two types of efficiency in 1909 called the Pareto efficiency in distribution and production. Pareto efficiency is said to be the state of production and distribution of goods and services at a maximum point of efficiency. A reallocation of resources from that point will either make someone better off or worse off. This concept was developed by Pareto in the context of microeconomics of production and distribution. However, in the field of macroeconomics, the Pareto efficiency theory may have different implications (not discussed here).

Conditions for Pareto efficiency in microeconomics: If resources are allocated to the point of equilibrium, they must fulfill the following criteria of Pareto efficiency.

1. Efficiency in allocative distribution: Price per unit (P) = Marginal utility (MU) = Marginal cost (MC)
2. Efficiency in allocative production: Price per unit (P) = Marginal revenue (MR) = Minimum average total cost (ATC)

Combining both the demand and supply sides of the two criteria, the complete Pareto condition can be rewritten with the following equation:

P = MU = MC = MR = Minimum ATC

Basic assumptions for the efficiency criteria for validity are

- perfect information about the goods and services to both consumers and producers,
- technology of production is the most efficient to produce at minimum average total cost, and
- no external costs are involved.

For example, consider the production and distribution of soybean oil and corn oil in the United States. The hypothetical demand curves for both markets are illustrated in Figure 3.1, with the assumption of identical cost structures in both production and technology. It is also assumed that MC = Minimum ATC at $200,000 per ton and marginal revenue is ignored for the sake of simplicity.

In Figure 3.1, the Pareto efficient point for soybean oil production and distribution is 500, and for corn oil, it is 1,200, with their corresponding prices and minimum average total costs at a and b. If some resources are taken away from soybean oil production to produce more corn oil, then the utility lost by soybean consumers at a price above $200 cannot be

Figure 3.1 Pareto Efficiency

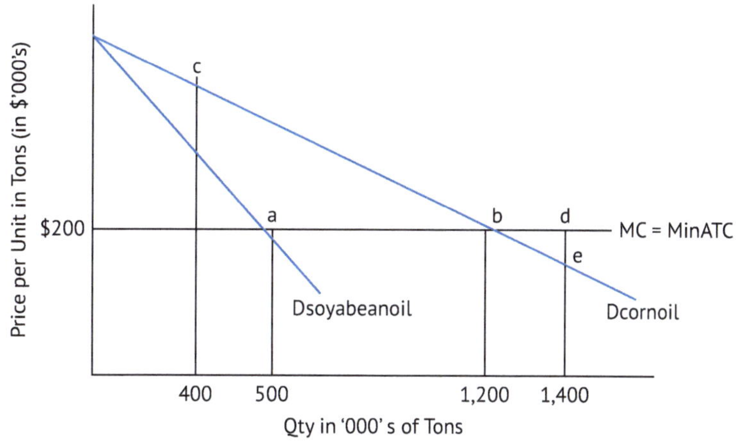

compensated by the lower price paid by corn oil consumers below $200. Of course, this simplification of the model structure is based on three assumptions mentioned earlier. Those assumptions are based on a perfectly competitive market structure called laissez-faire. However, under the conditions of imperfect market competition, such as a monopoly or oligopoly market power, Pareto efficiency conditions may not be the case. Since monopolies and oligopolies charge higher prices than marginal cost and marginal utility, the efficiency is lost. Even under conditions of perfect competition, the attainment of Pareto efficiency is not necessarily guaranteed for two reasons:

- The distribution of wealth and income may not be equitable.
- The economics of externality (negative and positive externalities) may affect the third parties in society who were not invited to the party of demand and supply equilibrium.

The first reason is common in every society; income distribution is rarely equitable. For example, if the government imposes high tax rates on higher income and wealthy individuals and corporations, and the extra tax revenue is spent on national defense and low-income welfare recipients, then the demand and cost structure illustrated in Figure 3.1 will shift to different positions. Under that scenario, Pareto efficiency may not be possible to attain. Other examples could be an unrestricted or unregulated logging industry or fishing industry that may cause negative externalities by deforestation or harming marine biology. In these examples, the social marginal cost of externality would be much higher than the conditions of Pareto efficiency criteria because the prices the industries charge do not necessarily reflect the true social scarcity of resources or cost to society. Industrial pollution is a classic example of such negative externality. To internalize these externalities, government regulations are needed so that marginal social benefit (MSB) is equally distributed to match with marginal social cost (MSC). The benefit of government intervention to internalize the externality is discussed in Section 3.4. Students will learn more technical detail with real-world examples of this logic in *Principles of Microeconomics*.

3.2. Foundation of the Free Market System: The Case for Laissez-Faire

The concept of a free market system dates back to the classical theory of demand and supply originally developed by Adam Smith in his famous book *The Wealth of Nations* published in 1776. The core principle of the free market system is known as laissez-faire meaning "leave the market alone." This principle implies that the equilibrium price and quantity determined by uninterrupted demand and supply (the foundation of free-market behavior) may be the most efficient point of resource allocation. This point of efficiency is supposed to provide the highest possible value. As discussed in Section 3.1, the efficiency condition of Pareto optimality as **MC = Price = MR = MU = Minimum ATC** is the primary argument in favor of laissez-faire principle. The advocacy of Adam Smith and subsequent classical economists for a free market system without government intervention is known as the theory of capitalism or the economic system of capitalism. The capitalist system of market behavior is also known as industrial capitalism—the system originally emerged from the **Industrial Revolution** in the United Kingdom during the second half of the eighteenth century.

The Industrial Revolution was primarily attributed to the invention of spinning jennies, spinning mules, and power looms in the textile industry during the 1760s. These technological breakthroughs transformed the social structure of Britain from a predominantly agrarian economy to an industry-based economy with an increase in labor productivity leading to improved living standards. This development was further enhanced by the invention of steam engine technology by English inventor Thomas Newcomen in 1712, which was further developed by Scottish inventor James Watt in the 1770s. Steam engine technology was an integral part of the Industrial Revolution in late eighteenth-century England, and it had a spillover effect on the rapid growth of industrial capitalism to other Western European neighbor nations, such as France, Belgium, and Germany. This spillover effect eventually exported to the northeastern region of the United States at the beginning of the twentieth century. The Second Industrial Revolution in the United States made America the industrial capital of the world. The power of free-market enterprise became the key driving force toward rapid economic growth and prosperity, with increasing living standards for workers and owners of industries on both sides of the Atlantic.

The economic boom and rise of living standards in Europe and the United States continued at a rapid rate during the first three decades of the twentieth century. However, the rapid industrialization without the US government's legislative control caused an economic boom-and-bust cycle in the late 1920s. The continued boom of the economy in the 1920s brought skyrocketing stock prices and enormous profits for financial and industrial corporations. In response to this rapid rate of industrial and manufacturing growth, consumers and savers invested their savings into stocks and bonds issued by corporations. As a result, the stock prices far exceeded their intrinsic value (the actual value as opposed to market value). The resulting speculative bubble on Wall Street eventually burst with the stock market crash of October 29, 1929. The stock market crash was mainly attributed to massive sales of stocks because of a loss of confidence in equity values, along with an excessive inventory of manufactured goods and appliances. The stock market crash was followed by massive unemployment and closure of thousands of banks and financial institutions across the United States. This was the beginning of the Great Depression of the 1930s, which lasted until 1939; it ended with the outbreak of World War II in Europe.

Despite the increase of the unemployment rate to over 25%, along with a significant decline in industrial production and massive bank failures between 1929 and 1931, then president Herbert Hoover still believed in free-market capitalism and did not intervene in the market to deal with the crisis. However, by the end of 1932, the US economy faced the worst economic depression in its history. Given the severity of the social and economic crisis, the Democratic presidential candidate, Franklin D. Roosevelt (as known as FDR), made campaign promise that the government would play an active role in ending the Great Depression. After winning the election, President Roosevelt declared his economic reform called the **New Deal** with the promise of full government intervention to end the economic crisis. The declaration of his New Deal was historically known as the birth of **Keynesian economics**, after the English economist John Maynard Keynes. Keynes actually pioneered the development of modern macroeconomics by calling for direct involvement of government fiscal and monetary policy prescriptions to save the economy from depression. The theories and applications of Keynesian economics were outlined in his book *The General Theory of Employment, Interest and Money* published in 1936. Keynes's recommendations were a major departure from the classical economic principle of laissez-faire. The case for government intervention is discussed in more detail in Section 3.3.

3.3. The Sources of Free-Market Failure and Their Effects on Society

It is evident from the discussion in Section 3.2 that the efficiency of the free market system measured by Pareto efficiency conditions is based on three restrictive assumptions: *perfect knowledge and information* about technology of production and products' quality and utility by both producers and consumers, *absence of external costs* of production and distribution, and *distribution of income* to labor and capital as equitable if not equal. However, those restrictive assumptions may not be valid most of the time. Therefore, the Pareto efficiency criteria do fail even under the free market system. The economic crisis of the Great Depression in the 1930s was an example of massive market failure in recent memory. Some of the key reasons for a market failure such as the Great Depression are as follows:

- The emergence of a market power, such as monopoly or oligopoly
- The rise of externalities, such as loss of consumer confidence or loss of profit
- Inventory accumulation of manufactured goods
- Information asymmetry and its effect on moral hazard

Given the factors for market failure, the economy loses its market efficiency. The loss of efficiency in production and distribution of income is expected to have negative effects on economic well-being for the whole society. Examples of some of those negative effects would be an increase in unemployment, decline in living standards, unequal distribution of income, social and political unrest, rise in crime, and uncertainty about the future. The foundation of modern macroeconomics developed by Keynes in the 1930s was the theory of economic policy in which an active role of government is recommended to fine-tune the market. The case for a government role is explained in Section 3.4.

3.4. The Case for Government Intervention in the Free Market System and Its Effects on Society

3.4.1. The Great Depression of the 1930s and FDR's New Deal

Keynes, the founder of modern macroeconomics, explained that the Great Depression of the 1930s was not caused by the failure of capitalism but was due to a deficiency in the aggregate demand in the free market system. To increase the aggregate demand, Keynes suggested that the government become involved in public-sector spending and thus create jobs. The details of the Keynesian macroeconomic model are discussed in Chapter 6. For now, it is important to mention that FDR adopted the active role of government intervention based on Keynesian theory in 1932 in his economic policy reform called the New Deal. The New Deal was the first experiment with a fiscal policy by the government to combat the Great Depression—the Keynesian economy was born. The key policy prescription of the New Deal was to invest heavily in physical infrastructure, such as roads and highways, hydraulic power plants, railways, and other transportation infrastructure, as well as modernizing airports and railway stations and building and repairing dams and bridges. In addition, new financial legislation was enacted to protect depositors' money in banks by creating the **Federal Deposit Insurance Corporation (FDIC)** and by separating investment banks from commercial banks so that personal savings could not be used in volatile and risky equity markets.

3.4.2. Market Power and the Antitrust Act

As discussed earlier, the existence of monopolies and oligopolies seems to have a negative effect on efficiency in the form of charging higher prices for consumer products, paying unfair wages, producing less, inefficient use of resources, and abnormal profits. To minimize these problems of market power, the government played a significant role by enacting antitrust legislation. The **Sherman Antitrust Act of 1890**, with several modifications in subsequent decades, has significantly reduced the externalities caused by market powers in the US economy.

3.4.3. Externalities and Government Legislation

Economists define externalities as the external cost or external benefit to a party caused by a system of production and distribution, making that party either better off or worse off without being paid or compensated for the loss or gain. This externality concept is also known as the spillover effect. The gain from the spillover effect is called **positive externality** and the loss from it is called **negative externality**. A classic example of negative externality is air pollution caused by the industrial use of fossil fuels, such as oil, coal, natural gas, and

Figure 3.2 Internalization of the Externality of Pollution

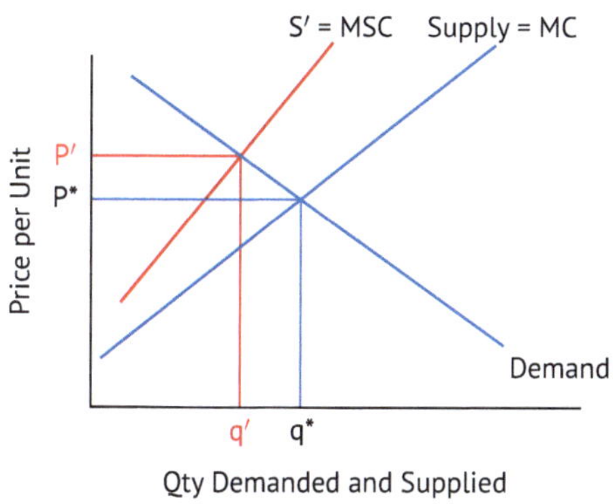

petroleum. Since increasing air pollution caused by emissions of carbon dioxide is blamed in part for global warming, the **Clean Air Act** passed by the US government enacted in the 1990s was a major initiative to internalize the level of externalities caused by rapid industrialization. Figure 3.2 is an example of the process to internalize the externalities of pollution through different legislative measures.

In Figure 3.2, suppose the supply curve and demand curve for a hypothetical market for X produces quantity q* with its equilibrium price at P*. The possible pollution caused by this equilibrium position of the market would be an example of negative externality in the form of emitting carbon dioxide. Since air pollution causes health hazards to all the people in the affected area, the equilibrium price and quantity combination at q* and P* do not reflect the true cost to society at that marginal value. Assuming that the demand side is equal to social marginal utility or marginal benefit, but the marginal cost of production on the supply side is less than the external cost to society, government legislation is needed to minimize the social marginal cost paid by both buyers and sellers in the market. By imposing government legislation that restricts the amount of pollution by producers, the supply curve can be shifted to the left until a new equilibrium is reached at the combination of P′ and q′, where MSB = MSC. This outcome from government intervention is called the internalization of externality.

There are a number of ways the government does internalize the externality of pollution or water contamination caused by rapid industrialization. Some of those actions include the imposition of pollution taxes, pollution quotas, marketable permits, and penalties. Although all of these legislative measures are not equally effective or efficient, it is imperative to implement these important measures to minimize market failure caused by externalities and thus maximize the social marginal benefit. Another example of negative externalities is overfishing in common-pool resources, such as in oceans, lakes, rivers, and ponds, which can harm marine biology and cause severe environmental degradation. Other examples of negative externalities are extraction of contaminated sludge and related by-products caused by steel mills, textile mills, oil refineries, chemical factories, fertilizer industries, nuclear waste, motor vehicles, and electricity grids—just to name a few.

The example of positive externality is the spillover benefit a society gets at a higher value than the equilibrium price determined by the market system. Investing in science and education is a great example of generating positive externality. Educated individuals and new scientific inventions and innovation generate more economic benefits to society as a whole when compared to the benefits received by individuals in the form of increased income or by institutions in the form of increased profits. Internalization of positive externality is different than what is illustrated for negative externality in Figure 3.2. In case of positive externality, the demand curve needs to be shifted to the right so that MSB = MSC—the quantity produced would increase at a higher social price. If positive externality comes from the cost side of competing corporations, then the S curve has to shift to the right with MSC = MSB at a lower social price and higher quantity of production. By the same token, if negative externality occurs on the demand side, then the demand curve has to be shifted to the left with a lower social price and less quantity of output produced. To summarize the process of internalization of externality by regulatory measures of the government, the four possible graphical illustrations can be made as follows:

- Negative externality in production: shift S curve to the left
- Negative externality in consumption: shift D curve to the left
- Positive externality in production: shift S curve to the right
- Positive externality in consumption: shift D curve to the right

The last section of this chapter lays out the arguments for and against government intervention in a free market system.

3.5. Pros and Cons of Government Intervention in the Free Market System

Based on the discussion in the previous four sections of this chapter, students should now be familiar with the theoretical foundations of the free market system called market capitalism. However, the theory of market capitalism is based on certain restrictive assumptions that may not be the case in real-world economics when the market fails to accomplish the objectives of economic outcomes under the utopian model of demand and supply behavior. Students have also learned how to measure the efficiency of production and distribution of output under those assumptions of the market system. However, those efficiencies cannot be achieved in cases of market failure.

Therefore, when the market fails because of the existence of the market powers and externalities discussed earlier, government intervention is recommended. However, the role of the government in cases of market failure is not to eliminate the market but to stimulate market activities by restoring consumer and investor confidence. That is the core foundation of modern macroeconomics. Despite the continued success of Keynesian economic policy adopted in most countries since 1936, the debate over the role of government and its effectiveness is still very much active in both academia and the political spectrum on both sides of the Atlantic. Highlights of the debate are summarized in Table 3.1.

The debate over the arguments for and against government intervention in a free market system has been going on since the publication of Adam Smith's book *The Wealth of Nations* in 1776. The concept of laissez-faire economics is still popular in the United States and some parts of Europe. As a matter of fact, this debate has split the political culture in both Europe and North America into two major ideological factions in the field of politics and political economy: the conservatives versus the liberals. The conservatives advocate for less and less government intervention for growth and production efficiency. On the other hand, the

Table 3.1: Pros and Cons of Government Intervention in a Free Market

Cases for Government Intervention	Cases Against Government Intervention
1. Assumptions of perfect competition are not realistic	1. Market failure is temporary, and the market will correct itself in the long run without government intervention
2. Market power makes allocation inefficient and distorts resource allocation	2. Market power is capable of maximizing efficiency in production and allocation of resources in the long run
3. Externalities must be internalized by government regulations to maximize the social marginal benefit and minimize the social marginal cost	3. Government regulations make production costs increase, cause cost inefficiencies, and reduce production and employment
4. Government policy helps distributional equity	4. Intervention of high taxes to pay for welfare reduces the incentive to work and invest
5. Restores consumer and investor confidence	5. Loss of confidence is temporary, and it restores in the long run
6. Government helps the poor and low income with welfare benefits as a social responsibility	6. Self-interest is the guiding principle to reduce poverty and increase productivity
7. Controls inflation and recession	7. It destabilizes the conditions of inflation and causes an unemployment crisis
8. Keynes argued that wage and price are sticky without government intervention during an economic crisis, all would be dead in the long run	8. Wage and price flexibility would restore full employment in a short period of time

liberals argue for more government involvement to combat inflation and recession, ensure safety of consumers, decrease poverty, reduce income inequality, and reduce discrimination based on ethnic and national origins. This ongoing debate shows no signs of slowing down anytime soon. In the United States, society as a whole is caught up in this political divide, overshadowing the real economic agenda. Nevertheless, the role of government policy is not expected to decline in the near future. Instead, it is expected to strengthen further to support the rapid rise of new technology and the knowledge-based economy to compete with emerging economies in Asia and the Pacific regions. Further details of this ongoing debate will be discussed in subsequent chapters of this text.

Chapter Summary

Section 3.1 introduced the criteria to measure the efficiency of allocating resources and its connection with equity. Efficiency in general is also categorized into two segments: efficiency in production and efficiency in distribution. The criteria for measuring these two types of efficiency are as follows:

1. Efficiency in allocative distribution: Price per unit (P) = Marginal Utility (MU) = Marginal cost (MC)
2. Efficiency in allocative production: Price per unit (P) = Marginal Revenue (MR) = Minimum average total cost (ATC)

Combining both the demand and supply sides of the two criteria, the complete Pareto condition can be rewritten with the following equation:

P = MU = MC = MR = Minimum ATC

Basic assumptions for the efficiency criteria for validity are

- perfect information about the goods and services to both consumers and producers,
- technology of production is the most efficient to produce at minimum ATC, and,
- no external costs are involved.

The real-world example of measuring these criteria is illustrated in Figure 3.1 in the context of soybean oil and corn oil production and distribution in the US market. However, it is also mentioned that even the state of perfect competition may not necessarily satisfy these criteria of measuring efficiency because of the existence of income and wealth inequality and the externality of production and consumption.

Section 3.2 focused on explaining the theoretical foundation of the free market system, known as laissez-faire or capitalism. This section introduced a bit of history on the concept of laissez-faire in reference to Adam Smith's theory of capitalism outlined in *The Wealth of Nations*. The theory of Smith's free market system also seems to be consistent with the efficiency criteria of P = MU = MC = MR = Minimum ATC discussed in Section 3.1. Historically speaking, the free market system of capitalism without government intervention actually emerged during the Industrial Revolution in England in the late 18th century. The spillover effect of England's Industrial Revolution paved the way for the Second Industrial Revolution in the United States during the twentieth century with continued expansion of economic growth and prosperity in most of the nations in Western Europe and North America until the Great Depression of the 1930s.

The Great Depression was primarily caused by excessive inventory of production, loss of profit and consumer confidence, information asymmetry of market values of equity and financial assets, and subsequent stock market crash in 1929. To cope with the Great Depression and an unemployment rate of 25%, then president Franklin D. Roosevelt adopted the Keynesian model of macroeconomics with active government intervention for economic recovery. The economic policy undertaken and implemented by FDR was dubbed the "New Deal" and marked the birth of Keynesian economics as an alternative to the laissez-faire doctrine of classical economics. This was the beginning of the modern macroeconomics institution that is still very much active today in 2019. Keynes explained that active government intervention in fine-tuning the economic depression was needed not because of the failure of capitalism but because of the demand deficiency in the market system. He advocated to boost the aggregate demand side by active fiscal policy of increasing government spending to create jobs for unemployed workers and thus rebound the economy.

Section 3.3 explained the sources of market failure that caused the Great Depression of the 1930s. The criteria of market efficiency described in Section 3.2 seemed to fail during the 1920s economic boom-and-bust cycle, as attributed to the following factors.

- The emergence of a market power, such as a monopoly or oligopoly
- The rise of externalities, such as the loss of consumer confidence or loss of profit
- Inventory accumulation of manufactured goods
- Information asymmetry and its effect on moral hazard

The foundation of modern macroeconomics developed by Keynes is the fiscal policy framework for fine-tuning market failure caused by the previously mentioned reasons that caused the Great Depression of 1930s. Section 3.4 explained the rationale for active economic policy by the government when addressing the issues of market failure.

Section 3.4 explained the Keynesian argument for the expansion of government spending to boost market demand. The Keynesian argument for expansionary fiscal policy in the form of massive government spending to create jobs highly dominated the economic policy framework under the New Deal in 1933. The New Deal is still the dominant blueprint of economic policy today not only for the US economic policy institution but also most of the countries in the world. The other legislative actions undertaken as part of the New Deal in the 1930s were the antitrust act against monopoly and oligopoly power of corporations, creation of the FDIC to insure bank deposits by the public, environmental measures to internalize the externality caused by pollution, and other related measures for economic growth and stability. The process of internalization of such externality caused by market power was explained and illustrated in Figure 3.2.

Section 3.5 explained the pros and cons of government intervention under the New Deal and afterward. Since the debate over the extent of government intervention in handling the business cycle fluctuations of market failure is far greater than ever, the arguments for and against government policy intervention are listed in Table 3.1. Students are encouraged to read the pros and cons thoroughly to understand the complexity of government intervention in a free market system composed of private enterprises like the one in the United States.

Application Activities

Q1. While defining the concept of market efficiency, briefly describe the theoretical basis for measuring efficiency under a perfectly competitive market.

Q2. What are the assumptions made in answering Q1? What happens if those assumptions are not valid?

Q3. What are the sources of market failure? Provide a real-world example.

Q4. What is the rationale for government intervention in economic and market activities?

Q5. Briefly describe the causes of the Great Depression of the 1930s.

Q6. What is Keynesian economics? How did it combat the Great Depression of the 1930s?

Hint: it is not necessary to mention any technical aspects of the model.

Q7. In your own opinion, provide at least two pros and two cons of government intervention in a free market system with examples.

Chapter 4

Application of Demand and Supply to Measure the Economics of the Retirement and Health-Care Industries with Case Studies in the US Economy

Learning Objectives

As they read the chapter, students will learn the following:

- Demand and supply model in microeconomics versus demand and supply model in macroeconomics
- Application of demand and supply of pensions for an aging population and its policy implications
- Examples of the general economics of the health-care industry and society
- Health-care industry in the context of macroeconomics

4.1. Demand and Supply Model in Microeconomics and Macroeconomics

4.1.1. Demand and Supply Model in Microeconomics

As explained in Chapter 2 with an example of the housing market in the city of Boston, the demand and supply behavior in microeconomics focuses on individual goods and services bought and sold in the market. Those goods and services have their own prices per unit determined by the interaction between market demand and market supply. In general, the demand and supply functions not only depend on the price of goods or services but also many other factors that indirectly or directly affect demand and supply. The functional relationship between quantity demanded for a commodity, say X, and quantity supplied of the same commodity X is given next.

Suppose you have a commodity X and its price/unit is Px; to determine the market equilibrium price and quantity based on basic principles of economics, you will use the law of demand and the law of supply.

Demand function Dx = f (Px, Py, Pz, income, taste, social and political status, war, etc.), where Px = price of x, Py = price of y, and Pz = price of z. Variables y and z could be substitutes and/or complementary goods.

Note: Dx = f(...) means the demand for commodity X is a function of ... as a general expression of the demand function.

Supply function Sx = g (Px, Py, Pz, cost of production, weather condition, war, income growth of consumers, technological advancement, expected profits, etc.)

Note: Sx = g(...) means the supply for commodity X is a function of ... as a general expression of the supply function.

The law of demand states that if Px increases, quantity demanded will decrease and vice versa, ceteris paribus (other variables like Py, Pz, ... stay the same). This means the D curve is downward sloping, and any price change would alter the quantity demanded in the opposite direction moving along the same D curve.

The law of supply states that if Px increases, quantity supplied will increase and vice versa, ceteris paribus (other variables like Py, Pz, ... stay with the same values). It means the S curve is upward sloping and any price change would alter the quantity supplied in the same direction moving along the same S curve.

It is important to note that when ceteris paribus assumption doesn't hold, changes in the D and S curves (as opposed to changes in quantity demanded and quantity supplied) mean shifting the D curve and/or S curve (instead of moving along the same curve). This means that the shift of the D and S curves does not happen by changing their prices but by changes in other factors, such as Py, Pz, or income (for a D-curve shift), and by changes in the cost of production, expected profits, tax policy, etc. (for an S-curve shift).

For a demand-side example, if X and Y are tea and coffee, respectively, then a change in Px will change the quantity demanded for tea (Dx), and it will move along the same D curve. But if the Py (price of coffee) changes, then Dx (for tea) will shift either left or right, depending on the direction of change for the price of coffee. In this case, X and Y are substitutes. For example, if price of tea increases, some tea drinkers may switch to drink coffee as a relatively inexpensive substitute. As a result, the demand for coffee will change by shifting to the right.

For a supply-side example, if the price of oranges changes, then the quantity of oranges supplied will move along the same S curve. But if inclement weather adversely affects orange production, then the supply curve will shift to the left. For tea or coffee case, if the cost of supplying coffee or tea increases, the supply will change by shifting to the left. In either case, the equilibrium price and quantity will change because of shifts in the demand or supply curve (or both) to end up with a new point of intersection between demand and supply.

Another real-world example would be the changes in the equilibrium prices of Starbucks (SB) coffee and Dunkin' Donuts (DD) coffee in the New England coffee market where these two top brands are close substitutes. On June 7, 2018, several news media outlets announced that SB raised the prices of its coffee drinks across the United States by 10 to 20 cents. The company explained that the price hike was due to the rise in operating costs. Given the explanation of demand and supply behavior, it is easy to expect that the price of DD coffee will increase as well. Although most customers of SB will not be swayed to go to DD, a considerable number of SB customers will change to DD coffee to adjust their expenses because of a limited budget. That means the demand curve for DD coffee is expected to shift out to the right given the supply curve of DD coffee. As a result, the new equilibrium price and quantity would be at a higher point of intersection between the new demand shift along the same supply curve.

Only the equilibrium point between supply and demand will clear the market. Every other point will either create a surplus or a shortage, and price movement will continue until the equilibrium point is reached. As the curve shifts, the equilibrium point moves from one point to another.

4.1.2. Aggregate Demand and Aggregate Supply Curve Model in Macroeconomics

Unlike the demand and supply structure defined and explained in microeconomics, demand and supply in macroeconomics are structured and analyzed differently. In macroeconomics, the demand and supply functions represent all goods and services produced and consumed in aggregate. That is why, instead of using the term demand and supply, economists use the terms aggregate demand (AD) and aggregate supply (AS) so that the model structure includes the transactions of all goods and services for the entire economy. To understand this distinction between the microeconomic and macroeconomic models, the conventional equations for AD and AS are stated next:

$$\mathbf{AD = C + I + G + (EX - IM),}$$

Where, C = Consumption expenditure

I = Investment expenditure

G = Government expenditure

EX = Exports expenditure demanded by buyers abroad

IM = Imports expenditure demanded by domestic buyers.

$$\textbf{AS = Gross Domestic Product (GDP)} = P_1Q_1 + P_2Q_2 + P_3Q_3 + \ldots + PnQn = \sum PiQi,$$

where i = 1 to n number of goods and services.

The aggregate supply equation involves adding the quantities of all final goods and services produced and then multiplying each by its respective per unit price for a particular calendar year; this results in the total market value of final goods and services produced. The prices for each of those final goods and services are considered to be the current market prices. However, the current market price is not the price level that is used in the AD-AS model structure. Economists instead use a pricing technique called price index or price level. The price level is an estimated index price determined by using a ratio of nominal GDP (NGDP; calculated by the AS equation at the current price) to real GDP (RGDP; calculated by using a base-year price). The base-year prices are selected by economists who consider a year in the most recent past when the price was normal without inflation increases.

For example, suppose in 2018 the NGDP estimated by the AS equation is about $20.5802 trillion and the RGDP estimated by using a base year of 2012 as $\sum(P_{2009} * Q_{2017})$ is $18.6382 trillion. Then the price index, which is also called the GDP deflator (GDPD), would be estimated as GDPD for 2018 = (NGDP/RGDP) *100 = (20,580,200/18,638,200) *100.

Or, GDPD for 2018 = 110.42

The index price is used as the price level indicator for the entire economy in the AD-AS model. If that index increases beyond a considerable level of the economy, then the economy is in a state of inflation. If the index starts declining, then the economy is in a state of deflation. Chapter 6 will provide a more detailed discussion of measuring inflation and deflation. For now, Figure 4.1 illustrates the AD-AS model of macroeconomics.

Figure 4.1 illustrates the basic structural model of macroeconomics. The vertical axis displays the price level, with 2012 as the base-year price. The price index equals 100 because NGDP and RGDP are identical for the base year. For 2018, the RGDP is $18.6382 ($Y_2$) trillion at the equilibrium point E_2, and RGDP in 2012 is $16.1970 ($Y_1$) trillion at the equilibrium point E_1. Figure 4.1 also explains how equilibrium RGDP can be increased by shifting the AD to the right by increasing any of the components of AD, such as C, I, G or (EX−IM) and thus creating employment opportunities (an increase in RGDP always creates more job opportunities and helps lower the unemployment rate). This expansion of the AD curve by shifting to the right is called Keynesian demand-side economic expansion through fiscal or monetary policy action. It is also possible to shift the AS curve to the right, called supply-side economics, to increase RGDP and thus create more jobs. The details of Keynesian demand-side macroeconomics and supply-side macroeconomics are discussed in Chapter 6.

Figure 4.1 AD-AS Supply Model

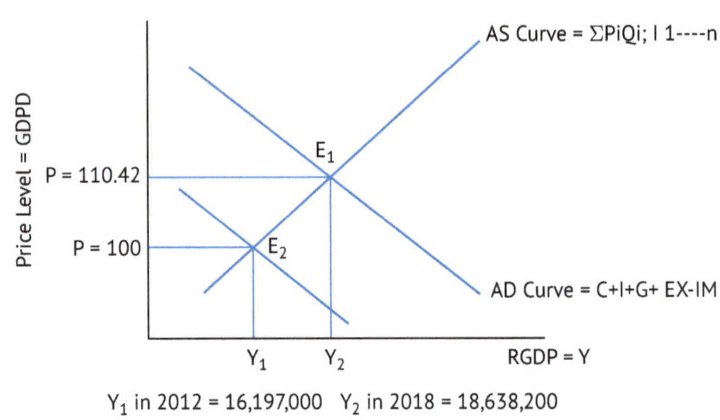

It is also worth noting that the approximate GDP contributions by each of the components of AD for the US economy are as follows:

C = Consumption expenditure = 67%
I = Investment expenditure = 18%
G = Government expenditure = 23%
EX–IM = Net export = −8%

From the relative contributions to GDP by each of the components of the AD for the over \$19 trillion economy, some implications can be made here. First, US consumers contribute more than two-thirds of the economy (67% of total GDP). Second, private investment and business contribution are much less than the government-sector contribution (18% vs. 23% respectively). Therefore, the US government plays a significant role in the entire economy for raising GDP. It also shows that over 108% of economic activities come from domestic sources, implying that the US economic structure is predominantly domestic based with relatively low dependence on foreign trade. The negative 8% net export balance indicates that the US economy imports much more than it exports. The economics of this Keynesian macroeconomic model and the role of the US fiscal budget expenses and tax policies are discussed in more detail in Chapters 6 and 9. The next section of this chapter focuses on the economics of the health-care industry as an important part of both microeconomics and macroeconomics because of the significant increases in health-care expenditure as a percent of GDP (17.9% of GDP in 2017) in the last few decades.[1] It is also predicted that the healthcare expenditure will reach up to 19.4% of GDP in the next decade,

4.2. Application of Demand and Supply of Health Care and Pensions for an Aging Population and Its Policy Implications

This section focuses on one of the fastest-growing sectors in the economy not only in the United States but also in almost every industrialized country in the world. In newly emerging economies, such as China and India, health care has become one of the top economic, social, and political agendas because of its importance to improving the status of human capital. The services under health care are multidimensional, and they include doctor's visits, surgical and preventive treatments, prescription drugs, cancer and cardiovascular treatments, vaccinations, and treatment of other epidemic diseases. These services are vital for good health, which contributes to the social and economic well-being of citizens. Maintenance of good health is also essential for improving the quality of education and productivity for the labor force, leading to faster economic growth and prosperity. For the United States, the total expenditures for health-care industries were estimated at 17.9% of GDP in 2017.[2] Table 4.1 indicates the rise of health-care expenses for the US economy since 1960.

The data in Table 4.1 indicate a significant rise in health-care expenditure, along with its rising contribution to total GDP between 1960 and 2017. For example, health-care expenditures increased from \$27 billion in 1960 to \$3.4921 trillion in 2017, which accounts for an increase of 12,833% over 66 years. The annual increase of NHE is rising more rapidly than the long-term GDP growth rate of 3%. Per capita increase of NHE in the same 66-year period

---

1 Office of the Actuary. "CMS Office of the Actuary Releases 2017-2026 Projections of National Health Expenditures." Centers for Medicare & Medicaid Services. February 14, 2018. https://www.cms.gov/newsroom/press-releases/cms-office-actuary-releases-2017-2026-projections-national-health-expenditures.

2 Ibid.

Table 4.1: US Health-Care Expenditure Data Since 1960

	1960	1980	2000	2017
National health-care expenditure (NHE) in billions	$27.2	$255.3	$1,369.1	$3,492.1
Population in millions	186	230	282	325
GDP in billions	543.3	2862.5	10,284.8	19,519.4
Annual % change in NHE	7.1 (between 1960 and 1961)	15.3	7.2	4.2
Per capita NHE	146	1,108	4,855	10,739
NHE as % of GDP	5.0	8.9	13.3	17.9

Source: https://www.cms.gov/Research-Statistics-Data-and-Systems/Statistics-Trends-and-Reports/NationalHealthExpendData/NationalHealthAccountsHistorical.html

shows an increase of 7,255%, from $146 in 1960 to $10,739 in 2017. The skyrocketing rise in health-care costs is also reflected in the percent share of GDP, increasing from 5% in 1960 to 17.9% in 2017 with over $4 trillion of the $19 trillion economy. Despite this significant share of GDP, the health-care system in the United States was not available to everyone until 2010 with the passage of landmark legislation—the Patient Protection and Affordable Care Act or simply the Affordable Care Act (ACA), which is also known as Obamacare because of the initiative undertaken by then president Barack Obama under intense opposition from Republican legislators in the US Congress.

Before the ACA legislation was signed into law in March 2010, there were over 45 million Americans without health insurance coverage, and over 80% of them were elderly citizens. The evidence presented by several studies indicates that the reason for such a vast portion of the population were without health insurance coverage was due to the high cost of insurance premiums for private individuals. Since the implementation of ACA with its mandatory provision to purchase health insurance with government subsidy, over 30 million Americans were covered by health insurance in eight years (2010–2018). Given the controversy and political rhetoric against Obamacare, there is a very active debate about whether to repeal Obamacare and replace it with an alternative or allow its expansion to include more uninsured Americans to guarantee health-care coverage. The two key points surrounding the controversy are the rising costs for federal and state governments to subsidize the coverage and the mandatory sign-up with a provision of penalties of about $700 per individual or 2.5% of income, whichever is lower, for not getting the coverage. Given this controversial issue on the universal health-care provision of the ACA, it is important to look at the current structure of health-care coverage and its payment systems to understand the significant role of both federal and state governments in covering the rising costs of health care.

After the ACA was implemented in 2010, the payment systems for health-care coverage in the United States were expanded by four main categories: employer-provided health-care coverage (34%), Medicare (age 65 and above; 20%), Medicaid (low-income individuals and families; 17%), and individual private out-of-pocket (11%). The sponsoring agencies for these four categories of coverage are the federal government and individuals (28%), private business enterprises (20%), and state and local governments (17%). The reasons for the continuing rise in health-care costs at a rate more than any other service in the US economy are as follows:

The rise of an aging population: According to data published by the Centers for Medicare and Medicaid Services, in 2016, over 55 million Americans were enrolled in Medicare (age 65+). The health-care cost of using special medical technology and medical equipment for the treatment of elderly patients was estimated to be about six times higher than for younger generations. With the baby boomer generation (born between 1946 and 1964) entering retirement in 2010, Medicare expenses are expected to increase in coming decades.

Improved health conditions and life expectancy at birth: With increases in life expectancy at birth and a significant reduction of infant mortality over the last 100 years, American life expectancy at birth has increased to over 80 years in 2016 as compared to 51 years in 1900.[3] The life expectancy for individuals with good health over 65 is over 85 years for males and over 90 years for females. The statistics clearly indicate that there will be a further rise in the cost of medical expenses for an increasing number of elderly citizens in the decades to come.

Decrease in out-of-pocket health-care expenses: The third-party payment system through health insurance companies for hospital care, doctor's visits, preventive care, and prescription drugs are considered to be one of the key reasons for the rising cost of health-care coverage. For example, employers in most cases pay around 80% of the total premium for their employees to purchase insurance coverage. The other 20% is paid by employees, who receive a tax deduction for the entire amount of their premiums. Under Medicare, Medicaid, and Obamacare, the cost is covered almost 100% by government agencies. This third-party payment process has significantly decreased out-of-pocket expenses from a 50% share in 1965 to only 11% in 2017.[4] The demand and supply behavior illustrated in Figure 4.2 helps explain how the rising cost of health-care services is partly attributed to the third-party payment system.

Figure 4.2 Demand and Supply Behavior of the Third-Party Payment System

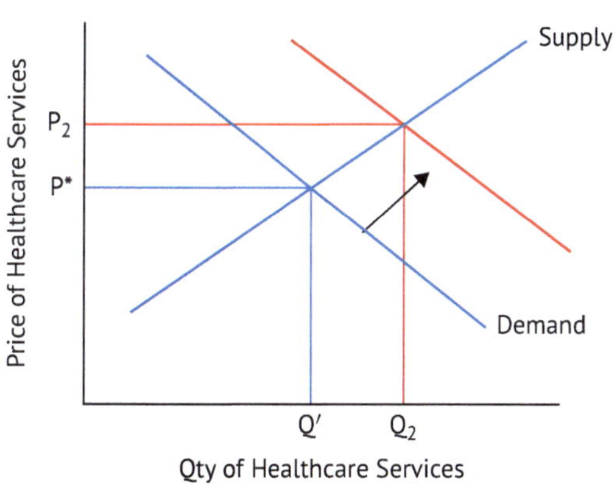

Figure 4.2 illustrates that with a full percentage of the out-of-pocket price at P*, individuals would receive a Q* level of health-care services. However, with a third-party payment system

3 "Social Security," Social Security History, accessed November 21, 2019, https://www.ssa.gov/history/lifeexpect.html)

4 Centers for Medicare and Medicaid Services

of almost 100% of costs covered by insurance companies, the demand for health-care services would shift to the right to settle at a higher equilibrium price and quantity of health-care services at P2 and Q2, respectively. The way insurance companies make a profit is by pooling hundreds and thousands of customers under the same plan and thereby minimizing the risk of reimbursing every individual. This is because only a small fraction of the insured in the pool requires extensive health-care services.

4.2.1. Policy Implications for Rising the Cost of Health Care

The previous explanations for the rapidly increasing trend of health-care costs since the 1960s help students of economics and business realize the importance of the health-care industry in the context of both microeconomics and macroeconomics. According to recent data from the US Bureau of Labor Statistics, the health-care industry and its related affiliations have become the largest employers in many states in the country. While there has been rapid growth in industries related to service and entertainment, knowledge-based research and development, and biotechnology, the health-care industry is expected to grow at a much faster rate than any other industry in the coming decades. In addition, the rising trend of an aging population with relatively good health means that the cost burden of providing health care to the elderly is expected to surpass the tax revenue of social security, Medicare, and Medicaid from the working population. The Congressional Budget Office (CBO) has predicted that much of the growing cost of Medicare and social security payments will be attributed to the aging baby boomer generation. The CBO has also predicted that the federal deficit may go up by 150% of GDP by 2047 if health-care pension costs plus debt service payments (interest payment on government debt) continue to rise at their current rates. This means that social security and Medicare funds are expected to run out by the year 2047. Therefore, it is important to examine the macroeconomic policy implications of health-care spending and pension funds before it is too late. More details of different aspects of policy strategy are discussed in later chapters; however, Section 4.3 will focus on positive and negative externalities of the existing health-care market in the United States.

4.3. Examples of General Economics of the Health-Care Industry

Since the health-care industry and its affiliated organizations contributed almost 18% of the total GDP of about $19 trillion in 2017, the market system of health-care services is far from perfect. Given the enormous size of the industry, along with highly regulated and government-sponsored programs, such as Medicare, Medicaid, and the ACA, the health-care industry in the United States is much more complicated than in any other industrialized country in the world. For example, Canada has a single-payer system paid by the government to all privately held health-care providers through very high taxes. On the other hand, the health-care system in the United Kingdom is fully socialized and provided directly by the government via high tax rates for the working labor force. Japan's health-care system—universal health-care—provides coverage for everyone and is sponsored by both government and private institutions. The system in Japan is very similar to the current US system. The only difference is the much higher premium paid by individuals in Japan. Given the complexity of US health-care economics, the insights provided next are from real-world examples of the theoretical understanding of the theory of positive and negative externalities discussed in Chapter 3.

4.3.1. Issues with Data Sharing and Information Asymmetry

Given the enormous burden of health-care costs in the United States, there is growing demand from both politicians and health-care consumers for better-quality services at lower costs. In economics, it is called measurable cost-effectiveness. Because of the complexity of the health-care system and the strict privacy legislation from the US government, data sharing and data availability are among the greatest challenges in health care. For example, information on sources regarding difficult diseases, such as cancer, cardiovascular issues, and deadly virus attacks on infants and the elderly, are not easy to collect in advance. Also, information regarding life expectancy at birth, infant mortality rates, occupational hazards, genetic diseases, substance abuse issues, and women's health are not accurate in most cases. Equipment, professional staff, and doctors are not equally distributed and placed to match patients' needs. The level of information availability and sharing also varies from region to region in the country. These ongoing problems with information gaps and information inaccuracy are called **information asymmetry**—a concept originally developed by George Akerlof in 1970 in the context of the used car market, where the information gap between buyers and sellers drives the price low, leaving behind only "lemons" (vehicles with significant mechanical issues).

The concept of information asymmetry is very much applicable to the health-care industry because the beneficiaries of health-care services know more about their health conditions than health insurance companies do. This information asymmetry causes problems not only for health-care providers and health insurance companies but also for all types of insurance providers. When there is a low level of information asymmetry, the expected profit by insurance companies can be more easily determined. However, the greater the information gap, the more degree of uncertainty insurance companies face in predicting their expected payoffs (revenue from premiums minus cost of claims). Unlike fire insurance for houses or auto insurance for cars (which are easy to predict with a low probability of loss), information asymmetry in health-care insurance is much higher. The two most common consequences of information asymmetry are **adverse selection** and **moral hazard**. These two consequences were the key factors for the financial collapse on Wall Street in 2008 and the rise of insurance costs in the health-care industry in recent decades. They are briefly explained with examples next.

Adverse selection in health-care industries. Because health-care service recipients are more knowledgeable about their health conditions than the insurance companies, the adverse selection of insured customers with more illnesses is highly likely. In that case, insurance companies may end up paying more medical claims than they receive from all premiums. If the premium were increased to cover the rising costs, it could cause more problems because customers with good health would forgo the purchase of insurance with higher premiums. As a result, adverse selection may cause more financial drain for insurance companies. To avoid the problem of adverse selection in the auto insurance industry, legislation mandating the purchase of auto insurance by all vehicle owners is a common practice in many states. A similar mandate was included in the ACA (Obamacare) discussed in the previous section. But the individual mandate under Obamacare has caused huge controversy nationwide, bringing the issue all the way to the Supreme Court.

Moral hazard in health-care industries. Moral hazard is a negative outcome on the financial condition of an industry caused by excessive adverse selections (explained earlier). For financial industry supporting Wall Street banks and holding companies, the rise in adverse selection from information asymmetry may cause financial collapse—an example of moral hazard. Adverse selection can lead to a similar result in the health-care industry. For example, mandatory health insurance under Obamacare has included over 30 million Americans who did not have health insurance coverage before the law went into effect in 2010. After the law was enacted, many of the insured individuals tended to change their behavior by making frequent visits to doctors, which they would not do without Obamacare coverage. There is also a likelihood of more individuals becoming ill because they may have less concern about health maintenance than they would have if they were uninsured. This change of behavior raises the cost of health care significantly for both insurance companies and government agencies. The moral hazard of Obamacare was never intended under the law, but it comes about as a result of adverse selection, which was unavoidable due to the mandatory purchase of insurance provision under the ACA. One way to deal with this problem is to increase the co-payments and deductibles, thereby slightly raising the costs paid by individuals.

Similar incidents might happen when there is an increase in the number of auto accidents after enacting a law that mandates all drivers wear seat belts. Although a mandatory seat belt law would not be intended to promote careless driving, the law could cause drivers to become less careful because of the perceived protection of wearing a seat belt. The increase in the number of car accidents after the implementation of the mandatory seatbelt law would be an example of moral hazard.

4.3.2. Positive and Negative Externalities in Health-Care Services

In addition to the concept of information asymmetry and its consequence of adverse selection and moral hazard explained in the previous section, there is another issue of distortion of resources discussed here using the demand and supply behavior of health-care services. The market imperfection in the health-care industry causes some forms of externalities. As students may recall, the concept of externalities and their examples were discussed in Section 3.4; similar examples of externalities are found in the health-care market. Sources of market imperfection in the health-care industry are information asymmetry, cost inefficiency, service inefficiency, third-party payments, and government subsidies. Because health-care services do not meet the two standards for defining a public good—non-exclusiveness and nonrivalry—there is much policy debate regarding whether the government should own and operate the entire health-care system. The answer to this debatable question can be understood better by explaining the external costs or gains incurred by the existing health-care system in the United States.

Positive externalities of US health-care programs. The programs offered by the Centers for Disease Control and Prevention to provide vaccinations and prevent seasonal flu and other viruses are examples of programs that create a positive externality. Private hospitals often collaborate with health insurance companies to provide routine annual or semiannual checkups for preventing any unpredictable diseases, such as cancer, cardiovascular problems, and high blood pressure. These programs are very popular with health-care consumers and provide positive externalities in a sense that the marginal social benefit of these programs far exceeds their actual marginal cost. Government-owned programs and routine checkups provided by private hospitals generate additional economic and social benefits to society by maintaining high productivity with better health and happiness while minimizing the out-of-pocket cost of preventive care for individuals. The government plays a significant role in internalizing this positive externality by expanding services through government funding. Figure 4.3 illustrates the internalization of positive externality.

Figure 4.3 Internalization of Positive Externality

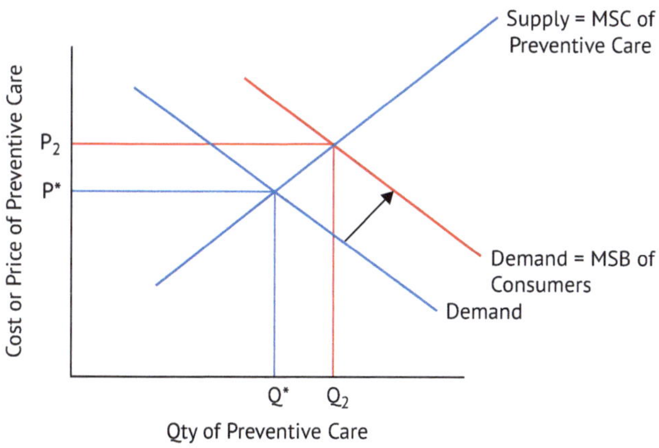

Negative externalities in the health-care industry. Similar to the positive externalities shown earlier, examples of negative externalities are also common in the health-care industry. For example, a prescription drug supplied by a monopoly pharmaceutical firm with no competitors may have many side effects. This medicine may present a negative health hazard to individuals; however, the individuals would have no alternatives. Government legislation of pharmaceutical firms and related biotechnology firms would help internalize this negative externality by shifting the S curve to the left where MSC = MSB, as illustrated in Figure 4.4.

Figure 4.4 Internalization of Negative Externality

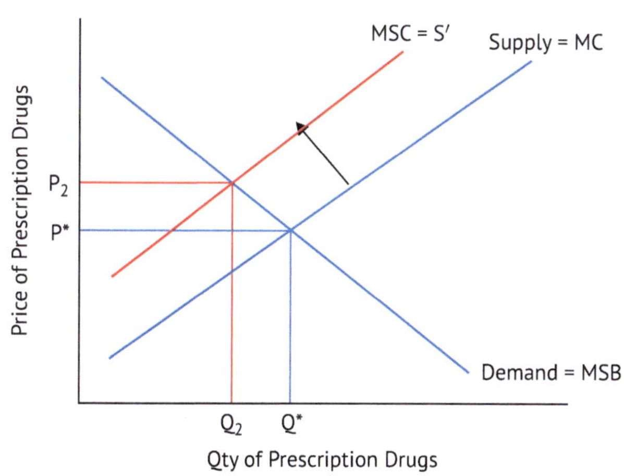

The two examples of externalities indicate how important government legislation is to internalizing externality. The role of the government is vital, even though health-care services are not pure public goods. Government legislation, subsidies, and direct coverage, such as Medicare and Medicaid (plus the Obamacae), would certainly improve the marginal social benefit and safety of health care while keeping the cost down and maximizing health-care services to society as a whole. In addition, given the basic necessity for prescription drugs and surgical procedures, fixed-income and low-income consumers need government intervention to internalize the externalities caused by overpricing or safety issues. This legislation is important, even if the majority of voters prefer market-based, health-care services.

4.4. The Health-Care Industry in the Context of Macroeconomics

As noted in previous sections of this chapter, the four components of the AD function of the macroeconomic model are consumption (C), investment expenditure (I), Government Expenditure (G), and net export (X–M). The share of health-care expenditure at 18% of total GDP goes into all four components of the GDP contribution. Therefore, the implications for government health-care policy involve the working mechanism of the AD-AS model of macroeconomics. A more detailed discussion on this topic is provided in Chapters 6 and 9. Readers need to be aware that the health-care policy implications of the government at both the federal and state levels are integral parts of the macroeconomic model and its application in the aging population in this century.

Chapter Summary

Section 4.1 has provided a distinction between the demand and supply behavior in microeconomics vis-à-vis the aggregate demand and aggregate supply model in macroeconomics. The demand and supply mechanism in the context of microeconomics was explained as an extension from its theoretical foundation introduced in Chapter 2. The example of price and quantity allocation of the housing market in the city of Boston was further explained in Section 4.1.1.

Section 4.1.2 introduced the macroeconomic model as AD = C + I +G + (EX–IM), where

C = Consumption expenditure
I = Investment expenditure
G = Government expenditure
EX = Exports expenditure demanded by buyers abroad
IM = Imports expenditure demanded by domestic buyers

$$\textbf{AS = Gross Domestic Product (GDP)} = P_1Q_1 + P_2Q_2 + P_3Q_3 + \ldots + P_nQ_n = \sum P_iQ_i,$$

where i = 1 to n number of goods and services. The estimation technique of GDP and the average price level (GDP deflator) were explained clearly in this section. Students are strongly encouraged to practice the numerical examples of indexing the price level provided in this section and to review the illustration depicted in Figure 4.1.

Section 4.2 focused on the economics of the health-care industry in the United States as one of the fastest-growing sectors in the economy and its growing importance to the improvement of the status of human capital. The discussion in this section was mainly based on the key importance of improving the health economics of the labor force and children as an integral part of good health, education, and labor productivity for sustainable economic growth. The total expenditures for the health-care industry were estimated at over 17% of GDP in 2017.[5] Table 4.1 summarized the rise of health-care expenses in the US economy since 1960. The reasons for the continued rise in health-care costs at a rate more than any other service in the US economy are given explained by three key sources as follows:

The rise of an aging population

Improved health conditions and life expectancy at birth

Decrease in out-of-pocket health-care expenses because of the third-party payment system

Figure 4.2 in this section illustrated the demand and supply behavior in the health-care industry, explaining how the rising cost of health-care services is partly attributed to the third-party payment system.

Section 4.3 provided several examples of the general economics of the health-care industry, including its contribution of 18% to the US GDP. In addition to private-sector, health-care funding, the key role of the government in providing funds for Medicare, Medicaid, and the ACA was discussed in more detail. Similar, but a little different, health-care systems in Canada, Japan, and the United Kingdom were also compared to the US health-care system. The issues with data sharing and patents' privacy were also introduced in this section with the related problem of information asymmetry (the information gap between health-care providers, health insurance companies, and patients). The effect of information asymmetry in the form of adverse selection and moral hazard was explained with examples in the context of the US health-care system. The application of positive and negative externalities was also explained. The process of internalization of positive and negative externalities of health-care expenses was discussed in detail with illustrations in Figures 4.3 and 4.4. It is strongly recommended that students review this part of the section with its important policy implications.

Section 4.4 briefly introduced the important consideration of health-care economics integrating into the macroeconomic framework so that health-care economics becomes an important part of the macroeconomic policy of the government at both federal and state levels.

5 Center for Medicare and Medicaid Services

Application Activities

Q1. Based on the concepts of the law of demand and the law of supply in microeconomics, explain the difference between changes in quantity demanded (and/or changes in quantity supplied) and changes in demand (and/or changes in supply). Provide a real-world example and draw a graph. Provide an explanation for the graph. No specific data is required for drawing the graph.

Q2. Based on your explanation in Q1, draw a hypothetical diagram of demand and supply for consumer goods in the US market. From the concept of demand and supply behavior in the marketplace, show and explain the effect of Donald Trump's imposition of tariffs on imported consumer goods from Canada, China, Mexico, and European Union (EU) countries. Specifically, explain (and show) who would actually end up paying for the tariffs and the changes in equilibrium price and quantities of imported goods and services in the US consumer market that would result.

Q3. How do you distinguish between the concepts of the D and S functions in microeconomics and the concepts of the AD and AS functions in macroeconomics? Why they are different?

Q4. Briefly explain how the problem with information asymmetry caused the financial collapse on Wall Street and financial trouble in the health-care service industry. Provide an example for each of these cases.

Q5. From your own real-life experience, provide an example of adverse selection and its possible moral hazard. How would it be possible to avoid or at least minimize the problem of adverse selection and moral hazard?

Q6. Make a list of the pros and cons of the individual mandate of Obamacare.

Q7. From your learning experience in this chapter and your additional reading on health-care economics for the United States, give at least three reasons why health-care economics should be considered an integral part of federal and state policies.

Chapter 5

Economics of the Stock Market, Bond Market, Loanable Funds, and Currency Market

The Wall Street Approach to Microeconomics and Macroeconomics

Learning Objectives

As they read the chapter, students will learn the following:

- Definition of the bond market, stock market, loanable funds market, and currency market
- Application of the demand and supply model in the government bond market and the corporate bond market
- Application of the demand and supply model in the stock market
- Application of the demand and supply model in the loanable funds market and the currency market

5.1. Understanding the Bond Market, Stock Market, Loanable Funds Market, and Currency Market

To understand the model of macroeconomics discussed in Chapter 6 fully, it will be useful to understand the financial markets. This chapter will begin with a discussion of bond market activities.

5.1.1. Bond Market: Corporate Bonds and Government Bonds

Corporate bonds are issued by major corporations to finance their operations by borrowing from individuals and institutional investors in the private sectors.

These bonds are debt securities issued with guaranteed fixed interest rates (called yield to maturity) with a stated face value (FV) and expiration of maturity at a future date. The law mandates that the issuer of the bonds pay their principal and interest under the terms and conditions of the bonds issued by the corporation. The US government also issues its own **Treasury securities** to public investors and foreign governments to borrow money to finance budget deficits and other government spending not covered by the tax revenue collected from individuals, businesses, and corporations. There are three broad categories of US Treasury securities: short-term securities issued with a maturity from 90 days to less than a year are called **Treasury bills** (TB), medium-term securities issued with a maturity between 1 year and 10 years are called **Treasury notes** (TN), and long-term securities with maturity beyond 10 years are called **Treasury bonds**. The volume of bond market transactions in both the corporate bond and Treasury securities markets is much larger than for the stock market and loanable funds market. Both corporate bonds and Treasury securities are traded during weekdays on Wall Street in New York City. The total volume of bonds outstanding in the US market is about $40 trillion, and the volume of the global bond market is over $100 trillion. On the other hand, the volume of total stocks outstanding in the US domestic market is less than $20 trillion with the volume of the global market at about $64 trillion.[1] The daily trading volume in the secondary market of bonds in the United States is estimated to be an average of $700 billion, as compared to the stock market at $200 billion.

Because of uncertainty during economic crises caused by business cycle fluctuations (states of recession and inflation), the corporate bond market is not immune to the risks of investment. The common risk factors of financial investments are default risk, liquidity risk, tax implications, and inflation risks. Because corporations can suffer from bankruptcy during economic downturns, investors in corporate bonds bear these four common risks, causing volatile patterns of price changes. On the other hand, government bonds issued by the US Treasury only bear the risk of inflation for long-term bonds. US Treasury bonds have zero default risk, zero liquidity risk (bondholders can cash in their bonds at any time before expiration), and very low taxes on interest earned. The general perception is that the US government can never default because it has no history of default and a long record of full employment and stability since 1945. This level of confidence makes US government bonds among the safest investments on Earth.

5.1.2. Stock Market

Unlike the bond market, the stock market is an equity market with no expiration or limit to terms of maturity. The stock market is created by an initial public offering (IPO) of common stocks by a public limited corporation to raise funds for operating expansions. Investment bankers usually purchase IPO stocks from the issuing corporations and sell them to the secondary markets for trading. The stockholders own a stake of the company's equity as a percent share of those stock holdings. If the company's expected profit goes up, so does the

---

1 "5 Bond Market Facts You Need to Know," The Motley Fool, https://www.fool.com/knowledge-center/5-bond-market-facts-you-need-to-know.aspx.

price of the stocks. On the other hand, when the corporations perform poorly with an expected decline in profits, the price of the stocks falls, and the stockholders lose their equity value. The process of these changes in demand and stock prices are seen in the news in the Dow Jones Industrial Average, the S&P 500, and the NASDAQ price index. Because the total shares of stocks traded in these secondary stock markets are fixed in supply, the supply curve is vertical. The change in equilibrium price happens by changes on the demand side only. The application of this stock market behavior is discussed in Section 5.2.

5.1.3. Loanable Funds Market

The loanable funds market refers to the capital investment market where all financial intermediaries provide loans to business investors and individual borrowers. They use the capital funds received from savers and other sources of surplus funds. These surplus capital funds are given as loans to business firms and individual borrowers in exchange for interest rates charged to borrowers. There are many types of loans: small business loans, car loans, construction loans, mortgage loans, credit card loans, vacation loans, personal loans, and student education loans, just to name a few. Therefore, the loanable funds market has various segments, each with its own demand and supply behavior with varying rates of interest. These interest rates are actually the price of loanable funds. The difference in interest rates for each of the segments is attributed to the difference in risk, volume, terms of maturity, and credit ratings of borrowers. The application of this market is explained in Section 5.4.2.

5.1.4. Currency Market

Unlike the bond market, stock market, and loanable funds market, the currency market is focused on the demand and supply of domestic legal tender currencies issued by a country's central bank against the currencies of other countries. For example, the trading of US goods and services against the goods and services of China creates demand and supply for the currencies of both countries (renminbi against US dollar) to exchange for exports and imports. The demand and supply for these currencies are influenced by demand for capital investments in both countries. If Chinese investors want to invest in US bonds, stocks, and real estate, they will need to purchase US dollars (US$) against their own currency, the renminbi (RMB). Given the supply of US$, the increase in demand for US$ will raise the value of US$ against RMB. This is called an increase in the exchange rate of US$ against RMB. Similarly, if American investors want to invest in China and buy more Chinese products, then the demand for RMB will increase and so will the value of RMB against the US$. The same exchange system in the currency market can be observed in trade relations between the United States and other countries. In Section 5.4.2, the specific model structure of currency markets is discussed.

5.2. Application of Demand and Supply Behavior in the Bond Market

Because the market behavior of both corporate bonds and government bonds works in the same pattern, except for the difference in risk factors, this section focuses on US Treasury securities for the sake of simplicity. There are two kinds of bonds issued by the US Treasury: coupon bonds and discount bonds. Coupon bonds work against the FV of bonds at a fixed rate of interest; the complicated equation is beyond the scope of this textbook. Therefore, the relationship between a bond price and its yield for a US Treasury security with a maturity of one year (a TN) is calculated by the equation that follows. This example is a typical discount bond issued by the US Treasury for all of its TBs and TNs to finance government budget deficits.

Yield = [(FVb–Pb)/Pb] * 100 ....Eqn (5.1)

where FV is the face value of a bond (stated on the face of a bond as a promissory note with terms of maturity), and Pb is the discounted price of the bond initially issued at the auction desk of the Federal Reserve Bank (the central bank).

Suppose a one-year TN is sold to an investor at the auction desk of the Federal Reserve Bank's Federal Open Market Committee (FOMC) at a discounted price of $940 with an FV of $1,000. The yield to maturity is estimated by plugging this information into the earlier equation (5.1).

Yield = (1,000 – 940)/940 * 100 = 60/940 * 100 = 6.38%, approximately

If the same note were issued at a higher price, say at $960 against its FV of $1,000, the estimated yield would be

Yield = (1,000 – 960)/960 *100 = 40/960 * 100 = 4.17%, approximately.

From the two numerical examples of two different prices for the same FV of TN, it is clear that the bond price and the yield always move in opposite directions. In other words, when the price of a TN increases, its yield decreases, and vice versa. Table 5.1 shows a typical Treasury market trading in the secondary market with an inverse relationship between bond prices and bond yields. The data in columns 2 and 3 show that as the price falls with different terms of maturity, the prices of bonds and their yields move in opposite directions.

It is also worth noting that the market volatility of the secondary market of bonds traded on the New York Stock Exchange and other exchange markets is only influenced by changes in demand for bonds with a fixed supply of total bonds outstanding. The supply of bond holdings typically stays unchanged in the secondary market; it is the demand side that fluctuates based on changes in several external and internal factors relating to business and economic expectations. Changes in factors influence the demand to shift to the left (because of negative expectations) or to the right (because of positive expectations). For example, suppose inflation is expected to rise in the near future because of the booming economy of 2018, and the unemployment rate is at an 18-year low of 3.7% in June 2019. This expected inflation would make the purchase of bonds less attractive to investors because the real value of interest rates, after adjustment for the expected inflation, will decline. This phenomenon is the real expected interest rate versus the nominal interest rate depicted in the following equation: the **Fisher equation** developed by American economist Irving Fisher in the early twentieth century.

Real expected Interest Rate = Nominal Interest Rate – Expected Inflation Rate ...Eqn (5.2)

Table 5.1: Bond Price and Yield for US Treasury Bonds

BONDS, RATES, AND CREDIT MARKET OVERVIEW 5:05 p.m. EDT 06/08/18 **Treasurys**		
	Price Change	**Yield (%)**
1-Month Bill*	−0/32	1.771
3-Month Bill*	0/32	1.933
6-Month Bill*	0/32	2.118
1-Year Note*	−0/32	2.289
2-Year Note*	−1/32	2.500
3-Year Note*	−2/32	2.636
5-Year Note*	−3/32	2.784
7-Year Note*	−5/32	2.897
10-Year Note*	−7/32	2.949
30-Year Bond*	−14/32	3.090

* At close
See Full Daily Closing Prices
Source: "Bonds & Rates," *The Wall Street Journal*, http://www.wsj.com/mdc/public/page/mdc_bonds.html?mod=mdc_topnav_2_3050

Equation (5.2) clearly indicates that with a zero expected inflation rate, the real expected interest is the same as the nominal interest rate. Because the interest rate charged under the loanable funds market is the nominal interest rate, changes in future or current inflation rates will change the value of real interest, which is the real purchasing power of interest earned. Based on this insight from the Fisher equation, investors find it useful to consider expected inflation when figuring out the real worth of interest rate when bonds are purchased at a fixed rate of return from future interest income. An example of this concept is demonstrated in the bond market model that follows.

Figure 5.1 Bond Market Behavior and Change Price and Yield

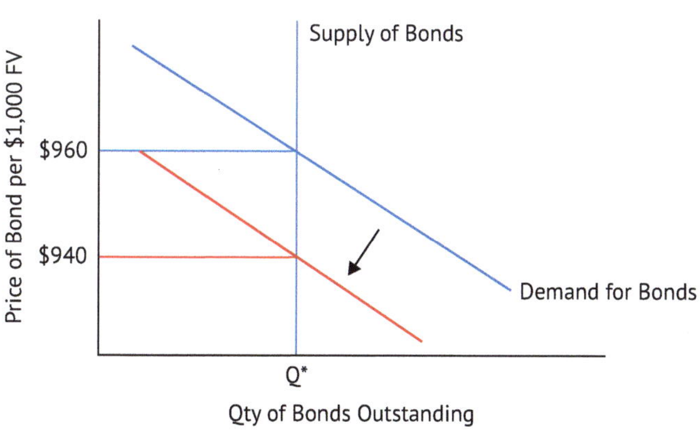

The resulting change in equilibrium price and quantity of bonds in the secondary market will be at a lower price and quantity, as illustrated in Figure 5.1. Because of a leftward shift of the demand curve for bonds, equilibrium price has declined from $960 per $1,000 FV bond to $940. As a result of this downward shift of the D curve, the bond yield will increase because bond price and yield always move in opposite directions (from equation (5.1) and Table 5.1).

5.3. Application of the Demand

and Supply Model in the Stock Market

As mentioned earlier, the stock market is an equity market with no expiration or maturity, and the stocks are actively traded in the secondary markets on Wall Street in everyday financial transactions. Stock market fluctuations are closely watched by all investors, policy makers, economists, business leaders, and professionals in the investment industry. This is because the rise and fall of stock market price indices have economic and business implications for expectations of employment, inflation, corporate profits, GDP growth, and investment returns. As explained earlier, a massive stock market crash causes panic to all economic agents, resulting in increasing uncertainty in the health and stability of the economy. Historically, many of the economic recession cycles, including the Great Depression, followed stock market crashes. The application of the stock market in macroeconomics is related to changes in macroeconomic variables, such as corporate earnings, corporate profits, unemployment rates, inflation rates, interest rates, expected inflation rates, inventories of durable goods, cars and real estate, and factory orders. Changes in these important macroeconomic variables are considered the key indicators for making forecasts of economic trends for the near future. Therefore, changes in these variables have an immediate effect on the trading mood of the stock market by shifting the demand curve of the equity market. The D curve shifts to the right when those changes have expected positive outcomes. On the other hand, the D curve shifts to the left when changes have expected negative outcomes.

Using the same example of inflation expectations in the bond market, suppose the FOMC, the Federal Reserve's policy-making body, projects that inflation will increase at a higher rate. This higher expected inflation rate may have a negative effect on real income and consumer expectations of future economic trends. That means that investors may perceive a downward trend of consumer spending habits on goods and services produced by corporations with large stock holdings in the stock market. If this downward expectation also causes an expected loss of corporate profits and earnings, then the demand for stock purchases will decline. This decline in demand will shift the demand curve to the left and thus lower the equilibrium price of stocks and equity values of the stocks. This process of real-world stock market behavior is depicted in Figure 5.2.

In the hypothetical diagram for the stock exchanges on the Dow Jones Industrial Average Index, the equilibrium price (before changes in profit expectations caused by expected inflation) is shown at the combination of P* and Q*. As explained earlier, the supply curve here is vertical because the total stock of common shares outstanding in the secondary market is unchanged. It is like an eBay market transaction of used products

Figure 5.2 Stock Market Behavior and Changes in Stock Price

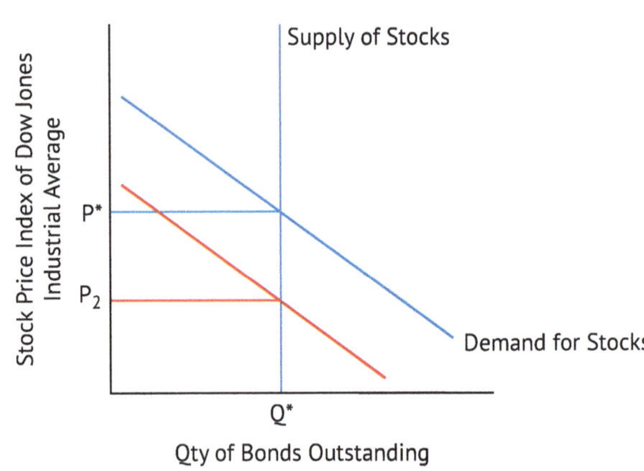

traded in the e-commerce market. The downward shift of the demand curve to the left lowered the equilibrium price to P_2. Students may use this model structure to look at changes in other macroeconomic variables (e.g., consumer confidence, interest rates, trade wars brought about by changes in government policies on tariffs on imported goods) to figure out which direction the D curve will shift and thus to easily determine the changes in equilibrium prices. The stock market volatility in both the Dow Jones and the S&P 500 Index in 2018 and 2019 was primarily attributed to the Trump administration's imposition of high tariffs on imported goods from China and EU countries.

5.4. Application of Demand and Supply in the Loanable Funds Market and Currency Market

Unlike the vertical supply curve in the bond and stock markets explained in Sections 5.2 and 5.3, the supply curve in loanable funds market is a standard upward-sloping curve because the quantity supplied in these two markets responds directly to changes in price (interest rate). More specifically, if the interest rate (the price of loanable funds) increases, then the quantity supplied of loanable funds will also increase and vice versa, ceteris paribus. The same principle of supply function applies to the currency market, as an increase in exchange rates will increase the quantity of currency supplied, and vice versa, ceteris paribus. On the demand side, the demand curve is downward sloping because of the inverse relationship between prices and quantity demanded in both markets, ceteris paribus. The real-world application of these two markets is illustrated and explained in Sections 5.4.1 and 5.4.2, respectively.

5.4.1. Demand and Supply Interaction in the Loanable Funds Market

Based on the principle of a downward-sloping demand curve and an upward-loping supply curve, the equilibrium interest rate and quantity demanded equal to quantity supplied is illustrated in Figure 5.3. This hypothetical model is an abstract theoretical example representing the overall complex nature of the loanable funds market. In reality, several financial products and assets, such as business, personal, credit card, car, and mortgage loans, to mention just a few, are traded between financial institutions and borrowers. However, the way the segmented loanable funds market works is not different than the hypothetical illustration shown in Figure 5.3.

Figure 5.3 Interest Rate and Quantity of LF Market

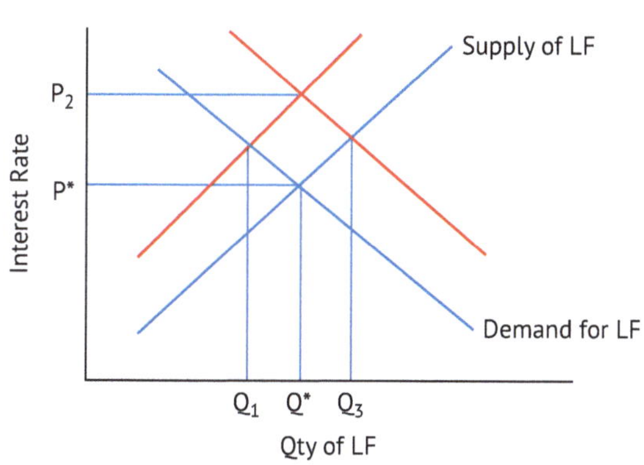

Figure 5.3 indicates the interaction between the D and S curves of the loanable funds market with the changes in external factors, such as the expected inflation rate. The demand curve represents the borrowers and the supply curve represents the lenders, with initial equilibrium interest rate and quantity at the point of

intersection between P* and Q*. If inflation is expected to rise, then the Fisher equation discussed in Section 5.2 will predict that real interest is expected to decline. The decrease in real interest is expected to impact expected real returns from lending negatively so that the S curve will shift to the left. On the other hand, a decrease in real interest rates would attract more borrowers to borrow loanable funds, and that would shift the D curve to the right. This process shifts D and S in opposite directions, as shown by the curves marked in red in Figure 5.3. It also indicates that because of the shift of these two curves in opposite directions, the new equilibrium interest rate will increase. However, it is not clear whether the quantity in loanable funds will increase, decrease, or remain unchanged. If the D curve shifts at a higher magnitude than that of the S curve, the quantity of loanable funds will increase, and vice versa. If the net effect is zero, meaning the magnitude of shifts cancel each other out, then the quantity will remain unchanged at a higher equilibrium interest rate. Having understood this analysis, the student may practice the same process by using other related macroeconomic variables to shift the curve(s) in the appropriate direction. The practice helps determine the changes in equilibrium interest and the quantity of loanable funds.

5.4.2. Application of Demand and Supply in the Currency Market

As explained in Section 5.1.4, the currency of any country is just like any other commodity that can be exchanged for the currency of another country to trade goods and services between them. The currency exchange rate is also determined by a free flow of demand and supply in the foreign exchange currency market traded through international banking divisions of major banks in every country. For example, the value of US dollars (US$) against euros or British pound or Japanese yen or Chinese renminbi (RMB) are determined by changes in demand and supply, which shift around the clock. This process of exchange rate determination is administered by foreign exchange rate specialists (called foreign exchange dealers) operating through computer-generated demand and supply software. The transactions are carried out in the same way that stock prices are determined—by dealer-operated demand and supply operations in the NASDAQ price index for high-technology company stocks. Figure 5.4 illustrates an example of a currency exchange market between US$ and euros under a free foreign exchange market of demand and supply.

In Figure 5.4, the euro/per US$ is the price of dollars against euros. The equilibrium exchange rate at point A, the point of intersection between D for US$ and S of US$ against the euro, determines the currency exchange of euros per unit of US$. Because the demand

Figure 5.4 Currency Exchange Market Equilibrium

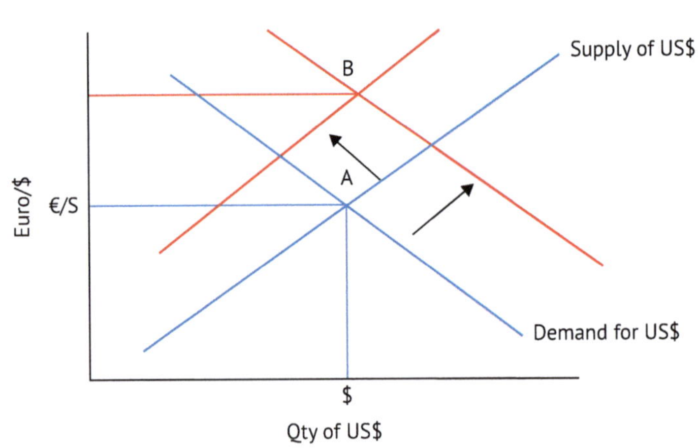

and supply of the currency market are constantly changing due to trading activities and capital inflow and outflow by investors in global markets, equilibrium exchange rates also change every minute. As indicated by the D curve shifting to the right and the S curve shifting to the left for the US currency market against the euro, the new equilibrium is at point B. Capital inflow by foreign investors to the US economy would shift the demand for US$ to the right. Keeping everything else constant, the exchange rate of US$ would increase. On the other hand, if foreign investors and domestic corporations take US$ out of the US market and invest in EU countries, then the demand for euros will increase, and the exchange rate of US$ will decrease. Changes in currency exchange rates have several trade and policy implications for macroeconomic stability and trade balance. More details on exchange rates controlled by government legislation versus flexible exchange rates (shown here in Figure 5.4) will be discussed in Chapters 14 and 15. At this point, it is important to know that increases in the exchange rate of US$ make US-produced exports and services more expensive to foreigners. At the same time, imports of goods and services from other countries to the United States become cheaper. As a result, net export causes a trade imbalance for the United States against other countries. The opposite happens to other trading partners. The direction of the trade balance is reversed when the currency exchange rate of US$ decreases against its trading partners. Again, the external factors that affect the exchange rates will be discussed in more detail in Chapters 14 and 15. Chapter 6 will begin with a discussion of the Keynesian macroeconomic model developed in the 1930s.

Chapter Summary

Section 5.1 introduced the conceptual differences in four types of financial markets. They are the bond, stock (also called equity market), loanable fund, and currency markets. The bond market is debt security with its expiration date in the future and a promised return of a fixed interest rate payment until maturity. Bonds are issued by corporations in the private sector and by the government. For the US government, the general term for government securities is Treasury securities, of which there are three types based on length of maturity. Short-term securities are called Treasury bills. Medium-term securities are called Treasury notes, and long-term securities are called Treasury bonds. The stock market is the equity market with no expiration issued by corporations to investors who purchase a stake in corporations' equity value. The equilibrium price of stocks fluctuates based on changes in the demand for stocks with a given supply of stocks in the secondary market. Changes in demand are influenced by several factors that directly or indirectly affect the stockholders' equity value. Both bonds (corporate and government) and stocks are traded daily on Wall Street in New York City. The interest rate differentials among different bonds are primarily attributed to the degree of risk factors, such as default risk, liquidity risk, tax consideration, and inflation risk. Details about these risks and the reason for very low risks for government bonds and thus very low yield were discussed with examples.

The loanable funds market is the market for financial lending and borrowing between banks and borrowers. The price for a loanable fund is the interest rate, which is determined by demand and supply interaction in the financial market. The currency market is the market for exchange-rate determination of domestic currency against the foreign currency it trades with. The exchange rate is determined by the demand and supply interaction between two countries' currencies.

Section 5.2 explained the theoretical foundation of the bond market for both corporate bonds and US Treasury bonds with the example of how the bond price and its interest rate (called the yield) are determined in the bond market transaction. A specific example of an inverse relationship between the bond price and the yield was given in equation (5.1) and illustrated the changes in price and yield in Figure 5.1.

Section 5.3 explained the theories and applications of stock market behavior with real-world examples of price determination of the Dow Jones Industrial Average Index traded daily on Wall Street. The changes in the equilibrium price index of the stock market composite index are influenced by the shift of the demand curve with the given total supply of common stocks outstanding. The process of changes in the equilibrium price by external and internal factors was explained with examples and illustrated in Figure 5.3.

Sections 5.4.1 and 5.4.2 explained the demand and supply behavior of the loanable funds market and the currency market, respectively. In the loanable funds market, the interaction between demand and supply determines the equilibrium interest rate. The changes in the equilibrium interest rate are influenced by other economic and financial factors that relate to the demand and supply of loanable funds. Demand for loanable funds represents the borrowers, and the supply for loanable funds represents the lenders. The detailed explanation of changes in equilibrium interest and quantity was given in this section and illustrated in Figure 5.3.

Currency market behavior was also introduced in this section, and an explanation of how the exchange rates fluctuate with domestic currency value against foreign currencies was provided. The changes in the equilibrium exchange rate that occur because of the changes in demand and supply of currency were illustrated in Figure 5.4. It is recommended that students make their own examples of currency market behavior and sources of constant change by identifying the relevant economic variables.

Application Activities

Q1. Briefly describe the difference in the bond market in general and the stock market in the context of investment and return. Why is corporate bond investment usually riskier than investing in US Treasury securities?

Q2. During a recession, the yield for corporate bonds tends to increase and the yield for US Treasury securities tends to decrease. Briefly explain why. Give a real-world example as part of your reasoning.

Q3. Estimate the rate of return (yield to maturity) if you as an investor purchase a one-year US TN at the market price of $955 with an FV of $1,000. Make sure you show the numerical estimation by using the yield equation.

Q4. Draw a hypothetical demand and supply curve for S&P 500 stocks and briefly explain the effects of unexpected increase in inflation rate caused by a sudden rise in energy prices.

Q5. Draw a demand and supply curve of the loanable funds market and explain the effects on equilibrium prices and quantities of loanable funds in response to the situation described in Q4.

Q6. Suppose the increase in tariffs on imports of goods and services from China and EU countries caused a capital flight of currency from the United States. Show the effects this would have on US exports, imports, and trade balances.

Chapter 6

Measures of Economic Performance for Macroeconomic Fundamentals

Nominal and Real GDP and Their Growth Rates, Inflation and Inflation Rates, and Unemployment Rates

Learning Objectives

As they read the chapter, students will learn the following:

- The concept of key macroeconomic variables: GDP, GDPD, unemployment and full employment, recession and inflation, stagflation, depression, and financial crisis
- Numerical data to measure key macroeconomic variables

6.1. Understanding the Fundamentals of Macroeconomics

Key macroeconomic variables are defined and briefly explained in this section.

Macroeconomic Variables:

NGDP and RGDP

Inflation index: GDP deflator (GDPD) and Consumer Price Index (CPI)

GDP per capita

RGDP growth rate and living standard

Unemployment and full employment

Recession, depression, inflation, and stagflation

In Section 4.2, the concepts of NGDP and RGDP were introduced briefly as part of the AS function of macroeconomics. In the same section, the components of AD were also introduced to determine the equilibrium GDP and price level. This section will discuss those key macroeconomic variables in more detail, along with real-world data. The connections among those variables and an explanation of the complete model structure will be presented in Section 6.2.

6.1.1. NGDP and RGDP

NGDP is the total market value of all final goods and services produced at current market prices in a particular calendar year. The reason for considering the market value of final goods and services is to avoid double counting the values of intermediate goods and services used in the process of delivering the final output of goods and services. For example, in the process of manufacturing an Apple MacBook, Apple uses software processing chips from Intel. It also purchases other intermediate ingredients to produce the final MacBook units for shipment to the distributors and Apple stores for sale. The cost of those chips and other ingredients were already added to the final value of the MacBook for sale. In calculating the total GDP, the cost paid by Apple to Intel and other vendors of intermediate goods as inputs in making the MacBook are already included in the final price of the MacBook. A similar example applies in manufacturing automobiles, airplanes, software operating systems, cell phones, and all other products and services at their final points of sale. The actual method of calculating NGDP is repeated next from Section 4.2 in Chapter 4.

$$\mathbf{NGDP = P_1Q_1 + P_2Q_2 + P_3Q_3 + \ldots + PnQn = \sum PiQi;}$$
$$\mathbf{i = 1 \text{ to } n \text{ number of goods and services}}$$

The equation is the estimated value of AS of all goods and services produced and measured in current prices. The per unit prices multiplied by the total quantity of final goods and services of each category produced for sale are added as the summation of the current value of all final goods and services. This summation of the current market value of each category gives the value of NGDP.

$$\mathbf{RGDP = P_{01}Q_1 + P_{02}Q_2 + P_{03}Q_3 + \ldots + P_{0n}Q_n = \sum P_0iQi;}$$
$$\mathbf{i = 1 \text{ to } n \text{ number of goods and services}}$$

RGDP in the equation is measured by using the base-year prices for each of the goods and services multiplied by the same quantities of current-year production. The base year is determined by selecting a previous year with no inflation. RGDP is also known as the GDP adjusted for inflation; it reflects the actual performance of economic growth without inflation (rising trends of price levels). In the equation, P_{01}, P_{02}, P_{03}, ... P_{0n} are the prices of the same goods and services for the base year considered as the normal prices without any inflation.

6.1.2. Inflation Index: GDPD and CPI

To measure the actual performance of the economy, it is important to understand the inflation index because the prices of goods and services continue to fluctuate over time regardless of the rise or fall of the actual production of goods and services. Because of continuous fluctuations in the prices of goods and services, the values measured in the NGDP equation do not reflect the real performance of the economy in terms of actual growth of production and services. Therefore, RGDP is used to adjust the inflation as an alternative measure of the real performance of the economy. However, the problem remains in understanding how well the whole economy is performing given the comparison between NGDP and RGDP. In addressing that important question, economists came up with a calculation for the inflation index to observe the rate of average inflation for the entire economy. In macroeconomics, there are two kinds of inflation indices: the GDPD and the CPI. These two indices are widely used for conducting research in economics and business, as well as for policy purposes. The measuring techniques of both of these indices are shown next.

GDPD = NGDP/RGDP * 100 for every year,

where NGDP is measured by using current-year prices and RGDP is measured in base-year prices. The example of this measure is restated here from Section 4.2.

Suppose in 2018, the NGDP estimated by the previous AS equation is about $20.5802 trillion and the RGDP estimated by using the base-year 2012 as $\sum(P_{2012} * Q_{2018})$ is $18.6382 trillion. Then the price index, called GDPD, would be estimated as

GDPD for 2018 = (NGDP/RGDP) * 100 = (20,580,200/18,638,200) * 100

or GDPD for 2018 = 1.104195 * 100 = 110.42.

Since the year 2012 is currently considered the base year, it is obvious that the NGDP and RGDP for the year 2012 are identical; therefore, the GDPD for the base-year 2012 = 100.

These two values of GDP are the inflation index used to calculate the growth of inflation between 2012 and 2018, as shown here.

Inflation rate between 2012 and 2018 = (GDPD for 2018–GDPD for 2012)/ (GDPD for 2012 * 100) = (110.42–100)/100 * 100 = 10.42%

The general equation to calculate the inflation rate by using the GDPD index is

Inflation rate = $(GDPD_t - GDPD_{t-1})/GDPD_{t-1} * 100$,

where t indicates the current-year GDPD and t-1 is the previous year GDPD. In the example, t was 2018 GDPD and t-1 was 2012 GDPD.

Later in this chapter, actual economic data for the US economy are used to estimate multi-year economic performances for GDP growth and inflation plus unemployment in a single table.

CPI is measured very differently than the GDPD. CPI is the weighted average price index for a select bundle of goods and services for metropolitan urban consumers only. This market basket is considered to be basic goods and services necessary for consumers living in metropolitan areas of the country regardless of their income levels.

> According to the US Bureau of Labor Statistics, "The CPIs are based on prices of food, clothing, shelter, fuels, transportation, doctors' and dentists' services, drugs, and other goods and services that people buy for day-to-day living. Prices are collected each month in 75 urban areas across the country from about 5,000 housing units and approximately 22,000 retail establishments (department stores, supermarkets, hospitals, filling stations, and other types of stores and service establishments). All taxes directly associated with the purchase and use of items are included in the index. Prices of fuels and a few other items are obtained every month in all 75 locations. Prices of most other commodities and services are collected every month in the three largest geographic areas and every other month in other areas. Prices of most goods and services are obtained by personal visits or telephone calls by the Bureau's trained representatives."[1]

Unlike the goods and services considered in the GDPD reflecting prices of all goods and services produced domestically, the CPI bundle of goods and services are selected for consumer items for typical households living in urban areas. Those items represent the basic needs of consumers, including both domestically produced and imported consumer items. CPI is widely used to measure the changes in the cost of living standard for households across the country, especially the cost of living and income comparison of urban residents. The CPI is used for major policy decisions, such as raising wages so that employees are able to maintain a minimum standard of living. The equation for calculating CPI is given here.

CPIt = CPI for a time period, say year t, = Pt (P0 * B/P0 * B) * 100,

where Pt is the current price of a market basket of goods and services, P_0 equals the prices of the base-year market basket of goods and services, and B equals the market basket for the base year.

The actual CPI estimation based on the equation is more complicated than students can observe here, and a detailed explanation of this measurable technique is beyond the scope of this level of study. For example, the numbers in parentheses are very complex calculations. However, it is also easy to observe from the simplified version of the equation that for the base year, Pt = P_0 and, therefore, CPI for the base year is always 100. The US Department of Labor Statistics is still using the year of 1983 as the base year.

The Department of Labor Statistics usually measures the CPI on a monthly basis using the previous equation. The actual monthly data is then annualized for forecasting purposes using the algebraic techniques shown in the example that follows.

Suppose actual monthly CPI data indicates an average price increase of 0.25% from the previous month, and then the monthly inflation rate of 0.0025 (0.01/4 = 0.0025) for that

1 "Consumer Price Index Summary," US Department of Labor Statistics, last modified September 12, 2019, https://www.bls.gov/news.release/cpi.nr0.htm.

month can be converted to the annualized inflation rate as $(1.0025)^{12}–1 = 1.0304 - 1 =$ 3.03%, approximately.

The inflation rate calculation from yearly CPI data is done using the following general equation:

Yearly inflation rate = (CPIt–CPIt-1)/CPIt-1] * 100,

where CPIt is the CPI for year t and CPIt-1 is the CPI for the previous year. For example, if the CPI data for 2017 and 2018 calculated by the US Department of Labor Statistics are, respectively, 245.12 and 251.10, then the actual inflation rate is estimated by using the previous equation for yearly inflation:

Inflation rate between 2017 and 2018 = [(251.10-245.12)/245.12] * 100 = 2.44%, approximately.

More yearly calculations of inflation rates using both the GDPD index and CPI are shown later in Table 6.1.

6.1.3. Shortcomings of CPI in Measuring the Inflation Rate

Despite the extensive use of CPI data in measuring the cost of living status of consumers, and thereby influencing policy measures for increasing wages and elderly benefits at both the state and federal levels, CPI data is far from accurate. For example, the weights assigned to each item in the market basket in the base year are not uniformly proportional to incomes of all consumers. They vary significantly by age, occupation, income, and lifestyle. There are always possible sampling errors in the way the survey is conducted when collecting the price data from retail stores. The items included in the basket also change over time; luxury goods become necessary consumer items—consider items such as cell phones, laptops, and internet access, which were not necessary items in the 1980s. The quality of different consumer items also varies widely, and it makes it very difficult, if not impossible, to adjust the prices collected.

6.1.4. GDP per Capita

GDP per capita is measured by total GDP per year divided by the population of that year. GDP per capita is an important indicator of a country's economic status and average living standard relative to other countries. Although per capita GDP data does not provide details of the income distributional pattern of a country, it does give a comparative outlook to classify all countries in the world as either low income, middle income, or upper-middle income. For example, the most recent data compiled by the World Bank indicate that in 2017, South Sudan had the lowest per capita income with $221, and the country with the highest per capita income was Luxembourg with about $107,000. The per capita income for the United States in 2017 was a little over $59,000.[2] However, to understand the economic well-being of all citizens of a specific country, information on income distributional patterns is needed.

---

2 "World Bank Country and Lending Groups," The World Group, http://data.worldbank.org/about/country-classifications.

It is called the **Gini coefficient**. Students are encouraged to youtube for learning the concept and technique of measuring income distribution known as the Gini Coefficient.

6.1.5. RGDP Growth Rate and Living Standard

As defined and calculated earlier, the RGDP is the preferred alternative to NGDP for understanding the actual performance of the economy over time adjusted for inflation. This is because RGDP calculation methods adjust inflation to reflect the growth of the real output of goods and services. After adjusting inflation, the rise in RGDP growth is a positive indicator of economic growth and employment opportunity for an economy. In general, a higher RGDP growth rate means greater income for working people and lower unemployment (or at least increased employment opportunities). With the increasing average income with the higher rate of RGDP growth, individuals are capable of spending and saving more as a way to improve their living standard. The key source of higher RGDP growth is an increase in labor productivity. High-income countries are rich not because they have luck or more natural resources but because of higher labor productivity than their counterparts in lower-income countries. Higher productivity is mainly attributed to the quality of higher education, skill of the workforce, technology, and effective institutions in production, service, and government sectors. The relevant equation to calculate RGDP growth rate is given next.

RGDP Growth Rate = delta Y/Y * 100 = ΔY/Y * 100 = (Yt–Yt-1)/Yt-1 * 100,

where delta is a change of RGDP values between two different periods, usually in the calendar year:

Y is the symbol for RGDP data; Yt = RGDP for year t; and Yt-1 = RGDP for the previous year.

For example, suppose the RGDP for the US economy in 2016 is $16.7162 trillion and for 2017 it is $17.0962 trillion, then the RGDP growth rate in 2017 from 2016 is estimated as follows:

RGDP growth rate in 2017 = [(17,096.2–16,716.2)/16,716.2] * 100 = 2.27%, approximately.

This rate of economic growth is a good indicator of a healthy economy in the context of the United States because the growth rate for achieving full employment in the United States cannot exceed 3% without accelerating inflation. This is because the minimum RGDP growth rate needed to achieve the full employment of an economy is derived from two important economic data points: labor force growth rate (ΔL/L) plus labor productivity growth rate (Y/L). For the United States, because of a chronic labor shortage, the annual labor force growth rate per year was at about 1% in 2017. With a relatively constant labor productivity growth rate of 2% per year, the minimum RGDP growth rate needed for achieving full employment is about 3% (1% + 2%) without accelerating the inflation rate. This minimum required RGDP growth of 3% indicates the level of constraint for the US economy to grow faster than 3%. If the economy actually hit the growth rate at or over 3%, inflation would be expected to kick in because of an acute shortage of labor force. On the other hand, China can increase its RGDP growth rate beyond the current rate of 7% per year because of its huge labor force entering the pool of individuals looking for jobs.

6.1.6. Unemployment and Full Employment

The measurement of unemployment and full employment is important to understand the state of the economy. The data on unemployment indicates whether the economy is creating new jobs and raising income. It also helps policy makers to take necessary actions if the unemployment rate is signaling an economic downturn. The equation for estimating unemployment is given next, followed by the most recent example for the US economy.

Unemployment Rate = (Total number unemployed/Total labor force) * 100

The labor force is defined as all persons of 16 years and older who are physically and mentally able to work and willing to work. Based on this definition of labor force, it is clear that not all citizens of the country who are aged 16 years and older are part of the labor force; some of them are voluntarily unemployed; some are full-time students; others are enrolled in job training or vocational training; some just don't want to work. As of June 2019, the total civilian labor force for the United States is about 163,351,000, and the number of people unemployed is about 6,063,000.[3] By plugging this information into the unemployment rate equation, the unemployment rate is estimated as

Unemployment Rate = (6,063,000/163,351,000) * 100 = 3.7%, approximately.

This low unemployment rate is considered the lowest unemployment rate in decades for the US economy. The economic implications of this low unemployment rate will be discussed after a review of the concept of full employment and recession.

Full employment occurs when anyone in the labor force looking for a job can find a job within a reasonable time period. That means job and labor markets have enough vacancies to offer jobs to all job seekers who are actively looking for work. However, it does not necessarily mean that job seekers will accept any job they are offered. Some people may not be willing to take a job if it does not fit into their skill level or the type of job they are looking for. For example, a software engineer may not accept or be willing to take job offers that do not match his or her expertise. Individuals may migrate from one state to another for many reasons, and there is generally a transition period while they look for a desirable job in their new location. People also lose their jobs temporarily because of technological shifts in production systems. These types of unemployment rates fall into a category called unemployment rate at full employment or natural rate of unemployment. There are two types of natural rates of unemployment: **frictional unemployment and structural unemployment.**

Frictional unemployment occurs when a job seeker is in between jobs or voluntarily quit his or her existing job to look for a better job to match his or her skill set. The unemployment in transition caused by interstate migration is also part of this type of unemployment. Relocation is a constant source of unemployment in the short run.

Structural unemployment is caused when corporations undertake technological changes to fit new production systems or are incapable of competing with rivals in an environment

---

3 "Employment Situation Summary Table A. Household Data, Seasonally Adjusted," U.S. Bureau of Labor Statistics. November 1, 2019. https://www.bls.gov/news.release/empsit.a.htm)

of new technology and innovation; this is a common occurrence in high technology–oriented economies, such as the United States and other highly industrialized countries.

Seasonal unemployment is another source of unemployment that fluctuates because of seasonal variations in different parts of the country. But recent data doesn't seem to show any significant issues for unemployment in the economy.

Economists consider **frictional and structural unemployment** to be integral parts of natural unemployment or unemployment that occurs at a time when the economy is in a state of full employment. In other words, unemployment rates will never be zero, even when the economy is considered to be in a state of full employment. This is because frictional and structural unemployment exist at a steady rate most of the time. This combined rate of unemployment is called the **nonaccelerating inflation rate of unemployment (NAIRU)**. Although there is constant controversy regarding the actual rate of unemployment that NAIRU represents, there is a consensus from the previous data regarding full employment and unemployment that the range of values of NAIRU falls between 4.5% and 5.5%.

The implication for NAIRU or the natural rate of unemployment is that the economy will be operating at this rate of unemployment at full employment without accelerating the rise of inflation. For example, if the actual unemployment rate falls below 4.5%, inflation will kick in because of a tight labor market, which gives employees bargaining power to raise their wages. Because of a shortage of labor, workers are hired by employers even if they lack the necessary skills, causing average rates of low productivity in the short run. This combination of increasing wages and low productivity would likely force employers and producers to pass along the increasing costs for final goods and services to the consumers. Further economic implications for inflation during an economic boom are discussed in later sections of this chapter.

6.1.7. Recession, Depression, Inflation, and Stagflation

An **economic recession** occurs when RGDP growth rate starts declining. The decrease in RGDP growth rate has three immediate consequences: increase in unemployment rates from job loss, increase in inventory of goods and services because of a decline in sales, and decline in price levels because of deficiency in AD expenditures. The domino effect of these three negative trends is the loss of confidence by consumers and investors in the economic health of the country for the near future. As a result, the stock price of the equity market falls and investors lose their equity values.

Economic depression is a state of severe recession that sustains for years—sometimes called a prolonged severe recession or depression. The Great Depression of the 1930s lasted for 10 years from 1929 to 1939, with a brief recovery started in the mid-1930s under the New Deal economic policy undertaken by President Roosevelt. The breakout of World War II in 1939 helped the struggling economy rebound almost overnight through reinvestment of the entire economy. There were a number of mild and short-lived recessions in the US economy in the 1970s, 1987, and 2001. However, the Great Recession of 2007–2008 that caused financial collapse and the housing market crash was very severe—the worst economic downturn since the Great Depression of the 1930s. The unemployment rate went up to almost 10%, and the

RGDP growth rate went into negative territory in 2008 and 2009. The aggressive application of Keynesian macroeconomic policy undertaken by President Obama in 2009 helped the economic recovery, which took about four years. The US economy has been growing at a steady rate since then, with an average RGDP growth rate of 2.5% and a continued decline in the unemployment rate to as low as 3.5% in September 2019. During the same period, the inflation rate stayed on the target rate of 2% plus set by the Federal Reserve's monetary policy.

Inflation occurs when price-level indicators, such as GDPD and/or CPI, continue to rise at a faster rate than the RGDP growth rate. For example, if the RGDP growth rate increases at 2.5% and inflation rises at a rate equal to or greater than 2.5%, the economy is considered to be in a state of inflation. This rate of inflation takes away real income from fixed-income wage earners; thus, the purchasing power of consumers declines because they can no longer buy the same amount of goods and services.

Stagflation, on the other hand, is caused by the simultaneous occurrence of inflation and deflation. This scenario of economic crisis usually happens because of a negative supply shock in the economy; the AS curve shifts left, causing a spike in the average price level, which leads to declining production and an increase in the unemployment rate. Stagflation is much more severe than just inflation because income and the purchasing power of households decline at the same time.

There are two sources of inflation in an economy: demand-side inflation and supply-side inflation. **Demand-side inflation** happens when the economy overheats with an excessive increase in AD during an economic boom. The excess of AD is more than needed for a full-employment state in the economy. This situation happens when actual unemployment rates fall below the natural rate of unemployment (NAIRU). As explained earlier, NAIRU is the unemployment rate at full employment without inflation. So when actual unemployment is equal to NAIRU, the economy is at full employment with no inflation. However, as the economy continues to expand beyond the level of full employment, actual unemployment falls below NAIRU and inflation is expected to kick in. As explained earlier, this demand-side inflation is caused in two ways: an increase in wages because of a tight labor market with shortages of labor; and a resulting decline in labor productivity because of relatively unskilled workers being hired for skilled employment. For example, in September 2019, unemployment data showed a rate of 3.5%, which was much lower than the lower-bound NAIRU range of 4.5 to 5.5%. This state of an overheating economy may cause demand-side inflation. The illustration of this scenario is shown in the next section of this chapter.

Supply-side inflation or stagflation (also called cost-push inflation) is caused by the negative supply shock of the economy. The sources of supply-side inflation are a combination of the rise in costs of production and a decline in productivity. This rare event happened in the US economy during the 1970s. It began with a recession at the end of the Vietnam War and was followed by oil price shock from an oil embargo imposed by Organization of Petroleum Exporting Countries (OPEC) in retaliation of US military assistance to Israel during the Arab-Israeli War. The drastic cut in oil production by the OPEC cartel suddenly spiked the crude oil price from $4 per barrel to $30 per barrel in one day. The worldwide hyperinflation caused by supply-side inflation and stagflation in the US economy lasted for over

10 years. The supply-side economic policy was a new idea developed by USC economist Arthur Laffer in the late 1970s to handle this crisis of stagflation. The policy recommendation of supply-side economics given by Laffer was eventually adopted by President Reagan in 1980. Reagan's supply-side economic policy is also known as **Reaganomics**. It is worth mentioning here that during a state of stagflation, the demand-side Keynesian economic policy doesn't seem to work effectively because expansion of AD during stagflation is expected to make the hyperinflation worse before achieving any positive results in production and unemployment. Section 6.3 will provide a graphical representation of the Keynesian macroeconomic model to achieve a deeper understanding of macroeconomic policy implications for stagflation. Before getting into that section, Section 6.2 focuses on actual data analyses of key macroeconomic variables for the US economy in recent years.

6.2. Numerical Data Analysis of Key Macroeconomic Variables

This section focuses on numerical data analysis of key macroeconomic variables for the US economy. In Sections 6.1.1 and 6.1.2, the relevant equations and numerical examples were discussed regarding how to measure NGDP and RGDP, GDP per capita, GDP growth rates, inflation rate (using GDPD and CPI indices), unemployment rate, and natural rate of unemployment (NAIRU). The following table contains the actual data of macroeconomic fundamentals for the US economy followed by data analysis.

Data analysis. From Table 6.1, students will be able to observe the actual data of three macroeconomic fundamentals: RGDP, unemployment rate, and inflation rate. The data in the table for all three variables are estimated in their respective growth rates from 2006 to 2017. Looking at the data of the RGDP column, students may observe that the RGDP and NGDP values are identical for 2012 because the former is calculated in 2012 base-year prices. As explained in earlier sections, the RGDP is adjusted for inflation by selecting a base-year price of 2012 as the most recent year of normal price levels before prices started to increase again because of the start of the economic recovery in 2009 and a slight decline of price level in 2011. This logic is confirmed and consistent with the price levels and inflation rates in columns 7 and 9 for 2012. The inflation rate calculated by using the GDPD index is 1.91% in column 6, and the inflation rate calculated by using CPI data for 2012 is 2.1% in column 9. These two rates in 2012 are showing the rising trend from their lowest rates in 2009 (0.762% and -0.4% respectively) because of the severe recession in 2009 followed by slow but steady recovery with sustained positive RGDP growth rate and declining unemployment rates through 2018. Looking at the trend of RGDP growth rate, students may notice the declining trend of negative growth in 2008 and 2009, with the unemployment rate rising to 5.8% and 9.3%, respectively, for the same period. The 2010 RGDP growth rate clearly shows an impressive rebound of economic growth in positive territory at 2.56%, followed by a decline in unemployment with a year lag in 2011. As the economy continued to grow positively with a rising RGDP growth rate, the unemployment rate continued to decline with a slow rise in inflation reflected in both the CPI and GDPD indices.

Table 6.1: Data of Macroeconomics Fundamentals for the United States 2006–2017

Year (1)	NGDP in 000s (2)	RGDP in 000s in 2009 Prices (3)	RGDP Growth Rate % (4)	GDPD = (2)/(3)*100 (5)	Inflation Rate % (6)	u-Rate % (7)	CPI (8)	Inflation Rate % (9)
2006	13,814.6	15,338.3	–	90.066	–	4.6	201.60	–
2007	14,451.9	15,626.0	1.88	92.486	2.687	4.6	207.30	2.8
2008	14,712.8	15,604.7	−0.14	94.284	1.944	5.8	215.30	3.8
2009	14,448.9	15,208.8	−2.54	95.003	0.762	9.3	214.53	−0.4
2010	14,992.1	15,598.8	2.56	96.110	1.165	9.6	218.05	1.6
2011	15,542.6	15,840.7	1.55	98.118	2.088	8.9	224.94	3.2
2012	16,197.0	16,197.0	2.25	100.000	1.917	8.1	229.59	2.1
2013	16,784.9	16,495.4	1.84	101.755	1.755	7.4	232.96	1.5
2014	17,527.3	16,912.0	2.53	103.638	1.850	6.2	236.74	1.6
2015	18,224.8	17,403.8	2.91	104.714	1.041	5.3	237.02	0.12
2016	18,715.0	17,688.9	1.64	105.801	1.034	4.9	240.01	1.26
2017	19,519.4	18,108.1	2.37	107.793	1.883	4.4	245.12	2.09
2018	20,580.2	18,638.2	2.93	110.419	2.435	3.9	251.10	2.43

Sources: GDP data from the US Bureau of Economic Analysis and unemployment and CPI data from the US Bureau of Labor Statistics

Note: Column (6): (GDPDt–GDPDt-1) * 100; Column (9): (CPIt–CPIt-1)/CPIt-1 * 100

The relationship among the three fundamentals of macroeconomics shown in the actual data clearly demonstrates the reliability of the basic theories of the macroeconomic model explained earlier—increased aggregate production will generate job opportunities by reducing the unemployment rate, and vice versa. The inflation rate changes in the table also indicate the consistency of the theoretical argument that as the economy grows faster and moves toward full employment, the inflation rate tends to increase a little faster as well. It is also worth observing that the inflation rate using GDPD and the inflation rate using CPI are different for almost every year except in 2018 when it shows the rates are almost identical. This identical inflation rate by two different indices is just a rare coincidence. Also, the rates move in the same direction for both GDP and CPI based inflation. Nonetheless, it is obvious that they should be different values because the measurement techniques and bundle of goods and services are different. Section 7.1 in Chapter 7 will focus on an illustration of the AD-AS model of Keynesian macroeconomics model with special reference to the US economy.

Chapter Summary

Section 6.1 provided the meaning and comparison of the following key macroeconomic variables.

NGDP and RGDP
Inflation index: GDPD and CPI
GDP per capita
RGDP growth rate and living standard
Unemployment and full employment
Recession, depression, inflation, and stagflation

$$\mathbf{NGDP = P_1Q_1 + P_2Q_2 + P_3Q_3 + ... + PnQn = \sum PiQi; i = 1 \text{ to } n \text{ number of goods and services}}$$

The equation is the estimated value of AS of all goods and services produced and measured at current prices. The per unit prices multiplied by total quantity of final goods and services of each category produced for sale are added as the summation of the current value of all final goods and services. This summation of the current market value of each category gives the value of NGDP.

$$\mathbf{RGDP = P_{01}Q_1 + P_{02}Q_2 + P_{03}Q_3 + ... + P_{0n}Q_n = \sum P_0iQi; i = 1 \text{ to } n \text{ number of goods and services}}$$

RGDP in the equation is measured by using the base-year prices for each of the goods and services multiplied by the same quantities of current-year production. The base year is determined by selecting a previous year with no inflation. RGDP is also known as the GDP adjusted for inflation; it reflects the actual performance of economic growth without inflation (rising trends of price levels). In the previous equation, P_{01}, P_{02}, P_{03}, ... P_{0n} are the prices of the same goods and services for the base year considered normal prices without any inflation. Numerical estimation of GDPD and RGDP and their growth rates between different time periods were provided.

Inflation Index GDPD = NGDP/RGDP * 100 for every year, where NGDP is measured by using current-year prices, and RGDP is measured in base-year prices. The numerical example for estimating the GDPD index was given in Section 6.1.

The inflation index as CPI is measured differently than the GDPD. CPI is the weighted average price index for a selected bundle of goods and services for metropolitan urban consumers only. This market basket is considered to be the basic goods and services necessary for consumers living in metropolitan areas of the country regardless of their income levels. The numerical example of estimating CPI is given in Section 6.1.

The inflation rate calculation from yearly CPI data is done using the general equation shown next with numerical estimation in Section 6.1.2.

Yearly inflation rate = (CPIt–CPIt-1)/CPIt-1] * 100 with numerical values

Where delta CPIt-CPIt-1 is the delta CPI between two time period divided by CPI of the previous period.

RGDP Growth Rate = delta Y/Y * 100 = ΔY/Y * 100 = (Yt–Yt-1)/Yt-1 * 100,

where delta is a change of RGDP values between two different time periods, usually in a calendar year; Y is the symbol for RGDP data; **Yt** equals RGDP for year t; **Yt-1** equals RGDP for the previous year. Numerical estimation is given in Section 6.1.5.

Unemployment Rate = (Total number unemployed/Total labor force) * 100

Numerical estimation of the actual unemployment rate and comparison with the full employment rate as the natural rate of unemployment were given in Section 6.1.6.

Section 6.1.7 provided the concepts of recession, inflation, stagflation, and depression with examples of business-cycle fluctuations and special references to the Great Depression of the 1930s, hyperinflation of the 1970s, and the Great Recession of 2007–2008.

Section 6.2 covered the data analysis of key macroeconomic variables, such as the RGDP growth rate, unemployment rate, and inflation rate with actual data for the US economy on RGDP, unemployment rate, and CPI between the period of 2006 and 2018. Using the equations for measuring RGDP growth rates, inflation rates, and unemployment rates in Section 6.1, Table 6.1 in Section 6.2 provided the actual estimation of growth rates for these three key macroeconomic variables between 2006 and 2018, followed by a numerical data analysis in the last two paragraphs of this section.

Application Activities

Use the information in the following table to answer the questions.

	Production			Prices		
	Year 1	**Year 2**	**Year 3**	**Year 1**	**Year 2**	**Year 3**
Good X	50	75	100	$1.00	$1.00	$1.20
Good Y	100	100	130	$0.60	$0.75	$1.00

Assume that this economy produces only two goods, Good X and Good Y.

Q1a. The value for this economy's NGDP in year 1 is _____.

Q1b. The value for this economy's NGDP in year 3 is _____.

Q1c. If year 1 is the base year, the value for this economy's RGDP in year 2 is ____.

Q1d. If year 1 is the base year, the value for this economy's GDPD in year 1 is___.

Q1e. If year 1 is the base year, the value for this economy's GDPD in year 1 is ____.

Q1f. If year 1 is the base year, the value for this economy's GDPD in year 2 is _____.

Q2. Given that the value of CPI in 2018 is 247.59 and the CPI for 2019 is expected to be 250. 75, calculate the expected inflation for 2019.

Q3. Assume your annual income in 2017 was $75,000 and the CPI for 2017 was 245.12. If you expect your annual income to increase to $85,000 in 2018 and CPI is expected to be 247.59 in 2018, estimate your expected increase in real income between 2017 and 2018.

Q4. You buy a car with a 5% interest rate per year with five years to pay off the car loan. Suppose the expected inflation is an average of 1.5% per year over the next five years. Using the Fisher equation for the difference between the nominal interest rate and real interest rate, explain whether you are better off or whether your lender is better off when you purchase your car with a five-year loan with a 5% interest rate.

Q5. Using Table 6.1, explain why the inflation rate calculated using CPI is different than the inflation rate calculated using GDPD in 2017 (the inflation rate is higher with CPI than with GDPD).

Q6. Explain why the positive growth rate of RGDP, which is already adjusted for inflation, doesn't necessarily reflect the true economic well-being of the society as a whole.

Q7. Explain briefly why actual unemployment is never zero, even when the economy is considered to be in a state of full employment.

Q8. Why do economists and business investors expect inflation to accelerate when actual unemployment falls below the natural rate of unemployment (NAIRU)?

Q9. What is the current actual unemployment rate for the US economy? Do you think the current unemployment rate is less than, equal to, or above NAIRU? Explain your answer.

Q10. Compare and contrast the concepts of demand-side inflation and supply-side inflation. Do you think supply-side inflation causes stagflation? If so, how do you describe its consequence in the economy?

Q11. What were the key sources of the Great Depression of the 1930s? How did the Keynesian economy address the situation for a quick recovery? Explain very briefly.

Q12. How can you distinguish between the theory of classical macroeconomics and Keynesian macroeconomics? Does US economic policy follow the Keynesian model, or does it follow the classical doctrine of economics?

Chapter 7

Understanding and Measuring Short-Run and Long-Run Economic Growth with Real-World Examples

Learning Objectives

As they read the chapter, students will learn the following:

- Concepts of short run and long run in macroeconomics
- Comparison between short-run and long-run AS curves and their implications
- Analysis of shapes of AD and AS curves in the short run and long run with economic implications

7.1. Aggregate Supply Model in the Short Run and Long Run

The concept of short run versus long run in economics is not tied to a calendar. Rather, short run refers to the time during which certain inputs in production processes are fixed. Long run is defined as a long enough period of time to change all inputs or factors of production into variables with no fixed costs or fixed capital.

In Chapter 6, students were introduced to the theoretical concepts of key macroeconomic variables and their relationships. Students have also seen how real-world data is consistent with fundamental economic theories. In this chapter, the focus is on the graphical illustration of those concepts so that students can make a successful transition from theory to data and from data back to theory.

Figure 7.1 illustrates the complete model of macroeconomics originally developed by Keynes in *The General Theory of Employment, Interest and Money* published in 1936. An effort has been made to include both short-run and long-run operating models of macroeconomics in Figure 7.1. Students will probably need to review the diagram and read the contents of explanations a few times to grasp the basic working mechanisms of this key foundation of macroeconomics. After reading and understanding the mechanism fully, it may also be a good idea to draw a similar diagram by their own and practice how to relate to theory and applications.

Figure 7.1 AD-AS Model of Keynesian Economics

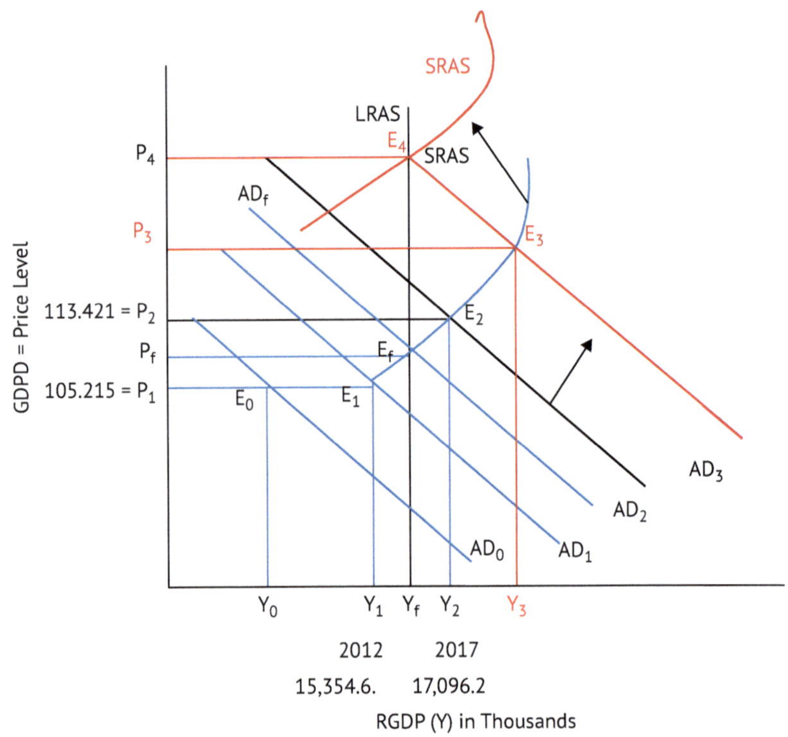

Note: SRAS is an acronym for short-run AS curve
LRAS is an acronym for long-run AS curve (the vertical line)
AD is an acronym for aggregate demand curve (assumed as linear for simplicity) = C + I + G + (EX–IM)
GDPD is an acronym for GDP deflator as a price index
RGDP is an acronym for real GDP, represented by the symbol Y

Figure 7.1 illustrates the basic macroeconomic model that reflects the entire economy on a single diagram, with short-run and long-run implications for price and output relationship. This model has several dimensions that can be explained from the perspectives of both theoretical and real-world macroeconomics. To explain the diagram systematically, students may start from both AD and AS curves to arrive at multiple combinations of the equilibrium price level and the RGDP at different points of intersection between AD and AS. For example, equilibrium point E_1 is a combination of GDPD of P_1 = 105.215 and RGDP of Y_1 = \$15.3546 trillion for a calendar year 1. This equilibrium point is a short-run equilibrium for RGDP and the price level at the point of intersection between the SRAS curve at below the full employment level of RGDP. The full employment level of RGDP is indicated by Y_f in the diagram at the equilibrium point E_f, where SRAS, AD_1, and LRAS curves intersect. This point of equilibrium is considered a state of full employment because both AD and SRAS curves cross the vertical LRAS curve. The LRAS curve is a hypothetical point of reference to indicate the desired position of the economic condition of RGDP at which anyone looking for a job can find a job—a state of full employment. It is also important to notice that Y_f sits somewhere between the 2015 and 2016 RGDP level because the actual unemployment rate in those two periods falls within the range of NAIRU (4.5%–5.5%). The actual unemployment rates for 2015 and 2016 are, respectively, 5.3% and 4.9%.

7.2. Comparison between Short-Run and Long-Run Aggregate Supply Curves and Their Implications

At the equilibrium point E_2 in Figure 7.1, the output and price combination, are shown as 113.421 and $17.0962 trillion, respectively. Since the actual unemployment rate for that year (say 2017) at 3.8% falls below the lower bound of NAIRU at 4.5%, it is reasonable to say that the state of the economy in 2017 is booming with a tight labor market condition. Therefore, the equilibrium point E_2 is placed to the right side of the LRAS curve, displaying the start of accelerated inflation with higher price levels than P_f at P_2. If the economy continues to expand, AD is expected to shift rightward from AD_2 along the steeper segment of the SRAS, as shown by AD_3.

To the left side of the vertical LRAS curve, equilibrium price and output combinations (such as E_0, E_1, and other possible points) are considered in a state of recession. Those equilibrium points are at lower levels of output than the desired level of output at Y_f along the vertical line of LRAS. It is also important to observe carefully that the shape of the perfectly horizontal segment of the SRAS curve (from P_0 to E_1) is a state of severe recession explained by Keynes in *The General Theory of Employment, Interest and Money*. He stated that wages and prices become sticky in a state of severe recession or depression because suppliers stop selling below the price at which they are not able to make any profits. At that price, the suppliers or employers are stuck with long-term contracts with employees (who still have their jobs) at fixed wage rates. Keynes explained further that this wage-price stickiness would keep the economy depressed for a very long time unless a government policy initiative was undertaken to boost the economy by shifting the AD curve rightward. The key implication for Keynes's policy prescription is that the increase in AD by government policy intervention would help expand output and job creation without increasing the price level or inflation, and thus boosting the economy to get back to full employment. The segment of SRAS between E_1 and E_f indicates that as the economic recovery comes close to the full employment level of RGDP (Y_f), the slope of the SRAS curve starts rising. This upward-sloping part of the AS curve implies that as the economy moves toward full employment, the decline in the unemployment rate comes close to NAIRU and, therefore, results in inflation caused by increased wages and other related costs of production.

On the other hand, when the economy keeps expanding beyond equilibrium points on the right side of LRAS curve (such as E2), the slope of the SRAS curve becomes steeper. This is due to the rise in labor costs in terms of wage increases in a tight labor market and the decline in productivity from unskilled labor. The process of this increasing MC of production faced by suppliers is clearly reflected in the increasingly positive slope of the SRAS curve. The SRAS curve is indeed the aggregate MC of the economy as a whole. The equilibrium price and output combinations in that segment of the SRAS curve also show that the rate of price level increase is greater than the rate of increase in output/RGDP, **$\Delta P/P > \Delta Y/Y$** (a state of accelerated inflation). Given this scenario, the long-run adjustment begins by shifting the SRAS to the left until the economy gets back to full employment (at E_4) at a higher price level (P_4), but it is also considered a normal price level in the long run. The speed of the leftward shift of the SRAS curve would depend on the net value of price-level changes based on the following equation.

$$\textbf{Change in price level} = \Delta P/P * 100 = (\Delta W/W) * 100 - (\Delta Y \Delta L) * 100,$$

where, W = Nominal wages for labor and L is labor inputs or labor hours.

This long-run adjustment process is shown by a leftward shift of the SRAS curve marked in red. In other words, the AD shift from E_0 to E_3 is the process of short-run movement, and the SRAS shift from E_3 to E_4 is a long-run adjustment. Section 7.3 provides an in-depth summary analysis of topics discussed in Section 6.2 and in this chapter.

7.3. Analysis of Shapes of Aggregate Demand and Aggregate Supply Curves in the Short Run and Long Run with Economic Implications

This section is an extension of the discussion from the previous two sections. We will further analyze the shape of the AS and AD curves of the macroeconomic model and examine their economic implications.

7.3.1. The Slope of the SRAS and LRAS Curves

Although many economics textbooks display SRAS supply as a linear upward-sloping curve, the real-world data on SRAS curves doesn't provide any indication of an upward-sloping SRAS line. Based on the law of diminishing returns in the short-run production function (with fixed capital input and labor hours of production as variable inputs), it has been proven that as more and more labor inputs are added with fixed capital and technology, the marginal labor productivity ($\Delta Q/\Delta L$) will eventually decline. With decreasing marginal productivity of labor, the MC of production starts increasing. The characteristic of this mirror image relationship between marginal productivity of labor and MC of production is called the principle of diminishing marginal returns in short-run production. The SRAS curve in macroeconomics is the added short-run MC curves. The added values of MC come from individual firms at different prices (MC = Price for efficiency condition of market equilibrium). Therefore, the upward-sloping shape of the SRAS curve is a true reflection of the law of diminishing returns. However, the upward-sloping curve doesn't necessarily have a constant slope because of disproportionate changes in output price and marginal output produced as the economy expands. Given the disproportionate rise in aggregate MC = Price level and aggregate output (Y), it is also true that the value of the slope of the SRAS curve is much lower at an output produced below the full employment level of Y. On the other hand, the slope of SRAS would rise at an increasing rate as the output level expands beyond the full employment level. Figure 7.2 shows a typical SRAS curve with real-world data.

Figure 7.2 SRAS Curve Behavior

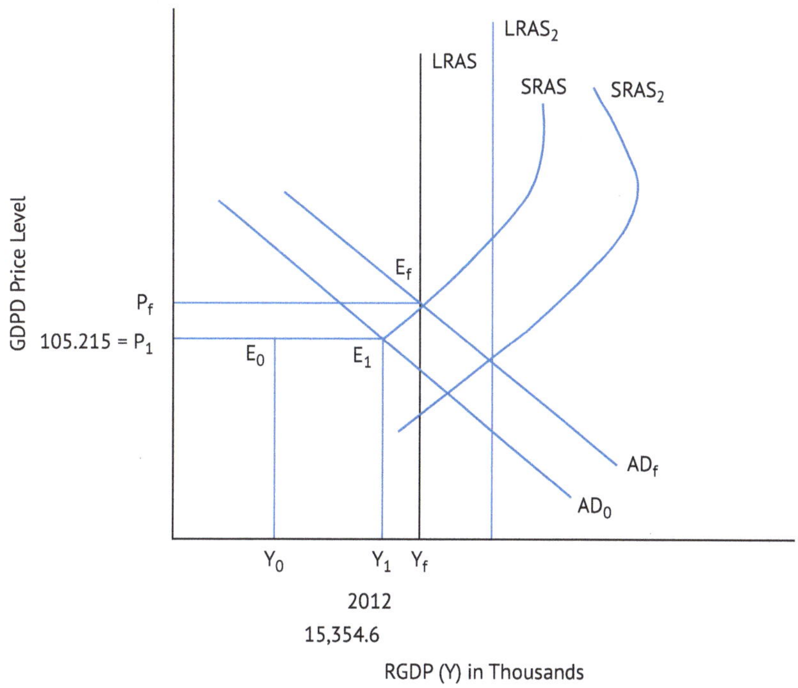

As explained in a similar graph in the previous section, the slope of the SRAS curve is relatively flat at output levels to the left of the full employment level (Y_f) and slopes upward at an increasing rate as the economy expands beyond the full employment level.

The slope of the LRAS curve illustrated in Figure 7.2 is perfectly vertical. The vertical shape of the LRAS curve assumes that, in the long run, the changes in the aggregate price level do not necessarily influence the level of RGDP. Therefore, any point of equilibrium combinations between RGDP and the price level along the LRAS curve are considered a state of full employment. For example, as shown in Figure 7.2, the equilibrium point at E_f as the point of intersection combining SRAS, AD_f, and LRAS is considered a state of full employment.

7.3.2. The Shift of SRAS and LRAS in the Very Long Run

To further understand the previously discussed economic implications for AS behavior, it is important to examine the changes in SRAS and LRAS when the assumption of fixed capital stock, technology, wage rate, labor productivity, and scientific discovery are not true in the very long run. This happens when these structural variables change over time, or all change occurs at the same time. For example, major technological innovation can improve existing production processes with better efficiency of productivity and cost-cutting. A new technological breakthrough in hardware and software industries may introduce new products and gadgets to the market, creating a new group of consumers and new investments for new jobs. The introduction of new prescription drugs and medical devices creates new industries in health care. New green technology can create major shifts in production processes for sustainable growth and development for future generations. The effect of these changes is a positive shift in the overall structure of the economy. Such structural changes not only shift the SRAS to the right but also shift the LRAS curve to the right, as shown in Figure 7.2, by shifting SRAS to $SRAS_2$ and LRAS to $LRAS_2$. The implications of these shifts in the very long run reflect a structural change in the economy, with significant increases in productivity, improved human capital and skill level of the labor force, and cost minimizations. The effect of these very-long-run changes must be reflected in a higher standard of living, better quality jobs, higher income, and a significant increase in the RGDP growth rate.

7.3.3. The Shift of the AD Curve and Economic Implications

This section is an extension of the earlier definition of AD and its components introduced in Section 4.1.2. The four components of AD expenditures [= C + I + G + (EX–IM)] are listed next with their respective categories of expenditure.

AD = C + I + G + (EX–IM) have the following subcategories of expenses:

C = Consumption expenditure = All household consumption expenditure on both durable and nondurable goods and services
I = Investment expenditure = New residential houses and business construction of buildings + machines and equipment for productions + increase in inventories
G = Government expenditure = All expenditure outlays spent by the federal and local governments for providing government-owned services that benefit society, including national defense, social welfare, food stamps, Medicaid, Medicare, roads, transportation and safety measures, payment to government employees, and other related public goods
EX = Expenditure on exports spent by foreign buyers on domestically produced goods and services
IM = Expenditure on foreign-produced goods and services bought by domestic residents

The equilibrium principle means the total of the AD-side components must be equal to the total supply-side (Y), which is also called total national income.

Y = Income side goes to wages, rents, profits, dividends, interest earned, capital depreciation, and taxes

The income categories can be simplified to C + S + T, where S = Saving and T = Taxes. That means, at equilibrium, S goes to investment (I) and tax goes to government spending (G).

The equation for complete equilibrium is Y = AD = C + I + G + (EX–IM) = C + S + T

The standard downward-sloping AD curve is subject to shift either rightward or leftward based on changes in any of the components of AD, such as changes in either C, I, G, or (EX–IM). The slope of the AD curve would depend on the price-level elasticity of AD, as price changes do influence the quantity demanded of expenditures. Given the slope of AD, changes in individual components of AD, say C, will shift AD to the right if C increases and shift to the left if C declines. Because GDP contribution of C components is almost two-thirds of the $20 trillion economy, factors such as taxes, consumer confidence, and changes in real income and wages significantly influence the shift of the AD curve.

Figure 7.3 Multiplier Effect on AD and Output

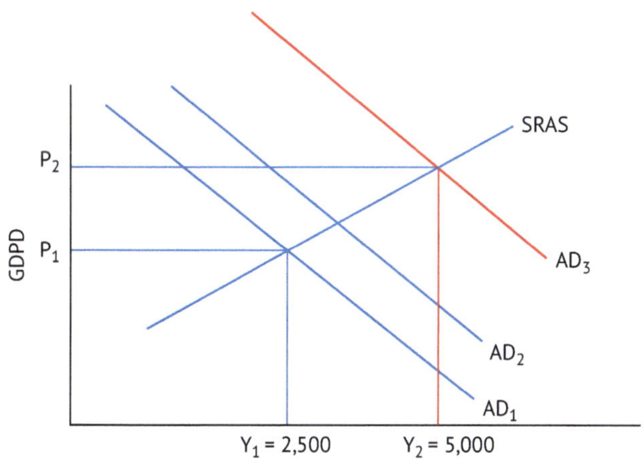

Note: Y_1 = 2,500 = AD_1; Y_2 = 2,500 + ΔG (= 500b) * 5 = $5,000

Investment expectations and government policy on G, profit tax, investment tax credits, dividend taxes, interest rate policy, and trade policy also shift the AD. With negative shock in those investment categories, AD would shift to the left and vice versa. An increase in government expenses and/or a decrease in taxes will increase AD by shifting to the right, and vice versa. Changes in variables, such as the exchange rate and income per capita or GDP growth, will affect the volume of EX and IM, shifting the AD. The illustration of this shift of the AD is shown in Figure 7.3 in Section 7.3.4 and explains the multiplier effect on changes in equilibrium RGDP.

7.3.4. Keynesian Multiplier and the Shift of AD

The shifts of AD described earlier are actually influenced by a multiple of the initial changes in those variables. This multiplied shift of AD is called the Keynesian multiplier. For example, suppose an initial expenditure of $500 billion is injected into the government expenditure program for upgrading the infrastructure of the economy. So, ΔG = $500. The AD curve will initially shift to the right by $500 billion. However, this expansion of government expenditure will create opportunities for contractors and consumers working on new infrastructure projects. Suppose that, after a 20% savings of gross income earned from this project, the consumption rate from this marginal income is 80%. In other words, the marginal consumption expenditure from this additional income by consumers from ΔG = $500b is calculated as

ΔC/ΔY = 0.8 called marginal propensity to consume (MPC), and

ΔS/ΔY = 0.2 called marginal propensity to save (MPS).

MPC + MPS = 1, always.

By using the values of MPC and MPS, suppose the multiplier is α. The value of multiplier α would be

$$\alpha = 1/(1-MPC) = 1/MPS = 1/1-0.8 = 1/0.2 = 5.$$

Therefore, the chain reaction of income and consumption generated by an initial $500 billion infrastructure expenditure by the government will increase the effect of AD by five times. Please note that the mathematical derivation of this multiplier is discussed in Chapter 8. For now, it is sufficient to understand that the multiplier in macroeconomics has the power to provide a boost to the economy that is much greater than the initial expenditure. For this example of $500 billion ΔG, the increase in RGDP = ΔY = multiplier * 500 = 5 * 500 = $2,500 billion. The process of this multiplier's effect on the economy is illustrated in Figure 7.3, where the multiplier effect is the increase of RGDP from Y1 to Y2 by a multiple of five times the initial investment of $500 billion in G.

Chapter Summary

Section 7.1 introduced the conceptual differences between the short-run and the long-run activities of macroeconomic variables by using the basic Keynesian macro-model of AD and AS. This section demonstrated the concept and application of equilibrium output (RGDP) as an actual level of production and its comparison with the desired level of full employment. The analysis of short-run fluctuation of equilibrium output and price level was explained in detail and illustrated in the diagram in Figure 7.1. Figure 7.1 also showed the transition of the adjustment of output, employment, and inflation from the short run to the long run when the economy is operating beyond the full employment level of output. It is strongly recommended that students read the explanation and relate that to the diagram drawn in Figure 7.1.

Section 7.2 discussed the economic and policy implications of SRAS and LRAS curves in understanding different dimensions of business cycle fluctuations and their impact on key macroeconomic variables of employment, output, and inflation. Figure 7.2 illustrated the behavior of the variables that change from short-run to long-run adjustments. The diagram in Figure 7.2 also illustrated the relationship between changes in labor wages and price level at different levels of business cycles and their policy implications.

Section 7.3.1 explained the implications for the shapes of SRAS and LRAS curves in regard to business-cycle fluctuations with interpretations of changes in output and price level in the short run and the long run.

Section 7.3.2 explained the key factors to shift the SRAS curve in the long run and the same for the LRAS curve in the very long run. Figure 7.2 also illustrated this movement from long run to very long run in response to the structural shift of the economy as a whole over time.

Section 7.3.3 introduced the factors that shift the AD curve. Changes in the key components of AD, such as consumption, investment, government expenses, and net export do shift the AD curve to determine changes in equilibrium output, employment, and price level. Figure 7.3 in Section 7.3.4 illustrated this shift of the AD curve through the effects of the multiplier process.

Section 7.3.4 introduced the concept of the multiplier and derived the mathematical equation of the Keynesian multiplier to explain the effect of the multiplier on changes in equilibrium RGDP when any of the components of AD plus other factors are changed to fine-tune the economy. A numerical example of the Keynesian multiplier equation was explained and estimated the Keynesian multiplier value as an example of the importance of the Keynesian multiplier in affecting the macroeconomic recovery from business-cycle fluctuations. Students are encouraged to practice the multiplier equation with other numerical examples offered in this subsection and illustrated in Figure 7.3.

Application Activities

Q1. Critically, but very briefly, explain why the minimum RGDP growth rate needed to achieve full employment for the United States is constrained by 3%. Give numerical examples by using relevant equations and compare them with other countries' positions.

Q2. Briefly explain why the shape of the SRAS curve is relatively flat during a severe recession and increasingly slopes upward as the economy reaches full employment and beyond.

Q3. Explain why the AD curve slopes downward.

Q4. Draw a hypothetical diagram for the AD-AS model you learned about in this chapter and indicate a situation with demand-side inflation. On the same diagram, indicate another situation with supply-side inflation.

Q5. What is the Keynesian multiplier and how does it expand the economy at the rate of the multiple of initial expenditure amount injected into the economy? Give a numerical example as part of your answer.

Q6. In Table 7.1, several factors are listed that shift the AD and/or AS curves to change the equilibrium price level and the RGDP. Read the descriptions of factors in the first column and then report their effects in the rest of the columns as indicated.

Table 7.1: Factors to Shift AD and AS Curves

Changes in Events	Shift of AD Right or Left	Shift of AS Right or Left	Change in Price Level and RGDP
Increase in oil price			
Increase in technology and productivity			
Increase in government spending			
Increase in taxes on wage earners			
Increase in consumer confidence			
Decrease in expected inflation			
Increase in currency exchange rate			

Chapter 8

The Real Sector Model of Keynesian Macroeconomics and Data Analysis

Learning Objectives

As they read the chapter, students will learn the following:

- Introduction to the foundations of the Keynesian macroeconomic model versus the classical theory of macroeconomics
- The AD and AS of Keynesian economics with the price level consideration
- The aggregate expenditure model (the demand) and aggregate production (the supply) of Keynesian economics without the price level consideration: the 45-degree equality line model

8.1. Introduction to the Foundations of the Keynesian Macroeconomic Model versus the Classical Theory of Macroeconomics

In addition to basic theories of macroeconomic foundations introduced earlier in Chapters 6 and 7, this chapter focuses on the complete model structure of Keynesian economics. It is a major departure from the classical school of thought in macroeconomics. Prior to the development of Keynesian economics in the 1930s, the theory and practice of macroeconomics were known as the classical theory of macroeconomics, originally developed by Adam Smith in his 1776 book titled *The Wealth of Nations*. The key theme of the classical view of macroeconomics is the process of a self-correcting mechanism of the free market system without government policy intervention. In his 1936 book titled *The General Theory of Employment, Interest and Money*, Keynes introduced his criticism of the self-correcting mechanism, arguing that a free market system fails to correct itself in a time of severe demand deficiency, which happened in the 1930s, resulting from an inventory accumulation of goods and services. With the rising trend of inventory accumulation and layoffs, production declined, and the unemployment rate climbed up to 25% during the Great Depression, with no sign of recovery through a self-correcting mechanism. The classical view of a self-correcting mechanism was based on the principle of wage and price flexibility in the labor market, which was rejected by Keynes with his theory of wage-price stickiness explained next.

Keynes's explanation of wage-price stickiness is based on the short-run fluctuation of labor market behavior during a severe recession. Keynes argued that wages and prices are not flexible when the average price level hits the lowest point during a prolonged recession. At that point, members of the labor force who are still working have a long-term contract with their employers on their wage rates and other fringe benefits. Until that long-term contract expires, the wage rates stay the same. Keynes concluded that with the reality of wage-price stickiness, the self-correcting mechanism of a free market system would fail to boost the AD in the long run, even at a very low price and wage combination (Keynes 1936, p. 257–271). Therefore, Keynes's solution for quick economic recovery was for active government policy to boost the AD in the short run. He also stressed the importance of active government intervention to avoid the possible grave danger of economic depression in the long term. As stated by Keynes,

> It follows, therefore, that if labour were to respond to conditions of gradually diminishing employment by offering its services at a diminishing money-wage, this would not, as a rule, have the effect of reducing real wages and might even have the effect of increasing them, through its adverse influence on the volume of output. The chief result of this policy would be to cause a great instability of prices, so violent perhaps as to make business calculations futile in an economic society functioning after the manner of that in which we live. To suppose that a flexible wage is right and proper adjunct of a system which on the whole is one of laissez-faire, is the opposite of the truth. It is only in a highly authoritarian society, where sudden, substantial, all-round changes could be decreed that a flexible wage-policy could function with success. One can imagine it in operation in Italy, Germany or Russia, but not in France, the United States or Great Britain.[1]

The Keynesian approach of government policy intervention in macroeconomics was developed in a manner in which the AD components involve active government participation in not only policy agenda but also in influencing economic expansion by increasing government spending and providing tax incentive policies for both private investments and wage earners. The AD equation [C + I + G + (EX–IM)] developed in the Keynesian framework indicates the power of government spending to boost the economy. The influence of aggregate consumption (C) and government spending (G) through appropriate fiscal policy is discussed in more detail in Chapter 9.

---

1 John Maynard Keynes, *The General Theory of Employment, Interest, and Money*, (New York: Prometheus Books, 1997), p. 269.

8.2. The Aggregate Demand and Aggregate Supply of Keynesian Economics with Price Level Consideration

The analysis of the Keynesian model can be made from two different approaches. One is the AD-AS model with price level considerations, as discussed in Chapters 6 and 7. The second approach is the aggregate expenditure (AE) model without the use of the price level, called **the real sector model**. Both of these approaches are important to understand not only for effective policy implications but also all dimensions of real-world macroeconomics. Figure 8.1 illustrates the AD-AS Keynesian model with its price level. It is important to note that this price-output model has been discussed in previous chapters. However, this section is an illustration of the same model with a focus on the analytical aspect of the model.

Figure 8.1 AD-AS with Price Level

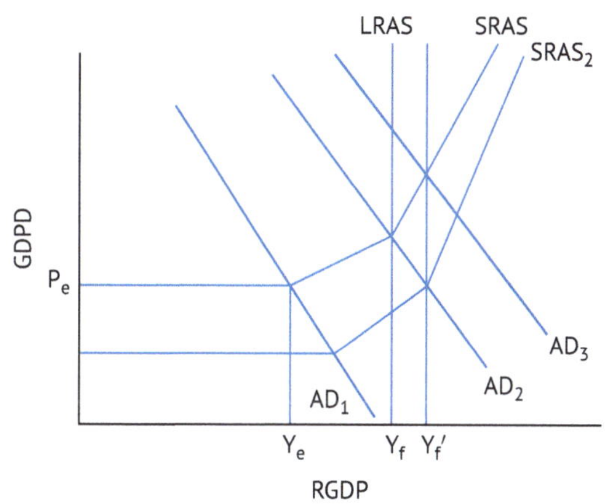

Figure 8.1 shows the price level (GDPD) as the vertical axis, and both AD and AS are labeled on the horizontal axis against the price level. The way the model structure works is explained by the AD and AS equations that follow.

AD = f (Price level, C, I, G, EX, IM, expected income, taxes, ...)

AS = g (Price level, cost of production, technology, expected profit, productivity, wages, capital stock, interest rate, tax policy on business and profit, ...)

The AD equation is a general expression of the functional relationship among variables in which the left side variable, AD, is expressed as a function of independent variables in the parentheses on the right-hand side of the equation.

The AS equation is also a general expression of the functional relationship between dependent variable AS on the left-hand side and independent variables in the parentheses on the right side of the equation.

In these two equations, changes in any of the independent variables on the right-hand side would influence the dependent variable (AD and/or AS) on the left-hand side. For example, if the price level in the AD equation increases, then the law of demand indicates that the quantity of components in AD would decrease, and vice versa, ceteris paribus. The ceteris paribus assumption here implies that, other than a change in the price level, all other independent variables will not change for the time being. This law of demand (the same law of demand in microeconomics) for the inverse relationship between AD and the price level explains why AD is downward sloping. For the AS function, if the price level increases, then the law of supply indicates that the quantity of goods and services produced in aggregate would also increase, and vice versa, ceteris paribus. This law of a direct relationship between the price level and the quantity of AS is illustrated as an upward-sloping curve (but not with a constant slope). Also, it is worth noting that the constant slope of AD curves is not really a realistic slope of the AD function. The straight-line AD curves are drawn just for simplicity without compromising the consistency of theorizing the model structure. The equilibrium for price level and RGDP is shown with the combination of Pe and Ye, respectively, at the point of intersection between AD_1 and SRAS.

Since this model structure has several independent variables to influence one dependent variable in both equations, the ceteris paribus assumption in both cases helps determine the equilibrium price level and quantity of RGDP. But a question remains: What happens when the ceteris paribus assumption does not hold true? In other words, what happens to the equilibrium price level and quantity of RGDP when variables other than the price level change. When they do change (they do actually change frequently), the initial equilibrium point changes by shifting either AD and/or AS curves in the appropriate direction (rightward shift or leftward shift) depending on the nature of changes. The general principle is that a change with a positive outcome will shift the AD or AS curve to the right and a change with negative effect will shift the curves leftward. For example, an increase in government spending would shift the AD curve to the right, say AD_2, with a new set of equilibrium prices and quantities at the point of intersection between SRAS and AD_2.

On the other hand, a technological advancement with better efficiency in production will increase labor productivity and may decrease the MC of production at the same time. Given this change in technology on the AS side, the positive impact would shift the AS curve to the right with a new equilibrium price level and quantity produced at the macro level. This scenario is shown in Figure 8.1 at the intersection between $SRAS_2$ and either of the three AD curves. Students may clearly observe here that, despite many independent variables in both equations, using the trick of shifting the AD or AS curves in response to any changes in independent variables can easily guide them through the process of determining new equilibrium combinations on a two-dimensional diagram. The mathematical jargon of this process is lengthy and much more complicated than is relevance here. That task is beyond the scope of this textbook.

It is worth mentioning that the determination of the equilibrium price and quantity was possible by labeling both dependent variables AD and AS on the same horizontal axis because both curves move in the opposite direction against price changes. In the next section, the model structure is discussed without the price level as an alternative approach to the price and quantity structure of the model.

8.3. The AE Model (the Demand) and Aggregate Production (the Supply) of Keynesian Economics without the Price Level Consideration: The 45-Degree Equality Line Model

The model discussed in this section is called the real sector model without considering price changes. The argument of analysis is the same as that made in Section 8.2, except with a different approach. This approach is more technical and objective than the purely philosophical aspects of the theory explained in Section 8.2. It is technical in the sense that this model is based on the application of elementary geometry and algebra. Students are expected to find this section easy to grasp as long as they are able to understand the basic concepts of the algebraic solution of two or more variables. The analysis also involves simple geometric logic regarding 90-degree angles versus 45-degree angles in two-dimensional graphs. It is also possible to refresh students' memories of elementary concepts of algebra and geometry for this application in economics through searches on Google and YouTube. The primary focus of this model is to analyze the AE side of macroeconomics—the core contribution made by Keynes in *The General Theory of Employment, Interest and Money*—for effective policy implications.

8.3.1. The AE Model of Keynesian Economics

The AE equation consists of four components:

AE = C + I + G + (EX − IM) ....Eqn (8.1)

Using the equation for the AE model of the macroeconomic framework developed by Keynes, a set of hypothetical data is applied next for the numerical estimation of equilibrium RGDP.

C = SR consumption expenditure = a + b Yd = a + b (Y − T) = 50 + 0.75 (Y − 20),

where a = Intercept (consumption of individuals even with no income), and

b = Marginal propensity to consume (MPC) = ΔC/ΔYd; ratio of change in C to change in disposable income

Yd = Disposable income = Gross income—Taxes (Y − T)

T = Total taxes = 20

I = Fixed investment expenditure = 100 (for sake of simplicity)

G = Fixed government expenditure decided by legislators = 150

EX = Export expenditure by domestic residents = 30

IM = Import expenditure by foreign buyers = 15

EX–IM = Net export = 15 (30 − 15)

Yf = Full employment level of RGDP (expected) = 1,600

At equilibrium.

Y = RGDP = AE = C + I + G + (EX − IM) ....Eqn (8.2)

Given the expenditure model and the assumed value of desired full employment at 1,600, students may practice the following algebraic solutions to determine equilibrium GDP followed by an illustration. This section explains the step-by-step process, starting with the consumption and savings functions.

8.3.2. The Equation for Consumption Expenditure

C = a + b Yd is a typical behavior of an individual or all individuals in the entire economy. This equation has two variables, C (dependent variable) and Yd (independent variable). It also has two parameters, a and b, which can be estimated by plugging in the observed values of C and Yd by conducting a sample survey from selected individuals. The estimated values of a and b explain the average behavior of consumers, where "a" is called the intercept—the level of consumption when income is equal to zero. With income greater than zero, the value of b (MPC) tells us what percentage of additional income a typical consumer will spend after paying taxes (Y − T = Yd) and what percentage of the same additional income will be saved.

For example, from the previous numerical values of the consumption equation, students can plug in the values given to derive the estimated consumption function and its corresponding savings function shown next:

$C = a + b (Y - T) = 50 + 0.75 (Y - 20)$, and
$S = Yd - C = Yd - (a + bYd) = Yd\text{-}a - bYd = --a + (1 - b)Yd = -50 + 0.25 (Y - 20)$.

From the consumption and savings equations, the derivation of MPC ($\Delta C/\Delta Yd$) and MPS ($\Delta S/\Delta Yd$) are estimated by using simple differentiations:

$MPC = \Delta C/\Delta Yd = \Delta(50 + bYd)/\Delta Yd = 0 + b = 0.75$; differentiation of a constant value 50 = zero,
$MPS = \Delta S/\Delta Yd = \Delta[(-50 + (1 - b)Yd)]/\Delta Yd = 1 - b = 1 - 0.75 = 0.25$.

The estimated values of MPC and MPS estimated are interpreted in the following manner: MPC = 0.75 means that an extra dollar of disposable income (after taxes) will influence a typical consumer to spend 75 cents and save 25 cents of a dollar earned after taxes paid. The combination of MPC and MPS will always be equal to one.

The numerical values of the schedule in Table 8.1 and the corresponding graph for the consumption and savings equations are presented in Figure 8.2 for further understanding of this important concept from a real-world perspective.

Table 8.1: Consumption and Savings Schedule

Disposable Income (Yd)	Consumption (C)	MPC	Savings	MPS
0	50	–	–50	–
100	125	0.75	–25	0.25
200	200	0.75	0	0.25
300	275	0.75	25	0.25
400	350	0.75	25	0.25

Table 8.1 represents the consumption and savings equations introduced earlier with the estimated value of MPC at 0.75 and the corresponding value of MPS at 0.25. The graphical

Figure 8.2 Consumption and Savings Curves

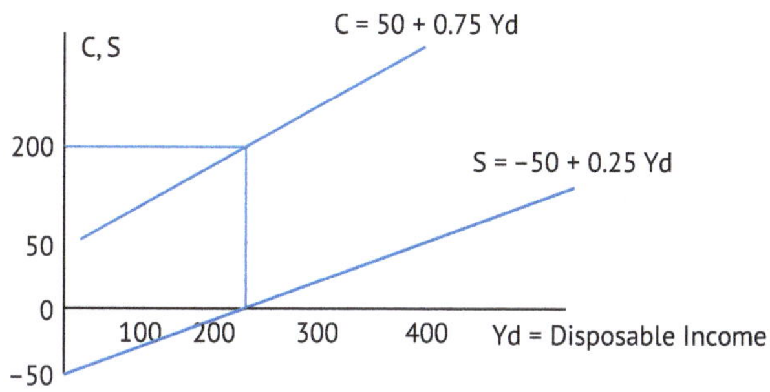

presentation of these consumption and savings values are illustrated in Figure 8.2, followed by a detailed explanation.

Figure 8.2 is a graphical representation of the consumption and savings equations with hypothetical values plugged into the equations and the graphs. Students may observe that the consumption curve started with +50 labeled on the vertical axis with a zero level of income, and the corresponding savings curve started with −50 from the lower segment of the vertical axis. The slope of the consumption curve is 0.75, and the slope of the savings curve is 0.25, moving upward as income starts increasing from zero to 100, 200, 300, and 400, displayed on the horizontal axis. It is also shown that when income is at 200, consumption and income are at 200 with zero savings. The negative savings appears before the 200 level of income and positive saving appears after the 200 level of income.

This hypothetical consumption-and-savings model is the observed behavior of a typical consumer, as such, it is an individual or aggregate consumption scenario for the entire economy. However, the values of MPC and MPS are not identical for all individuals and widely vary from the national average depending on income levels, lifestyles, and other obligations.

For example, MPC in the short run for the US economy varies between 0.90 and 0.98, with 0.98 for the baby boomer generation (some have already started to retire since 2010). That means the workers of the baby boomer generation do not seem to be saving, and they will probably never save. There are two main reasons for such a low rate of saving by the baby boomer generation: they are the highest income earners in the entire labor force, and they have other tangible wealth and assets accumulated to rely on during retirement. The assets and wealth-generating income are in addition to the cash flow they receive from their regular income. Some experts also explain this high MPC as an indicator of good health without any plans to retire anytime soon. Nonetheless, the overall value of MPC for US consumers is much higher than in many industrialized countries. Many experts have concluded that the high MPC for American consumers is mainly attributed to economic stability, with a full employment record most of the time since the 1940s. Another reason could be a generous social safety net in the form of social security payments, Medicare, Medicaid, unemployment insurance, subsidized housing, and food programs for low-income families.

Nonetheless, the Keynesian expenditure multiplier measured by **1/(1–MPC)** implies that the higher the MPC, the higher the multiplier to boost the economy faster. For example, with MPC = 0.9, the multiplier is 10, [(1/(1 − 0.9) = 1/0.1 = 10]. Although the realistic multiplier may not be so robust, the power of the multiplier basically comes from the high value of MPC. With over two-thirds of the GDP contribution made by consumers, the high MPC value actually has a profound influence on GDP growth for the US economy through the multiplier process.

The consumption function is altered by changes in tax policy, expected income, and other external factors that directly or indirectly influence its parameters (intercept and MPC). The long-run MPC value is a little different than the short-run MPC value. The long-run MPC does not have the intercept because zero income is not considered a relevant parameter in the long-run consumption function.

8.3.3. Investment Function

For the simplicity of the expenditure model in Section 8.1, the investment equation is assumed to be fixed for short-run analysis. However, real-world investment function is usually downward sloping because investment is inversely related to changes in interest rates. In *The General Theory of Employment, Interest and Money*, Keynes explained the power of interest rate behavior in a comprehensive manner. Since interest rates are one of the key driving forces to influence the financial markets on Wall Street, the economics of interest rate behavior is discussed in more detail in the money market and monetary policy sections in Chapter 10. At this point, investment is considered fixed with the assumption that the interest rate is constant for the short run. The relevant hypothetical graphs for the investment curve for both constant and variable interest rates are illustrated in Figure 8.3.

Figure 8.3 Investment Curve

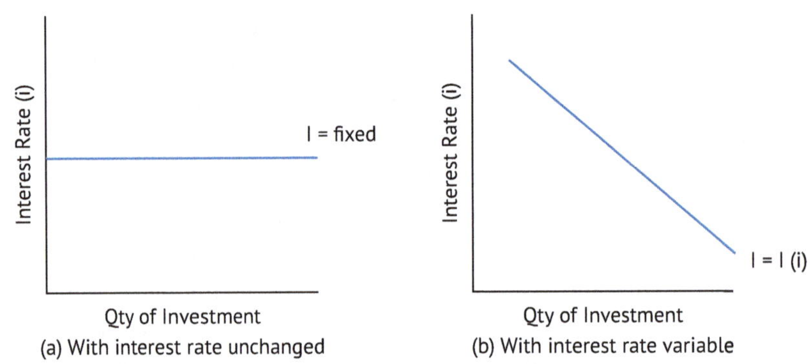

With investment as a function of interest rates and other external variables, panel (a) in Figure 8.3 shows the horizontal investment curve with the assumption of a fixed interest rate in the short run. Panel (b) shows the downward-sloping investment curve with variable interest rates, which is inversely related—meaning that as interest rates increase, investment volume will decrease, and vice versa, ceteris paribus. However, if the ceteris paribus assumption does not hold true, changes in business expectations, inflation, profit, or government policy would shift the curve to the right or to the left depending on the nature of changes. For this chapter, interest is assumed to be fixed.

8.3.4. Government Expenditure

The G component of the AE equation is an external factor that is solely decided by the political actions undertaken by the legislators of the government. The value G is changed by political decision through the legislative voting process.

8.3.5. Net Export (EX—IM)

The last of the four components of the AE equation—export (EX) minus import (IM)—is discussed here to help the student become familiar with its contribution to RGDP. The details of this segment of the AE are discussed in Chapters 14 and 15 under the economics of foreign trade and globalization. In this model, the introduction of this foreign trade component provides students with exposure to observe the important role that the trade sector plays in the economy at the rapid pace of globalization. Exports and imports are mainly influenced by two main variables, as shown in the general equations that follow.

EX = EX (e, Y^f), where e is the currency exchange rate, and Y^f is the income of foreign countries doing the trade.
IM = IM (e, Y^d), where e is the exchange rate, and Y^d is domestic income or RGDP.

The changes in e, Y^f, and Y^d affect the volume of exports and imports either positively or negatively depending on the direction of change. For example, if the exchange rate increases for the US$ against a foreign currency, the quantity of exports will decrease, and the quantity of imports will increase because exporting US-produced goods will become more expensive to foreign buyers, and imports will be cheaper for American residents. The opposite will happen if the exchange rate for the US$ decreases. On the income side, if foreigners' income increases, exports of US goods will increase, and vice versa. Likewise, if the domestic income increases, imports will increase, and vice versa. The net effect of the foreign trade balance depends on the relative volume of exports and imports for a particular year that varies from year to year. For the United States, there has been a chronic trade deficit for decades because the US export volume is always less than imports for a number of reasons, which are discussed in Chapters 14 and 15. For the simplicity of this model, it is assumed that there is no change in exchange rates, domestic income, and foreign income. That means the number of exports and imports are considered fixed, with no influence from changes in exchange rates and incomes. The next section covers the algebraic solutions of this real-sector macroeconomic model.

8.3.6. Determination of Equilibrium RGDP Without the Price Level

Given the information for the macro model in Section 8.3.1 and the introduction of each of the components of the AE equation in Sections 8.3.2 through 8.3.5, the equilibrium condition to determine RGDP and AE is expressed as the equality between AE and Y as shown in Eqn 8.2 below.

Y = C + I + G + (EX − IM), ...Eqn (8.2)

where the left-hand side in output = RGDP, and the right-hand side items are expenditure-side components. Plugging in the numerical values assigned in Section 8.3.1, the algebraic solution is derived next:

Y = a + b (Y−T) + I + G + (EX−IM)
= 50 + 0.75 (Y − 20) + 100 + 150 + (30 − 15) = 330 −15 + 0.75Y − 0.75 * 20
= 330 − 15 − 15 + 0.75Y.

The only variable, Y, in this reduced equation can be solved by moving 0.75Y to the left-hand side of the equation.

$Y - 0.75Y = 300$ or
$Y(1 - .75) = 300$; now taking the common factor $(1-0.75)$ to the right-hand side, it can be rearranged as
$Y = [1/(1-0.75)] * 300 = 4 * 300 = 1{,}200$, **where [1/(1−0.75)] is called the Keynesian multiplier.**

Y = 1,200 is the estimated equilibrium GDP for this model; it is also important to understand the derivation process of the Keynesian multiplier [1/(1−0.75)] = 1/MPS] from the same solution of the model. Because the value of MPC is given as 0.75, the multiplier is 1/MPS = 1/0.25 = 4. Now suppose the MPC was a different value than 0.75, say 0.80, and then the multiplier would rise to 5 (1/0.2 = 5). That means the higher the MPC, the larger the value of the multiplier, and the lower the MPC, the smaller the multiplier. If the MPC is 0.9, which is normal for US consumers, then the multiplier will increase to a whopping 10. As mentioned before, the high MPC for American consumers works very well for the economy when policy makers increase G (government expenditure) and/or decrease taxes. The **tax multiplier** is estimated a bit differently than the expenditure multiplier, as shown next.

To derive the tax multiplier, instead of keeping the tax amount fixed, it is treated as a one-time variable decided by the government. The relevant equation for the tax multiplier is shown here. Suppose tax is decreased by the government from T1 to T2, and the change in tax is ΔT. Plugging this into the reduced form of the equilibrium equation that follows, and the tax multiplier is derived as

$$\Delta Y = 1/(1\text{-}MPC) * (-MPC) * (\Delta T).$$

Note that −**MPC**, which comes from $C = a + b(Y-T)$ or $\Delta C = -MPC * \Delta T = b\Delta Y$ as already moved to the left-hand side of the equation.

$$\Delta Y = [-MPC/(1-MPC)]^* \Delta T,$$

where $[-MPC/(1-MPC)]^* = -MPC/MPS$ is the derived **tax multiplier.** Now suppose that the tax amount is reduced by the government to 10 from 20 in the above model. Then the change in equilibrium GDP would be as follows:

$\Delta Y = -\mathbf{MPC/MPS * (-\Delta 10) = (-0.75/0.25) * (-10) = (-3)^* (-10) = +30}$ (tax reduction is a negative tax, so, ΔT is negative to maintain the consistency of the value of the tax changes).

Adding this increase in RGDP to the initial equilibrium 1,200, the total GDP after-tax reduction of 10 would be 1,200 + 30 = 1,230. Using a similar algebraic trick, students may practice increasing the value of each of the AE components in the earlier model to estimate the equilibrium RGDP. One more task here is to illustrate the earlier calculations of RGDP by using a 45-degree equality line and examine its relationship with full-employment RGDP. Figure 8.4 illustrates the graphical representation of this AE model estimation.

Figure 8.4 AE Model and Macroeconomic Equilibrium

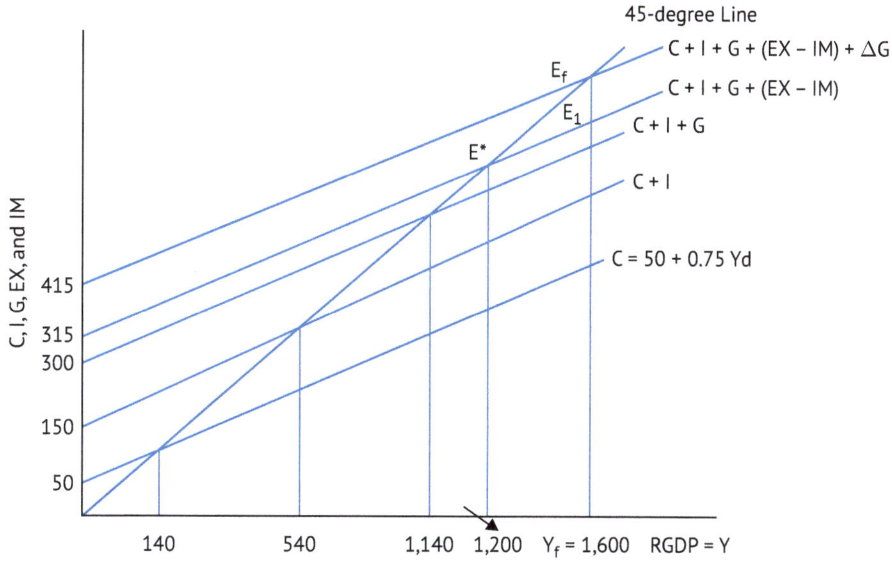

The solution for the equilibrium RGDP for this section is displayed in Figure 8.4 to visualize the whole real sector model, with the horizontal axis labeled for RGDP or supply-side and the vertical axis labeled for all four components of AE or the AD side. The 45-degree equality line is drawn with its slope equal to one to display all possible equilibrium levels of GDP at the points of intersection between the AE line and the 45-degree equality line. The reason for drawing this equality line is to use a simple geometric trick to determine the equilibrium level of RGDP to be sitting always on this equality line. The slope of this 45-degree equality line is always equal to one and, therefore, the consumption expenditure line with its slope less than one (the MPC is assumed to be less than one) will always cut through the 45-degree line to determine the point of RGDP equilibrium. That means from any point on this line, the vertical line drawn to the horizontal axis and to the vertical axis must be equal (AE = Y = RGDP). Thus the equilibrium RGDP estimated for 1,200 is at point E*, where the AE [equal to C + I + G + (EX – IM)] intersects with the equality line. Students may also notice that other components of the AE equation are also drawn separately with their respective values on the vertical axis and corresponding equilibrium RGDP on the horizontal axis, using the same expenditure multiplier of 1/(1 – MPC) = 1/(1 – 0.75) = 4. For example, using C = 50 + 0.75 (Y – 20), the value of Y is estimated to be 140, as labeled on the horizontal axis. The estimation method is Y = 1/(1 – 0.75) *(50 – 0.75 * 20) = 4 * (50 – 15) = 4 * 35 = 140. Students may practice the estimation of 540, 1,140, or any number by using the same estimation method.

The last step of this section is to move the economy from its equilibrium point at 1,200 to full employment at 1,600. Students may recall in the model structure that the full employment level of RGDP is assumed to be at 1,600. Given this full-employment RGDP, the RGDP gap and recessionary gap from this set of information are defined as follows:

RGDP gap = Full employment RGDP—Actual or equilibrium RGDP

= 1,600—1,200 = 400.

Recessionary gap = (RGDP gap)/(expenditure multiplier) = 400/4 = 100.

In Figure 8.4, the point of intersection for the full-employment level of RGDP is plotted at E_f, where the AE cuts through the 45-degree line with RGDP at 1,600 on the horizontal axis. The RGDP gap is between points E* and E_1 = 400. The corresponding recessionary gap is the vertical distance between E_f and E_1 = 100. With a multiplier value of 4, the RGDP gap of 400 can be closed by the additional investment of 100 either by increasing government expenditure or any other components of AE. For example, the AE line labeled C + I + G + (EX–IM) + ΔG expands the economy from a state of recession at 1,200 to the full-employment level of RGDP at 1,600 by adding government spending estimated by the shortcut equation as follows:

ΔY = (Expenditure multiplier) * (Recessionary gap) = 4 * 100 = 400.

Total RGDP is now = 1,200 + 400 = 1,600.

Mission accomplished!

The fiscal policy implications of using taxes and government spending as policy tools are discussed in more detail in the next chapter, with an analysis of the budget deficit and public debt and their financing mechanism.

Chapter Summary

Section 8.1 introduced the basic foundation of the Keynesian model of macroeconomics as a major development over the weakness of the classical macroeconomics model when the market mechanism under laissez-faire fails to operate efficiently. The Keynesian approach of government policy intervention in macroeconomics was developed in *The General Theory of Employment, Interest and Money*. The way Keynes developed and explained the key components of AD involving active government participation is not only a policy agenda but also influences economic expansion by increasing government spending and providing tax incentive policies for both private investments and wage earners. The AD equation (C + I + G + (EX–IM)) developed in the Keynesian framework indicates the power of government spending to boost the economy. The influence of aggregate consumption (C) and government spending (G) through appropriate fiscal policy is discussed in more detail in Chapter 9. The last two sections of this chapter explained the mechanism to determine equilibrium RGDP by considering price level to change as well as the same to determine without considering the price level. The former approach is the AD-AS model we have already discussed in early chapters, while the latter approach is known as the real sector model with the use of a 45-degree equality line.

Section 8.2 revisited the AD-AS model structure of macroeconomics with price level as the key variable to change in the determination of output (RGDP) and price level. Figure 8.1 illustrates the AD-AS Keynesian model with its price level on the vertical axis, and both AD and AS are labeled on the horizontal axis against the price level. It is important to note that this price-output model has been discussed in Chapters 6 and 7. However, this section is an illustration of the same model with a focus on the analytical aspect of the model without changes in the price level. The discussion in this section was primarily focused on analyzing the changes in equilibrium because of changes in other macroeconomics-related variables than its own price level. The changes in other variables usually shift the AD and/or AS curve to reach out to a new equilibrium level of output and prices. Students are encouraged to practice this section by drawing hypothetical diagrams of using a similar method and critically observe the mechanism of change in the output and price level attributed to other variables and their policy implications.

Section 8.3 introduced the real sector model of macroeconomics without the price level originally developed by Keynes in the 1930s. The real sector model structure incorporates all four components of AE as the demand side for the entire economy. These components of AE are expressed as follows:

$$\mathbf{AE = C + I + G + (EX{-}IM), \;\ldots\ldots\ldots\ldots Eqn\ (8.1)}$$

where C = Consumption expenditure,
I = Investment expenditure,
G = Government expenditure, and,
EX − IM = Export minus export as net export.

Section 8.3.1 explained each of these four components in regard to how the changes in these components affect the changes in the AE curve to affect production, jobs, and inflation. The equilibrium condition for the real sector economy was also introduced as follows:

$$\mathbf{Y = AE = C + I + G + EX - IM,}$$

where Y = Total output produced called RGDP.

Section 8.3.2 introduced the theoretical model of the consumption function as follows:

$$\mathbf{C = a + b(Y - T),}$$

where a and b are parameters, and C and Y − T are consumption expenditure and disposable income, respectively. The detail of this consumption equation and its corresponding saving function $\mathbf{S = -a + (1 - b)\ (Y - T)}$ are discussed with numerical data and the graph in Table 8.1 and Figure 8.2, respectively. The concept of MPC and marginal propensity to save (MPS) were also explained in this section with numerical examples.

Section 8.3.3 introduced the investment component of the AE model with two alternative ways to explain the behavior of investment in macroeconomics. The first one is assumed to be a fixed investment with no change in the interest rate, and the second option is to assume the interest rate as a variable that will affect the investment portfolio. Figure 8.3 illustrates these two types of investment curve with a horizontal investment curve for the fixed interest rate and a downward-sloping investment curve for the variable interest rate.

Section 8.3.4 introduced the contribution of government expenditure to add to the economy. But government expenditure is considered a fixed amount at any moment in time because the government decides the maximum amount to allocate once a year.

Section 8.3.5 explained the contributions to RGDP (Y) made by the foreign trade component of AE equation. This component is expressed as follows:

EX – IM, with

EX = EX (e, Yf), where e is the currency exchange rate, and Y^f is the income of foreign countries doing the trade.

IM = IM (e, Yd), where e is the exchange rate, and Y^d is domestic income or RGDP.

Section 8.3.6 presented the combined model structure to determine the equilibrium RGDP by using the real sector and numerical values for each of the components of AE. The importance of the Keynesian expenditure multiplier (1/MPS) and tax multiplier (–MPC/MPS) was explained in this section as significant contributions to Keynesian macroeconomics to fine-tune the economy through government involvement in the market system during recession and inflation. The numerical examples were given to estimate the equilibrium RGDP systematically without considering the price level. This method of estimation is also illustrated in Figure 8.4 with a more detailed explanation of policy implication for government spending and tax policy. Students are strongly recommended to practice this model structure by choosing different numerical values to repeat the process. It is important to note that the numerical estimations of equilibrium RGDP from equation (8.2) and their illustration in Figure 8.4 reflect the real-world policy perspectives of government involvement in active fiscal policy actions to achieve full employment.

Application Activities

Use the following macroeconomic model to answer questions Q1 through Q11:

$$C = 115 + 0.75Yd,$$

where C = Consumption function; Yd (Y − T) = Disposable income

I = 150; I = Investment

G = 200; G = Government expenditure

T = 100; T = Tax revenue

X = 40; X = Export

M = 30; M = Import

Also assume that Yf = Full employment GDP (potential GDP) = 2,000

Q1. Estimate the equilibrium GDP level (income, Ye).

Q2. Estimate the level of aggregate consumption (C).

Q3. Estimate the level of aggregate saving (S).

Q4. The MPC and MPS for the economy are, respectively, ________ and ________.

Q5. The expenditure multiplier for the economy is ________.

Q6. The tax multiplier for the economy is ________.

Q7. Given the value of the full-employment level of GDP, the GDP gap is ________.

Q8. The government spending needed to bridge the GDP gap you found in Q7 would be ________.

Q9. If the export value increases to 60 because of a decrease in the value of US$, other things staying the same, then the answer to Q1 would be ________.

Q10. In addition to an increase of export value in Q9, if the import value decreases to 20 for the same reason, other things remaining the same, then the answer to Q1 would be ________.

Q11. In Q8, the GDP gap and recessionary gap are, respectively, ________ and ________.

Q12. Illustrate your answers from Q1 through Q8 in a graph of 45-degree equality line, similar to Figure 8.4 in Section 8.3.6.

Chapter 9

Macroeconomic Policies

Fiscal Policy and Monetary Policy

Learning Objectives

As they read the chapter, students will learn the following:

- The causes of free-market failure and rationale for policy actions as opposed to the classical view of laissez-faire
- Working mechanism of fiscal policy under Keynesian perspectives
- Working mechanism of monetary policy under Keynesian perspectives

9.1. The Causes of Free-Market Failure and Rationale for Policy Actions as Opposed to the Classical View of Laissez-Faire

In Chapter 8, we introduced the Keynesian macroeconomics foundation, with its significant departure from the classical theory of macroeconomics. Keynes convinced policy makers and his peers in academia that the Great Depression, the worst financial and economic crisis in the twentieth century, was mainly attributed to the deficiency in AD under the free market system. The theoretical contributions made by Keynes toward the deficiency of AD greatly influenced the adoption of the fiscal policy presented by President Roosevelt in 1933. Based on the Keynesian macroeconomic model, President Roosevelt incorporated a massive fiscal spending budget into his 1933 economic recovery plan called the New Deal. The New Deal was a major public policy initiative to establish the role of government in handling the severe economic depression at the time. Although there has been ongoing political and intellectual debate as to whether the New Deal based on the Keynesian model was actually effective, there is a consensus by many economists that the slow recovery was due to the aggressive fiscal policy measures undertaken by FDR through the New Deal.[1] However, it was also argued that the application of Keynesian economics did not fully recover the US economy from the Great Depression until the outbreak of World War II in 1939, when the US economy was fully reinvested to its full potential.

A similar economic crisis emerged again in the US economy during the Great Recession of 2007–2008, when the financial and real estate markets collapsed to their worst levels since the Great Depression of the 1930s. The severity of the Great Recession resulted in a negative GDP growth rate of over 4% and the unemployment rate rising to almost 10% in 2009.[2] Given the urgency of the economic and financial crisis at the time, President Obama initiated a massive fiscal spending and tax-cut program under the American Recovery and Reinvestment Act (ARRA) of 2009, with total government spending of over $800 billion, the highest government spending package since the end of World War II in 1945.[3]

The stimulus package established by the ARRA seemed to have a positive effect on a slow recovery; the recession ended by December 2009, new jobs were created, and the GDP growth rate increased in subsequent years. The relevant data in Table 9.1 indicate that the recovery process continued consistently, with a sustained positive RGDP growth rate and declining unemployment rate since then. The data also show that the actual unemployment rate declined to its natural rate of unemployment by 2016. Although the recovery process was slow—over seven years to reach full employment—the growth rate was steady and sustainable, with very little fluctuation over the years under consideration. The actual unemployment rate in 2017 and 2019 at 4.4% and 3.8%, respectively, reflect a state of economic boom because 3.8% unemployment rate in 2019 is the lowest unemployment rate in the last 40 years. The RGDP growth rate at 2.9% in 2018 also indicates a steady rate of growth for sustainable full employment since 2016.

---

1 Hubbard, R.G and O'Brien, A.P. (2019). *Macroeconomics*, 7th edition, Pearson Publishing.

2 "U.S. Bureau of Economic Analysis (BEA)." U.S. Bureau of Economic Analysis (BEA). Accessed November 22, 2019. https://www.bea.gov/. and "U.S. Bureau of Labor Statistics." U.S. Bureau of Labor Statistics. U.S. Bureau of Labor Statistics, November 20, 2019. https://www.bls.gov/.

3 Green brenda checkmark

Citation successfully created!

My Citation List

Create another citation

Copy all

Save

Download

Chicago-16th

"Congressional Budget Office." Congressional Budget Office. Accessed November 22, 2019. https://www.cbo.gov/.

Table 9.1: RGDP Growth Rate and Unemployment Rate, 2006–2018

Year	RGDP Growth Rate	Unemployment Rate	Comments
2006	2.67%	4.6%	State of full employment
2007	1.78%	4.6%	RGDP delinked, no change in unemployment rate but a state of full employment
2008	−0.29%	5.8%	Negative GDP growth rate and unemployment rate rose
2009	−2.77%	9.3%	Severe recession and high rate of unemployment
2010	2.53%	9.6%	Recovery started with positive GDP growth but still high unemployment rate
2011	1.60%	8.9%	Setback in growth rate, unemployment rate declining
2012	2.22%	8.1%	Recovery continued
2013	1.68%	7.4%	RGDP declined a little but unemployment rate continued to decline
2014	2.57%	6.2%	Recovery started picking up
2015	2.86%	5.3%	Unemployment continued declining
2016	1.49%	4.9%	Reach full employment, took over seven years to achieve full recovery
2017	2.27%	4.4%	State of full employment, same as 2006
2018	2.9%	3.8%	State of economic boom with the lowest unemployment rate in 40 years

Sources: For RGDP growth rate, US Bureau of Economic Analysis and for unemployment rate, US Bureau of Labor Statistics.

Between the 1930s and 2008, the US economy experienced ups and downs from business-cycle fluctuations, such as the stagflation (simultaneous rise of inflation and unemployment) in the 1970s caused by an oil embargo imposed by OPEC and the relatively short-lived recessions in 1991 and 2001. In those situations, the government was also proactive in fine-tuning the economic recovery during cyclical downturns. Therefore, the history of economic policy actions suggests that active fiscal policy measures undertaken by US government agencies over the last 75 years have been very effective in keeping the economy at its full-employment level for most of this time period. The US government also has a legal responsibility to fine-tune economic fluctuation, which is mandated by the Employment Act of 1946 enacted by the US Congress. Note that the Full Employment Act of 1945 was later passed as the Employment Act of 1946. (The word "full" was excluded in the final passage of the act.) The act was further amended in 1978 and titled the Full Employment and Balanced Growth Act. In the next section of this chapter, we will discuss the application of fiscal policy and monetary policy, two major policy-making strategies in the US government.

9.2. Working Mechanism of Fiscal Policy under Keynesian Perspectives

9.2.1. Fiscal Policy Process

There are three key objectives of fiscal policy, as implied from the Employment Act of 1946:

Achieve and maintain full employment
Achieve and maintain maximum possible national output
Achieve and maintain price stability

To fulfill the three objectives, the following fiscal policy tools are used:
Government spending (G) and
Tax policy (T)

The fiscal policy tools are actively used at the federal level to fulfill the policy objectives outlined earlier. In addition to these basic tools of fiscal policy, federal government agencies may also use some other discretionary policies as needed. Those additional discretionary fiscal measures in the areas of national defense, environmental regulations, emergencies caused by natural calamities, and climate change are part of the discretionary spending that goes beyond the fiscal policy guidelines of the government. Nevertheless, the fiscal policy action of the US government is also primarily guided by the discretionary principle of Keynesian macroeconomic foundations. The only departure from Keynesian guidelines was the introduction of a **supply-side economic policy** first implemented by President Reagan in the 1980s. The use of supply-side economics is still in the works at times, depending on which political party is in power. The Republican Party is usually in favor of the supply-side policies whenever appropriate. The theories and practices of supply-side economics will be discussed later in this chapter. For now, this section will explain the working mechanism of fiscal policy as an extended process from the previous chapter.

9.2.2. Expansionary Fiscal Policy

Expansionary fiscal policy is designed to boost the AE [AD or AE = C + I + G + (EX−IM)] by either increasing government expenditure (G) or reducing taxes (T) or both. Expansionary fiscal policy is a discretionary policy measure usually undertaken during a state of recession. During a recession, the decline of consumption (C) and investment (I) causes the decline of AE and thus lowers production and raises the unemployment rate. To reverse this economic downturn, an increase in G and a reduction of T are expected to increase the AE to rebound the economy from a recession. The Keynesian macroeconomic model (as introduced in the previous chapter) was developed with the multiplier process to boost the AE, as shown next:

Expenditure multiplier process. Suppose the AE equation that follows is used by fiscal policy makers to expand the AE by increasing government expenditure (G) by a certain amount (see Chapter 8 for a discussion of the multiplier process).

AE = C + I + G = a + b (Y–T) + I + G (skip the export and import component for now) ..Eqn (9.1)

Suppose at equilibrium, AS of output Y = a + b (Y–T) + I + G. ....Eqn (9.2)

By algebraic manipulation shown in Chapter 8, equation (9.2) can be rewritten as

Y = [(1/(1–b)] * [a–bT + I + G], ...Eqn (9.3)

where Y is an independent variable and (1/1–b) is the expenditure multiplier, T = taxes, I = investment, and G = government expenditure.

Now assume the values of the parameter, a, the MPC b, T, and I stay the same. The only change is to increase G by its discretionary fiscal expansion. So, the increase in G by a certain amount will increase the value of output Y by the value of the multiplier (1/1–b), as shown in equation (9.3).

Delta Y = [(1/(1–b)] * [Delta G] ....Eqn (9.4)

What happened to the rest of the components of equation (9.3)? Because it is assumed that the other components stay constant; the delta of those constants multiplied by the multiplier would be zero. The derivative of constant terms is always equal to zero.

Now, it is clear from equation (9.4) that any amount of increase in government spending would increase the value of output (RGDP) by a multiple of the original increase in government spending. For example, suppose the value of the MPC (b) = 0.8 and delta G as an initial increase in government spending of $100 billion. Then the increase in output would be as estimated next.

Delta Y = [1/(1–0.8)] * $100B = 5 * 100 = $500 billion increase in RGDP value, the RGDP has increased by 5 times of initial increase in government increase.

Tax multiplier process. As in the earlier process, the effect of tax reduction is shown next by using the value of the tax multiplier (see Chapter 8 for a discussion of the tax multiplier).

Instead of changing G in the expenditure multiplier case, assume that only the tax component will change and that all other right-hand side components in equation (9.3) are unchanged or constants.

Given the assumption of changing taxes only, equation (9.3) can be rewritten as shown in equation (9.5).

Delta Y = [(–b/(1–b)] * [Delta T] ....Eqn (9.5)

Note: Delta Y = (–b * Delta T)/(1–b) or –b/(1–b) * Delta T,

Where **–b/1–b** is the tax multiplier, or **–MPC/(1–MPC) = –MPC/MPS = Tax multiplier.**

Remember that the negative sign of the tax multiplier is the adjustment process of the consumption equation explaining that change in income/output and change in taxes always move in opposite directions. For example, tax reduction is a negative tax. Therefore, a negative tax amount multiplied by a negative sign of the tax multiplier will result in a positive increase in output, and vice versa. A numerical example of such a tax reduction is shown next.

Suppose that instead of increasing government spending of $100 billion, the government decides to give a tax rebate totaling the same amount to eligible taxpayers by sending rebate checks to the recipients. The increase of output estimated from this would be (assuming the MPC is the same at 0.8)

$$\Delta Y = -b/(1-b) * -\Delta T = -MPC/(1-MPC) * (-\Delta T) = (-MPC/MPS) * (-\Delta T)$$
$$= (-0.8/0.2) * (-\$100b) = (-4) * (-\$100b) = \$400 \text{ billion.}$$

Please note that MPC + MPS = 1. So, if MPC is 0.8, MPS = 1−0.8 = 0.2.

It is important to observe that despite the same amount of tax reduction of $100 billion, the increase in output is $400 billion instead of the $500 billion shown in the case of the expenditure multiplier. This is due to the fact that the tax multiplier is smaller than the expenditure multiplier. The economic reasoning is very simple: tax rebates given out to consumers are not fully spent because the MPC is less than one. On the other hand, the increase in government spending of the same amount is fully applied toward the full effect of the expenditure multiplier. Students may use different numerical examples by assuming different MPC values and will be able to distinguish between policy effects caused by government spending versus tax policy.

Conversely, **contractionary fiscal policy** actions are undertaken during a state of inflation. To combat inflation, the fiscal policy makers in the government either reduce government spending (G) or increase taxes (T) or both. The process of contractionary fiscal policy measures is just the opposite of the expansionary fiscal policy measures just explained above. The next section of this chapter explains the monetary policy objectives and their policy tools for fine-tuning the economy during a recession, inflation, or stagflation (stagflation is the simultaneous occurrence of inflation and unemployment).

9.3. Working Mechanism of Monetary Policy under Keynesian Perspectives

9.3.1. Monetary Policy Process

The objectives of monetary policy are listed next (they are very similar to the objectives of fiscal policy):

Achieve and maintain full employment

Achieve and maintain maximum possible national output

Achieve and maintain price stability

Achieve interest rate stability

Achieve foreign exchange rate stability

To fulfill the objectives of monetary policy, the Federal Reserve Board (whose nickname is the Fed; the central policy-making board of the central bank of the United States) uses the following key monetary policy tools:

Reserve requirements

Discount rates

Open market operations

In addition to the three conventional policy tools, the Fed also uses nonconventional policy targets, such as the **federal funds rate**. The federal funds rate is the regulated interest rate at which the depository institutions (commercial banks and other financial institutions) lend their balances at the Federal fund rate to other depository institutions overnight. The working mechanism and the financial effect of changes to the federal funds rate will be discussed after an explanation of the three monetary policy tools. For more information on the monetary policy process of the Fed, students are encouraged to visit the website of the Federal Reserve at https://www.federalreserve.gov/monetarypolicy/fomc.htm.

9.3.2. Reserve Requirements

The **reserve requirement** is a regulated (by the Fed) percentage of every deposit of money in financial institutions by each depositor. A portion of deposits must be kept in reserve by depository institutions. This regulatory requirement is particularly applied to checking and savings accounts; rates differ up to a maximum of 10% of each deposit. If the Fed wants to increase the reserve and money supply in the banking and financial system of the economy, the reserve requirement must be decreased; to decrease the reserve/money supply, the reserve requirement has to be increased. Decreasing the reserve requirement increases excess reserve (total reserve minus required reserve) and increases the lending capacity of the banks to their clients. This process increases multiple deposits to increase the money supply in the economy. Conversely, increasing the reserve requirement reduces the excess reserve and lending capacity by the banks to their clients, and thus the money supply decreases. However, the Fed rarely uses this policy tool because alternative tools are more effective for achieving the goal of stability. More details of this process are explained in Chapter 10.

9.3.3. Discount Rate

The **discount rate** is the rate the Fed charges depository institutions to lend money directly as needed. The Fed is always there to provide loans whenever the depository institutions need liquidity for their day-to-day business operations. This interest rate is controlled by the Fed at a very low discount rate. When the Fed raises the discount rate, it implies that the Fed is raising the overall interest rate to reduce the reserve and money supply in the financial system of the economy. On the other hand, the Fed's reduction of the discount rate implies the Fed's intention to increase the reserve and thus increase the money supply in the economy. Both reserve requirements and discount rates are controlled by the Board of Governors of the Fed. This process is discussed in more detail in Chapter 10.

9.3.4. Open Market Operations

This monetary policy tool is a day-to-day function controlled by the **federal open market committee (FOMC)** of the Fed. The FOMC has oversight over the purchase and sale of US Treasury securities to security dealers (the major bond investors and foreign governments) conducted each day at the Federal Reserve Bank of New York. The FOMC works as the agent for the US Treasury in buying and selling US government bonds to investors. Selling bonds to bond investors means these investors are lending their money to the US government, which is borrowing at a certain interest rate to finance recurring budget deficits. Buying bonds means the US government pays off some of its debts to the bondholders with surplus tax revenue. US Treasury securities comprise three types of securities with different terms of maturity: short-term securities, Treasury Bills (TBs); medium-term securities, Treasury Notes (TNs); and long-term securities, Treasury Bonds (TBs).

In addition to conducting the open market operations of the Fed for Treasury securities, the Fed can also effectively use these policy tools to change the circulation of the aggregate money supply and interest to achieve its monetary policy objectives. These processes—expansionary and contractionary monetary policies—are briefly explained next.

9.3.5. Expansionary Monetary Policy

During a recession, the Fed usually conducts expansionary monetary policy to increase AD through increasing aggregate money supply and thus to decrease interest rates. In this process, the Fed needs to buy back a significant volume of Treasury securities held by the bond investors to increase bank deposits. When the Fed buys back those securities, the bondholders receive their principal and interest payments. They deposit the proceeds in their bank accounts, and deposits increase, along with the reserve and lending capacity of the depository institutions. The increase in reserve and lending increases the money supply and thus decreases interest rates. A decrease in interest rates increases investments (I) and consumption (C) from the public and thus increases AE to increase output and employment. More details of this transmission process from the money market to the goods market are provided in Chapter 10.

9.3.6. Contractionary Monetary Policy

During inflation, the Fed usually conducts contractionary monetary policy by selling US Treasury securities to bond investors. The Fed receives money from the investors in exchange for securities sold. These transactions reduce bank deposits/reserves and the lending capacity of depository institutions and thus decrease the aggregate money supply. The effect of a decrease in money supply is the opposite of the effect of the expansionary monetary policy described earlier- increase interest rates and thus decrease investment and consumption by the public.. This negative effect slows down the economic expansion to decrease output, employment, and inflation.

9.3.7. Federal Funds Rate

The Fed considers the federal funds rate to be the most effective policy in fine-tuning the economy when it encounters recession or inflation. During a recession, the Fed lowers the federal funds rate to decrease all other short-term and long-term interest rates. A reduction of the federal funds rate triggers changes in foreign exchange rates, inflation rates, credits, and lending. The chain of effects transmits to the goods market to increase investment, employment, and output. On the other hand, during inflation, the Fed can raise the federal funds rate to reverse the transmission process to slow down economic expansion to control inflation. The relative effectiveness of this monetary policy target is discussed in more detail in Chapter 10. The implications for both fiscal policy and monetary policy actions will be explained in the next few chapters.

Chapter Summary

Section 9.1 discussed the sources of market failure that causes business-cycle fluctuation in the form of a recession, inflation, and stagflation. The market failure that caused the Great Depression of the 1930s occurred during the time that Keynes rejected the notion of the laissez-faire doctrine of classical economic theories. Keynesian macroeconomic theory called for active government policy in coping with the business-cycle fluctuations for quick recovery of the economy. Therefore, the Keynesian economic foundations were a major departure from the classical economics principle of leaving the market alone for self-correcting process of the business cycle fluctuation. Keynes argued that the primary cause of the Great Depression was the deficiency in AD and, therefore, the US economy needed government intervention to boost the AD side of the macroeconomics. The New Deal of 1933 undertaken by President Roosevelt was the first implementation of Keynesian economics as a recovery plan during the Great Depression. The effectiveness of the New Deal and full adaptation of Keynesian economic policy in subsequent decades was a major public policy change in the United States and most of the industrial nations in the twentieth century. Keynesian economic policy was also implemented effectively during 2009 by President Obama to coping up with the 2008 Great Recession. There was only one time of departure from Keynesian economic policy in 1980, when President Reagan implemented the so-called supply-side economic policy in the face of stagflation caused by the 1970s oil price crisis (causing hyperinflation). Table 9.1 showed the data of the RGDP growth rate and the unemployment rate for the US economy during the period from 2006 to 2018. The data indicate the consistency of Keynesian economic theories and policy recommendations for active fiscal and monetary policy for economic recovery from the severe recession in 2008.

Section 9.2 discussed the working mechanism of fiscal policy under the Keynesian framework. There are three key objectives of fiscal policy, as implied by the Full Employment Act of 1946:

Achieve and maintain full employment

Achieve and maintain maximum possible national output

Achieve and maintain price stability

To fulfill the three objectives, the fiscal policy tools are as follows:

Government spending (G)

Tax policy (T)

Section 9.2.2 explained the mechanism of conducting expansionary fiscal policy during a recession by increasing government spending or decreasing taxes or both. The Keynesian multiplier process is used in this section with numerical examples so that students can easily make the connection between theory and practice for government policy implications.

Section 9.3 introduced the role of monetary policy in combatting recession and inflation. The monetary policy action is also based on the Keynesian framework with the following objectives and policy tools.

Objectives:

Achieve and maintain full employment

Achieve and maintain maximum possible national output

Achieve and maintain price stability

Achieve interest rate stability

Achieve foreign exchange rate stability

Tools:

To fulfill the objectives of monetary policy, the Fed uses the following key monetary policy tools:

Reserve requirements

Discount rates

Open market operations

Sections 9.3.2 through 9.3.5 explained each of the monetary policy tools and their effectiveness in the case of the expansionary monetary policy during a recession. For more information on the Fed's use of monetary policy tools, students are encouraged to visit the following URL on the Federal Reserve home page, https://www.federalreserve.gov/monetarypolicy/fomc.htm.

Section 9.3.6 introduced the Fed's contractionary monetary policy actions and its effectiveness during inflation.

Section 9.3.7 explained the Fed's frequently used monetary policy target, called federal fund rate for effective monetary policy targeting of interest rates movement. Controlling the federal fund rate is also considered one of the best alternatives to conventional monetary policy tools, such as discount rate or reserve requirements.

Application Activities

Q1. By using the fiscal policy tools explained in this chapter, explain the possible fiscal policy actions of the government and their effect on output and employment during a recession.

Q2. Explain possible fiscal policy actions of the government and their effect on output and employment during a period of inflation.

Q3. Explain why a tax rebate increases output less than increasing government spending by the same amount. Give an example of both for comparison.

Q4. Distinguish between fiscal policy and monetary policy actions undertaken by two different government agencies. Do they complement one another, or do they conflict? Briefly explain why or why not.

Q5. What is the open market operation of the Fed? How do the open market operations work, and what are the effects on the money supply and the economy?

Q6. What is the federal funds rate, and why are changes in the federal funds rate considered more effective than other policy options for achieving monetary objectives?

Q7. Suppose the state of the US economy in 2019 is very strong, with the lowest unemployment rate in decades. Given this scenario, what courses of policy action would the Fed be expected to take in using the federal funds rate? Explain briefly.

Q8. Why does the Fed rarely change the existing reserve requirements?

Chapter 10

Foundations of Money Demand and Money Supply and Policy Implications

Learning Objectives

As they read the chapter, students will learn the following:

- Theories of the money demand and money supply process
- The money supply process and measures of money supply aggregates
- The Fed—the central bank of the United States—and its functions and control of the money supply
- The Fed's control of money supply and the process of money creation through lending from commercial banks
- The theories of money demand under Keynesian economics: money demand as a function of interest rate and income
- Determinations of money market equilibrium under Keynesian theories of money and interest

10. Theories of Money Demand and Money Supply

The foundation of Keynesian macroeconomic theories and applications has been divided into two major segments: the **goods market** and the **money market**. Chapters 6, 7, and 8 discussed the foundations of the goods market. Chapter 9 introduced the macroeconomic policy for both the goods market and the money market under fiscal and monetary policies. This chapter and the next few chapters are focused on the foundations of the money market and its policy implications. Like the theories of

AD and AS in the goods market, Keynes also developed the theories of money demand and money supply to influence the changes in the interest rate, employment, and output. The sections that follow will discuss both demand and supply theories of the money market, the determination of the equilibrium interest rate, and implications of the Fed's monetary policy.

10.1. Money Supply Process and Measures of Money Supply Aggregates

Money is a financial asset—the only legal tender currency issued by the Fed to the public—that provides the common medium of exchange for buying and selling other goods and services in the marketplace and for the payment of debt (government or private). In a broad sense, money could be considered any form of asset that is acceptable to perform transactions among buyers and sellers successful. For example, besides the legal tender of notes and coins, other forms of assets, such as Bitcoins (digital currencies), credit cards, digital payment applications (PayPal, Apple Pay, Alipay, WeChatPay), promissory notes, bonds, stocks, precious metals, or similar assets are also being exchanged against goods and services when making market transactions. However, regardless of what alternative methods of payments are made, all transactions are valued against money issued by a central bank (the Fed, for example, in the US market). The money is actually solely controlled by the central bank. In the US economy, the money supply process through depository institutions has a significant effect on the activities of the goods market. For example, the lending activities of depository institutions are important to create multiples of actual legal tender currencies issued by the central bank. This process of the multiple creation of money in banking systems boosts the AD side of the goods market. The transmission process of such money creation is discussed in later sections of this chapter. There are actually three key functions of money.

10.1.1. Functions of Money

Medium of exchange
Unit of account
Store of value

As explained earlier in this section, all transactions of goods and services are basically bought and sold against the money in the market. The payment made in a market transaction is powered by money—it is called the **medium of exchange** because the key function of money is to buy or sell goods and services in the marketplace. The **unit of account** function of money is the monetary value or price tag per unit of goods and services. It is the amount that suppliers ask for in exchange for a good or service, assuming that the buyers will accept the price tag to make the transaction happen. The **store of value** function of money is the transformation of money into other forms of financial assets to generate more income or money in the future. This function of money occurs when individuals or firms invest liquid money into other forms of assets with expected future returns. Examples of the store of value function of money are investment decisions economic agents make by buying stocks, bonds, precious metals, real estate, and other forms of assets. The purpose of this function is to generate more earnings because of the expected positive returns from the investments.

10.1.2. Types of Money Supply Aggregates

Because money is the primary source of measuring the aggregate values of GDP, the quantity of money circulated or issued by the central bank is important in measuring the value of real goods and services produced and sold in the market. The way the money moves from one type of transaction to another in the form of medium of exchange and store of value is the key driving force for creating multiple of original amounts of money or currency issued by the Fed. All electronic and actual cash transactions of money in these two functions move through the lending process of depository institutions. This movement of money from hand to hand in the banking systems of checking and savings accounts creates much more volume of money in bank ledgers than actual volume of paper currency issued by the Fed. The process of such multiple creations of money by the banking system is explained in the next section. The aggregate measures of money supply are categorized by three types based on their liquidity; these are listed next, with M_1 as the most liquid money supply aggregate.

$$\mathbf{M_1 = Currency\ (C) + Checking\ account\ deposits,}$$

where C is the currency held by the households and business institutions outside the bank deposits.

Checking accounts are the deposit accounts in the banks opened by households and business entities to deposit and withdraw their cash as needed.

As of June 2019, the total M_1 measured by the Fed equals $3,823.9 billion.

$$\mathbf{M_2 = M_1 + Savings\ deposits + Certificate\ of\ deposits\ (CDs)\ less\ than\ \$100{,}000\ denomination + Money\ market\ accounts}$$

As of June 2019, the total M_2 measured by the Fed equals $14,770.6 billion.[1]

10.1.3. Other Measures of the Money Supply Process

Although in 2006, the Fed stopped tracking and publishing other forms of less liquid money supply aggregates, such as M_3 (other liquid assets that fall outside of the M_2 definition of money), many economists argue for the inclusion of other near money assets. The components of near money other than M_2 are financial assets, such as short-term Treasury bonds, commercial papers, Bitcoins, and money market mutual fund accounts. It is also important to note here that the Fed ignores other forms of near money assets for three reasons: First, the list of assets is not actually liquid money, such as credit cards and short term bonds. Second, the Fed no longer uses M_1 or M_2 as a policy target for conducting monetary policy; instead, it sets ST interest targets in the federal funds market as a more effective policy option. Third,

---

1 Sources of the Fed's M_1 and M_2 monetary measures are found at https://www.federalreserve.gov/releases/h6/current/h6.pdf.

collecting, tracking, and publishing the data on other near money, such as M_3, is not only very complex but also the Fed found that it was not cost-effective. This complex nature of measuring financial assets is beyond the scope of this introductory course on economics. As recognized by Baumol and Blinder in their macroeconomics textbook, "Money consists only of coins, paper money, and checkable deposits."[2]

10.2. The Fed—The Central Bank of the United States and Its Functions and Control of the Money Supply

10.2.1. Structure and Functions of the Fed

The **Fed** is the central bank of the United States established in 1913 by the US Congress. It was given full authority to control the money supply and conduct monetary policy for economic stability. The Fed Board of Governors consists of seven members. The Fed chair is now Jerome "Jay" Powell. These governing members of the board are appointed by the US president. The president nominates the Fed chair from among the members of the board for a term of four years, to be approved by the US Senate. The chair of the Fed is one of the most powerful money managers in the world because any decisions made by him/her on changes in interest rate policy will have a significant effect on macroeconomic variables and financial institutions not only in the US economy but also the rest of the global economy.

A powerful wing of monetary policy-making activities in the Fed is FOMC. FOMC consists of 12 members: the 7 members of the Fed Board of Governors, the president of the Federal Reserve Bank of New York, and rotating positions held by presidents of 4 of the 12 branches of the Federal Reserve Bank located across the country. The monetary policy actions taken by FOMC are fully independent of US government fiscal policy conducted by the executive branch (the White House) and legislative branch (the US Congress) of the federal government. Unlike many other nations' central banks, FOMC of the Fed is mandated by law to carry out the monetary policy actions they find appropriate to maintain full employment and price stability in the economy. Unlike members of Congress, the members of FOMC are not publicly elected officials. That helps FOMC maintain its independence to make economic policy decisions without pressure from the legislative or executive branches of the government. This independence also helps the Fed avoid any possible conflicts of interest between economic policy and political agenda. However, the independence of the Fed in conducting monetary policy is not free from controversy. Many political pundits argue that the Fed has too much independence to truly reflect the interest of the people during times of crisis (Baumol and Blinder 2015, p. 262–263). On the other hand, the majority of economists and Wall Street moguls, apparently, favor the current independence of the Fed. Nevertheless, the debate over this controversy is ongoing.

---

2 William J. Baumol, Alan S. Blinder, and John L. Solow, *Macroeconomics: Principles and Policy* (Boston, MA: Cengage Learning, 2020))

10.2.2. Key Functions of the Fed

The key functions of the Fed are briefly stated next:

1. **Issuing** US legal tender to control the money supply by adjusting the GDP growth rate
2. **Implementing** regulatory compliance by all banks and financial institutions
3. **Clearing checks** deposited into private banks by households and business entities
4. **Conducting regional economic research** in each of the twelve Federal Reserve Bank branches across the country
5. **Controlling interest rates** and thus money supply to maintain economic stability
6. **Setting short-term interest rate targets in the federal funds** market to indirectly control lending and borrowing by major financial institutions and Wall Street
7. **Lending money to commercial member banks** at a discounted interest rate to meet their liquidity needs
8. **Controlling foreign exchange rates** by indirectly manipulating the demand and supply of domestic currency in foreign exchange markets
9. **Conducting open market operations (OMO)** to control bank reserves and bank lending, thus controlling the aggregate money supply process and interest rates
10. **Implementing reserve requirement policies** for depository institutions

The listed activities listed are also a part of the monetary policy actions by the Fed, especially items 5, 6, 7, 8, 9, and 10. These issues were discussed in Chapter 9. Items 1, 2, 3, and 4 are mostly performed by the 12 regional branches of the Fed.[3]

10.3. The Fed's Control of the Money Supply and the Process of Money Creation through the Lending Processes of Commercial Banks

The Fed's control of the money supply by increasing or decreasing AS of money was discussed in Chapter 9. In that discussion, the three key monetary policy tools—reserve requirements, discount rate, and OMO—were introduced, with their power to influence the changes in money supply and interest rates. Chapter 9 explained the importance of the Fed's interest rate target in the federal funds market and its effect on the money supply and interest rates in the market. This section of Chapter 10 will provide technical aspects of theories and applications of the Fed's money creation process through its use of monetary policy tools and interest rate targets in the banking system. Before getting into an example of money creation through a typical bank's balance sheet, it is important to introduce the concepts of bank reserve (assets) and deposits (liabilities) and their relationship to a bank's lending and money creation.

---

3 For more detailed information about the Fed's functions and responsibilities, students are can visit the Fed's website at https://www.federalreserve.gov/aboutthefed.htm.

10.3.1. Bank Reserve

Bank reserve is the cash held by a bank on the asset side of the bank's balance sheet, including cash in the vault and other reserve accounts, such as **required reserve (RR)** and **excess reserve (ER)**. These reserve accounts are called noninterest-bearing assets until the banks move some of them to interest-bearing assets, such as loans to clients, Treasury securities, or other short-term and long-term financial investments with expected future returns. **RR** is a percentage of every deposit in checking and savings accounts (the rates are different for those accounts with very low minimum balance requirements). The **ER** is the difference between total deposits and minimum RR. For example, if the reserve requirement is 10% for checking accounts, then a deposit of $1,000 by a depositor will be subject to a RR of $100, leaving an ER of $900.

Bank deposits are deposits made with the banks by individuals, households, and business entities in the form of checking deposits, saving deposits, CDs (certificate of deposits), and other money market accounts. Checking account deposits are normally noninterest-bearing deposits because banks do not offer interest rates on checking accounts. Savings deposits have a low interest rate, and the rates vary depending on the terms of maturity and minimum balance required. The same rule applies to other deposits, such as CDs and money market accounts with relatively higher interest rates offered by banks. These deposits are the *liabilities* of the banks because banks owe this cash to their depositors on demand for withdrawal or when terms of maturity expire. However, the banks usually convert these deposits into assets under reserve accounts. These deposits become *assets* when they are entered into the reserve accounts of bank ledgers. Using a typical balance sheet of a hypothetical bank, the process of money creation in a bank's lending system is explained next. All three monetary policy tools and their correlation with money creation will be examined afterwards.

10.3.2. Money Creation by a Bank's Lending and Reserve Requirements

Assume the **minimum reserve requirement** of the Fed on every deposit in checking accounts is 10%. Using Table 10.1 as a typical bank's balance sheet, the process of money creation with the reserve requirement is provided in a few steps for a hypothetical bank, say the Bostonian Bank.

Table 10.1: The Bostonian Bank

Assets	Liabilities and Net Worth
Cash in vault $0	Checking account deposits **$1,000**
Total reserve (TR) **$1,000**	Savings account deposits $0
Required Reserve (RR) **$100**	CDs $0
Excess Reserve (ER) **$900**	Money market accounts $0
Other assets $0	Other deposit accounts $0
Loans $0	Net worth of capital (equity) $0
Total assets: **$1,000**	Total liabilities: **$1,000**

Notice in Table 10.1 that the portfolios of both assets and liabilities are hypothetical balance sheets, with the initial deposit in checking accounts on the liability side assumed to be $1,000. With the *reserve requirement of 10%* (assumed here), the Required Reserve (RR) of $100 and Excess Reserve (ER) of the remaining $900 are converted from checking account deposits of $1,000 and listed on the assets side of the balance sheet. Although other portfolios have actual dollar amounts in real-world banking, for the simplicity of focusing on money creation by reserve requirements only, zero is placed in all other line items in the balance sheet. The balance sheet also has to comply with the general accounting principles of bookkeeping—equality is necessary between total assets and total liabilities, as shown on the bottom row of Table 10.1. To comply with the Fed's regulations, the bank is able to make loans up to $900 (the full amount of ER) and must keep a RR of $100 with its reserve account with the Fed's balance sheet (not shown here). The next step is to start lending the full amount of $900 ER to see the process of **multiple money creation**.

Suppose the Bostonian Bank has decided to lend the full amount of ER of $900 to its best client to earn some interest instead of keeping the amount idle as a noninterest-bearing reserve. This lending decision will change the portfolios, as shown in Table 10.2.

Table 10.2: The Bostonian Bank

Assets	Liabilities and Net Worth
Cash in vault $0	Checking account deposits **$1,000**
TR **$100**	Savings account deposits $0
RR **$100**	CDs $0
ER **$0**	Money market accounts $0
Other assets $0	Other deposit accounts $0
Loans **$900**	Net worth of capital (equity) $0
Total assets: **$1,000**	Total liabilities: **$1,000**

The only changes happened on the asset side of the balance sheet by transferring ER of $900 to the loans portfolio, as the Bostonian Bank lent out its full amount of ER. Typically, banks try to economize the ER amount by lending the full amount to its clients. However, it is also important to keep enough liquidity to meet the demand for withdrawals made by depositors. Liquidity management is a different part of a bank's business and is not relevant to this topic. The total amount of assets and liabilities stay the same for now. However, these amounts will change with increased money creation from the newly created loans by the Bostonian Bank. This further change in money creation is shown in Table 10.3.

Table 10.3: The Bostonian Bank

Assets	Liabilities and Net Worth
Cash in vault $0	Checking account deposits **$1,000** **Adding deposit $900**
TR **$1,000**	Savings account deposits $0
RR **$100 + $90 = $190**	CDs $0
ER **$810**	Money market accounts $0
Other assets $0	Other deposit accounts $0
Loans **$900**	Net worth of capital (equity) $0
Total assets: **$1,900**	Total liabilities: **$1,900**

Table 10.3 shows an increase in deposits of $900 made by borrowers on the liability side. The new deposit of $900 has become subject to the RR ratio of 10% and thus converts to an ER of $810 and a RR of $90, adding to the existing portfolio of ER and RR on the asset side of the balance sheet. Now TR has become $1,000, with an ER of $810 and an RR of $190. Notice that money creation in the lending process has increased by $900 in deposits, providing the bank with an additional $810 as ER that can be offered in loans. This second round of lending creation is shown in Table 10.4.

Table 10.4: The Bostonian Bank

Assets	Liabilities and Net Worth
Cash in vault $0	Checking account deposits **$1,000** **Adding deposit $900+$810**
TR **$1,000**	Savings account deposits $0
RR **$100 + $90 + 81 = $271**	CDs $0
ER **$0**	Money market accounts $0
Other assets $0	Other deposit accounts $0
Loans **$900 + $810 = $1,710**	Net worth of capital (equity) $0
Total assets: **$2,710**	Total liabilities: **$2,710**

With a new ER of $810, the total available for lending has become $1,710, an increase of $810 from the initial $900. This process will continue until the ER is fully exhausted in this chain effect of multiple lending creation from an initial deposit of $1,000. The maximum amount of potential deposit creation and corresponding lending (or credit) creation is calculated next by using the equation of geometric progression from the required minimum ratio of 10%. This process derives the money multiplier for maximum money creation shown in equation (10.1).

The money multiplier for the transaction = 1/Reserve requirement
= 1/0.1 = 10. ....Eqn (10.1)

The derivation of this simplified money multiplier is shown next from the concept of geometric progression.

Notice that in the previous tables, lending and deposit transactions are increasing by 90% of the initial deposit of $1,000 because of the fixed minimum reserve requirement of 10%. If this process goes on for infinite geometric progressions, then the chain effect of this deposit creation (D) would be as shown in equation (10.2).

$$1 + D + D^2 + D^3 + \ldots + = 1/1 - D \ldots, \quad \ldots\ldots\ldots\ldots \text{Eqn (10.2)}$$

where D is the ER ratio of 90% for each deposit. The actual application of this equation can be extended from the earlier tables:

Deposits are 1,000 + 900 + 810 + ...

$$= 1{,}000 \text{ X } (1 + 0.9 + 0.81 + \ldots +)$$

$$= 1{,}000 \text{ X } (1 + 0.9 + 0.9^2 + \ldots +)$$

$$= 1{,}000 \text{ X } [\ 1/(1 - 0.9)]$$

= 1,000 X (1/0.1) = Total maximum possible deposit creation
= $1,000 *10 = $10,000. ....Eqn (10.3)

The simplified money multiplier as derived here in equation (10.3) is

1/Reserve Requirement = 1/0.1 = 10.

With the same process, and using an initial ER of $900, the total maximum lending creation is estimated in equation (10.4):

Total potential lending amount = Money multiplier * Initial ER
= 1/0.1 * 900 = $9,000 ....Eqn (10.4)

It is also important to note that the previous estimation of money creation is a simplified version of a vast complex of trillions of dollars of deposits and lending in the entire banking system. From a real-world perspective, there is no single deposit to exhaust after all ER is lent out. Multiple deposits take place from multiple sources, along with the process of lending to millions of clients every day. Banks also do not necessarily lend out all of their ER every time. The presence of transaction leakage in a bank's lending and reserve deposits commonly has a lesser effect on deposit and lending creation than estimated in equations (10.3) and equation (10.4). Regardless of the volume and complicated nature of bank deposits and lending, using this simplified model helps students understand the power of the Fed to manipulate the volume of reserve and money supply by changing the reserve requirement. This money supply process controlled by the Fed is explained next for policy implications.

Suppose the Fed would like to lower interest rates by increasing the money supply (usually the policy action during a recession) by changing its reserve requirements from this assumed 10%. To do so, the Fed has to reduce the reserve requirement, say from 10% to 8%. This reduction of reserve requirements would have a significant effect on deposit and lending creation by increasing both money multiplier and ER, as shown next:

Deposit creation = New money multiplier * Initial deposit = 1/0.08 * 1,000 = 12.5 * 1,000

= 12,500

Lending creation = New money multiplier * Initial ER = 1/0.08 * 920 = 12.5 * 920 = 11,500

Conversely, if the Fed would like to reduce the money supply to combat inflation by reducing the bank reserve and lending creation, it has to increase the reserve requirement. The Fed, however, does not intend to use this powerful monetary policy tool unless other options do not work. The Fed has not changed its current reserve requirement for decades. Changing the discount rate, federal funds rate, and daily activities of OMO works very well in allowing the Fed to achieve its goals of economic stability. The money creation process by these alternative policy tools and targets are discussed in the following subsections.

10.3.3. Money Creation Using the Fed's Discount Rate and Federal Funds Rate Policy

The Fed occasionally uses the discount rate to increase or decrease the bank reserve and money supply. The **discount rate** is the low interest rate the Fed charges on short-term loans given to depository institutions to meet their liquidity needs. During a recession, the Fed lowers the discount rate, along with decreasing the federal funds rate to increase bank reserve. The spread between the discount rate and the federal funds rate is in a range between 0.5% and 1% set by the Fed, with the discount rate higher than the federal funds rate. The reason for setting the discount rate above the federal funds rate is to indirectly discourage banks from borrowing from the Fed. During inflation, the Fed increases the discount rate and federal funds rate simultaneously to maintain price stability. The Fed's changes in the discount rate and federal funds rate immediately affects other interest rates, such as mortgage, car loan, prime rate, and personal loan rates. It is also important to note that the effect of changes in the discount rate on bank reserves is very insignificant under economic circumstances. The reason for its very minor effect is the Fed's reluctance to provide loans to banks unless needed for emergency liquidity during a severe recession or a massive withdrawal by clients (called a run on the bank and usually occurs because of a rumor about the bank's financial insolvency). On the other hand, changing the federal funds rate is an effective tool for making changes in bank reserve and money supply. The federal funds rate is discussed in later sections of this chapter.

10.3.4. Money Creation Using the Fed's OMO

OMO refers to the Fed purchasing and selling US Treasury securities in open markets of major financial institutions and foreign governments. It is administered by the Federal Reserve Bank of New York on every business day. About 30 major financial institutions located in New York City and representatives for selected foreign governments participate in the buying and selling auctions of the Fed's OMO every business day. The primary purpose of this activity is for the Fed to act as the banker of the US Treasury to borrow money (by selling Treasury securities) and pay off debts (by purchasing Treasury securities) for the US government. Selling Treasury securities means borrowing for the US government to pay government spending bills not immediately covered by tax revenue. Purchasing Treasury securities held by open market financial institutions means retiring or paying off some existing government debts with surplus revenue or the Fed's own surplus funds. The activities by the OMO are one of the Fed's most important monetary policy tools for not only paying off funds for the US Treasury but also for maintaining economic stability by changing bank reserves and money supply to affect interest rates and investment in the entire economy. The process of money supply created by the Fed's OMO is explained in Table 10.5 with the help of a hypothetical bank's balance sheet.

The Fed frequently uses OMO as one of the most effective monetary tools to influence the money supply and interest rate. To lower interest rates in the economy, the Fed can indirectly expand deposits and reserves in the banking system by purchasing Treasury securities, as illustrated in Table 10.5.

Table 10.5: The Bostonian Bank

Assets	**Liabilities and Net Worth**
Cash in vault $0	Checking account deposits **No change** **Adding deposit $0**
TR **$0**	Savings account deposits $0
RR **$100 million**	CDs $0
ER **$0**	Money market accounts $0
Other assets Treasury securities $100 million	Other deposit accounts $0
Loans **No change**	Net worth of capital (equity) No change
Total assets: **No change**	Total liabilities: **No change**

Assume that the reserve requirement is still 10% and that Bostonian Bank has used up all ER for lending. If the Fed purchases Treasury securities of $100 million from Bostonian Bank by crediting the reserve amount with the Fed from the Bostonian Bank, the above RR of $100 million will change from RR to ER. Such a change in portfolio from the Fed's purchase of Treasury securities or mortgage-backed securities is shown next (keeping everything else unchanged in the balance sheet in Table 10.5).

First Step of Portfolio Change

Assets	Liabilities
RR: +$100 million	Deposits: No change
ER: $100 million	
Treasury Securities: –$100 million	
Loans: No change	

Suppose that Bostonian Bank uses this newly created ER of $100 million to lend out to its clients. The resulting change in the bank reserve is shown in the "Second Step of Portfolio Change."

Second Step of Portfolio Change

Assets	Liabilities
RR: $100 million	Deposits: No change
ER: –$100 million	
Securities: No change	
Loans:	+$100 million

Now suppose the borrowers of $100 million worth of loans made by the bank deposited the money into checking accounts with this bank (they can, however, deposit with any other bank). This deposit will create the next round of money creation shown in the "Third Step of Portfolio Change."

Third Step of Portfolio Change

Assets	Liabilities
RR: $100 million + 10 million	Deposits: +$100 million
ER: $90 million	
Loans:	+$100 million

Now the bank lends $90 million of ER to another client; the change in the balance sheet is shown in the "Fourth Step of Portfolio Change."

Fourth Step of Portfolio Change

Assets	Liabilities
RR: $100 million +10 million	Deposits: +100 million + $90
ER:–$90 million	
Loans:	+$90 million

The process of the multiple creation of money will continue until the newly created ER is fully exhausted. Using the simplified money multiplier from equation (10.1) in the previous section, the total potential money creation from this purchase of Treasury securities of $100 million is estimated next:

Total potential reserve creation = Money multiplier * Initial purchase of Treasury securities

= (1/0.1) * $100 million = 10 * $100 million = $1,000 million or $1 billion.

It is also important to note that this $1 billion money creation is the maximum possible deposit creation in the banking system, assuming no ER is left and no borrowers held any currency. If that is not the case, the money creation shown earlier would be a lower amount. Therefore, it is expected to see the decline of maximum possible money creation for the factors listed next. These common factors in the banking industry cannot be controlled by the Fed.

Banks' willingness to keep more ER than just the RR in their portfolios
Transfer of funds from checking to savings or CDs by clients
Household and business demand for currency held in cash

The Fed can also reduce a bank's reserves and thus lower the money supply to raise the interest rate by selling Treasury securities to the open market of financial institutions. The process of decreasing reserve and money supply will simply be the reverse of money creation discussed above. The Fed usually sells Treasury securities to borrow money for the US budget deficit. Selling Treasury securities is part of a tight monetary policy to combat inflation during an economic boom. On the other hand, the purchase of Treasury securities and/or mortgage-backed securities is an act of expansionary monetary policy to combat a recession during an economic downturn.

10.3.5. Federal Funds Rate Target and Money Creation by the Fed

This section focuses on the concept of the federal funds market and the Fed's OMO to control the short-term interest rate within the federal funds market and overall interest rate in the entire financial market. As mentioned previously, the federal funds market is the borrowing and lending market of key financial institutions on Wall Street, where the banks borrow and lend funds overnight to meet their liquidity needs for daily operations. The interaction between the demand and supply of federal funds market activities by the banks determines the equilibrium interest rate of the federal funds market. To maintain desirable interest rate stability in the short run, the Fed uses its regulatory authority of targeting the federal funds rate to influence the direction of the federal funds interest rate. The OMO activity of the Fed can also influence the demand and supply behavior of the federal funds market by changing bank reserves in the banking system, as will be discussed in Section 10.3.7. The working mechanism of the demand and supply model and the role of the federal funds market target are discussed next.

10.3.6. The Federal Funds Market and Its Applications

The hypothetical demand and supply model of the federal funds market is illustrated in Figure 10.1, starting with an initial equilibrium interest rate and quantity demanded/supplied.

Figure 10.1 indicates the downward-sloping demand curve representing the borrowers and the upward-sloping supply curve representing the lenders within the banks of the federal funds market. The usual shapes of the demand and supply curves of federal funds are due to the basic principle of buyer and seller interest, similar to the behavior of the goods market. The borrowers will borrow more funds if the interest rate is lower, and vice versa, ceteris paribus. The lenders, on the other hand, will lend more funds if the interest rate is higher, and vice versa, ceteris paribus. The borrowers may also borrow funds from alternative sources, such as the Fed's discount window, issuing corporate bonds or stocks to the public, opening up CDs, other money market accounts, and money market mutual funds markets, to attract potential savers. Similarly, the lenders may lend to other clients outside the financial market such as in the US Treasury, companies in other service and manufacturing industries, and international business entities.

Figure 10.1 Federal Funds Market Behavior

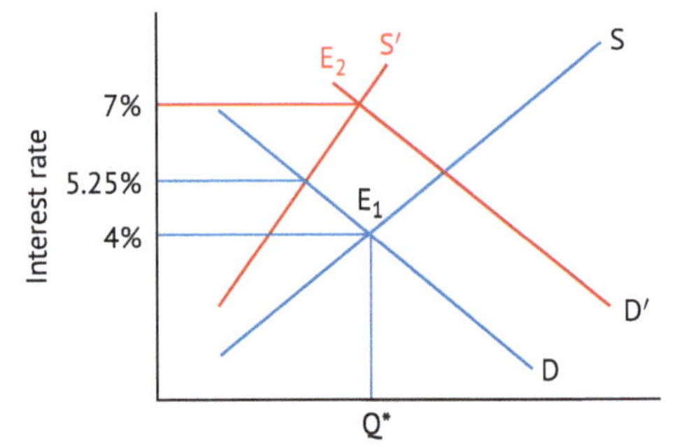

10.3.7. The Process of Changing Equilibrium Interest Rates in the Federal Funds Market

There are several factors other than the federal funds interest rate itself that affect the demand and supply conditions of the federal funds market. In the previous paragraph, only a change in the federal funds interest rate was considered in determining the equilibrium point shown as E_1 in Figure 10.1. To determine this initial equilibrium interest rate at 4%, for example, the restrictive assumption made was ceteris paribus (other factors remaining the same). However, when this restrictive assumption of ceteris paribus is not valid, then the demand and supply curves themselves will tend to change by shifting to the right or left, depending on the direction of changes in other factors. The other possible factors that shift the demand and supply curves are as follows:

- **ERs in bank portfolios**
- **Shortage of reserves in bank portfolios**
- **State of the economy (recession, inflation, full employment, economic boom)**
- **Transfer of depository funds from one deposit account to another**
- **Unexpected increase/decrease of withdrawals and deposits in deposit accounts**
- **Capital inflow and outflow from outside or inside the country**

With excess reserves (ERs) in the banking system, the S curve of federal funds shifts to the right, and a simultaneous shift of the D curve occurs in the opposite direction (to the left). As a result, the equilibrium interest rates in the federal funds market increase, as shown in Figure 10.1 at E_2. Because the federal funds market activities involve both lenders and borrowers within the same limited market, the shift of demand and supply happens simultaneously but in opposite directions. For example, when there is a shortage of federal funds, demand shifts to the right and supply shifts to the left.

The state of the economy influences the shift of the D and S curves of the federal funds market in a similar fashion. For example, during a recession, the supply of funds exceeds the demand for funds and thus lowers the equilibrium interest rates. On the other hand, during an economic boom, banks' desire for making loans increases and thus demand exceeds supply, causing a rise in interest rates. Transferring funds from different deposit accounts also creates similar shifts in demand and supply. An increase in currency held by the public and/or more deposits in checking accounts decreases ERs for lending. Therefore, supply shifts to the left and demand shifts to the right cause interest rates to rise. Capital outflow from domestic financial institutions to foreign banks also causes a decline in supply and thus raises interest rates. Given the circumstances of change in other factors, the new equilibrium interest rates may not necessarily be the point of equilibrium the Fed desires to see. The next section explains how the Fed's OMO activity can reverse an undesirable equilibrium, allowing the Fed to achieve its federal funds rate target.

10.3.8. The Role of the Fed in Controlling the Federal Funds Rate by OMO

Without the Fed's intervention in the federal funds market, the changes in equilibrium interest rates described earlier may not necessarily serve the best interests of the economy because such changes might be too high or too low for economic stability and sustained growth. The strategic policy action of the Fed is to intervene in the free flow of demand and supply by setting up a regulatory action called the federal funds rate target or short-term interest rate target. For example, during a recession, the Fed usually lowers this target, along with the discount rate, to boost the AD, leading to a quick economic recovery. Conversely, during an economic boom, the Fed raises its interest rate target to combat the expected inflation.

However, setting the federal funds target doesn't guarantee the successful achievement of the target without using the indirect method of OMO, the Fed's monetary policy tool. To make sure the Fed's target is achieved, the Fed's open market committee buys or sells enough Treasury securities in the financial market to change the reserve position in financial market portfolios. For example, suppose the Fed has set a target rate at 5.25% (as in Figure 10.1), but the demand and supply changes of the federal funds market increased the actual equilibrium interest rate to 7%. To bring this undesirable interest rate from 7% to 5.25%, the Fed may buy Treasury securities or mortgage-backed securities from the investors and increase the bank reserves. As a result, the S curve will start shifting to the right with a simultaneous shift of the demand curve to the left. The Fed will continue to conduct open market purchases of securities and/or mortgage-backed securities until the actual interest rate falls to its target rate. The Fed can do the opposite by selling Treasury securities or mortgage-backed securities when the actual equilibrium rate drops below the target rate.[4]

The next section of this chapter will introduce theories regarding the demand side of the money market originally developed by Keynes in the 1930s.

10.4. Theories of Money Demand under Keynesian Economics: Interest Rate and Income as Determinants of Money Demand

In Sections 10.1 and 10.2, a detailed discussion was provided regarding how to measure aggregate money supply and categorize it based on the liquidity (how quickly an asset can be converted into liquid cash). In Section 10.3, the process of money creation in the banking system was explained by using all monetary policy tools of the Fed. In this last section of the chapter, the theories of money demand (also called liquidity preference) and its practices are introduced. Keynes originally introduced his revolutionary concept of liquidity preference, called the theory of money demand, in 1936 in his book titled *The General Theory of Money, Interest and Employment.* The Keynesian theory of money demand was based on real-world observation to determine how much money households and business entities hold in the form of liquid cash or near cash at any moment in time when interest rates and other related variables, such as income, change. This theoretical foundation of money demand and its applications are explained next.

10.4.1. Money Demand Function and Changes in the Interest Rate

Because money is just like any other commodity, except that money is used to buy and sell other commodities and services, money has its own price tag—the opportunity cost of holding money idle or in the form of cash or near cash. This opportunity cost of holding money idle is also considered the price tag for using or not using money—called the interest rate. When the interest rate rises (other factors staying the same), the opportunity cost of holding money in the form of cash or near cash tends to increase, and vice versa. Therefore, the quantity of money demand and interest rate changes are inversely related, with interest rate as an independent variable and quantity of money demanded as a dependent variable, ceteris paribus. In equation (10.5), the money demand function is defined as interest rate (i), a determinant of money demand.

---

4 For more detailed information about the Fed's OMO activity to control the federal funds rate, students may be interested in visiting the links listed next: http://www.federalreserve.gov/pf/pf.htm
For advanced study, visit https://www.newyorkfed.org/education/Fed21/index.html
Speech by Governor Lael Brainard on June 2, 2015: http://www.federalreserve.gov/newsevents/speech/brainard20150602a.htm
Wall Street Journal article: http://www.wsj.com/mdc/public/page/2_3022-bondbnchmrk.html?mod=mdc_bnd_pglnk

Md = F (i, ...), ...Eqn (10.5)

where Md = Money demand and i = Interest rates, F is a general expression stating interest rate is the determinant of money demand.

The inverse relationship between the quantity of money demanded and interest rate changes is illustrated as the downward-sloping demand curve for money in Figure 10.2. This hypothetical demand curve indicates that when interest increases, the demand for money decreases, and vice versa, ceteris paribus.

Figure 10.2 Money Demand Curve

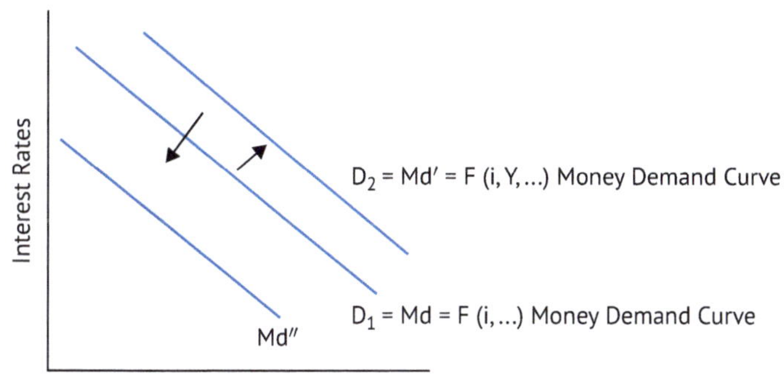

Figure 10.2 indicates that changes to the interest rate on the vertical axis will change the quantity of money demanded in the opposite direction moving along the same D curve, say D_1. However, there are other factors of money demand that shift the whole money demand function, usually called changes in money demand instead of changes in quantity of money demand. The other important factors causing shifts of the entire money demand curve are changes in RGDP, inflation rate, technological changes in financial and monetary institutions, monetary policy changes at the Fed, and other related policy actions. For example, if RGDP is added to the money demand function shown in equation (10.5), the modified money demand function can be rewritten as equation (10.6), with Y as RGDP.

Md = F (i, Y, ...) ....Eqn (10.6)

Keynes argued that equation (10.6) was a basic model of liquidity preference theory, where quantity of money demand and interest rate are inversely related; ceteris paribus. But when ceteris paribus assumption is not held, changes in other important variable such as income (Y) will cause the change in money demand function. Keynes explained further that given any level of interest rate, if income rises, the money demand curve will shift to rightward. On the other hand, if income falls, the money demand curve will shift leftward.

It is also worth noting that it is not necessarily the case of proportionate increase in money demand when income goes up by certain percent. Money demand will change proportionally to changes in income (Y) only if the slope of the money demand function is constant and is equal to one, which is not always the case.

Suppose RGDP increases by 3% to support the purchasing power and other financial and economic needs of citizens. That 3% increase in national income is expected to cause a similar rate of increase in money demand. That means money demand will shift to the right, illustrated in Figure 10.2 as Md'. Similarly, if the RGDP decreases, the Md curve will shift to the left, as indicated by Md" in Figure 10.2. Other factors, such as technological changes in digital payment systems (e.g., PayPal, ATM/debit cards, Apple Pay, Alipay, WeChatPay), and extensive use of traditional credit cards and online banking have significantly reduced the demand for holding cash for day-to-day transactions. Therefore, the demand for money in liquid form seems to have reduced significantly in recent years. Changes in banking regulations on depository institutions also cause changes in the opportunity cost of holding money idle, thus shifting the money demand function.

10.5. Determinations of Money Market Equilibrium under Keynesian Theories of Money and Interest

10.5.1. Determination of Short-Run Interest Rate Equilibrium

The short-run interest is usually the interest rate on notes with a maturity of one year or less. The equilibrium interest rate is determined at the point of intersection between the vertical money supply curve and the downward-sloping money demand curve developed by Keynes (1936). Figure 10.3 illustrates the equilibrium interest rate where quantity of Md is equal to quantity of Ms.

Figure 10.3 Money Market Equilibrium in the Short Run

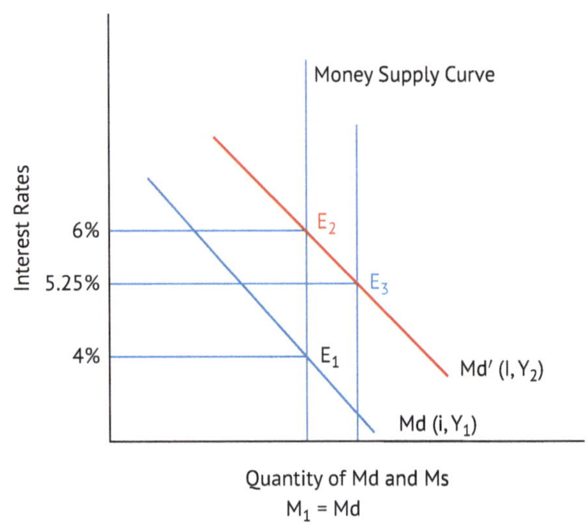

The money supply curve is vertical because aggregate money supply as M_1 or M_2 is solely controlled by the Fed (explained in Chapter 9). Rewriting the money demand equation (equation (10.6) from Section 10.4) and using the money supply Ms as a fixed aggregate money supply, say M_1, the equilibrium condition of the money market is given equation (10.7).

At equilibrium, Md (i, Y) = Ms ....Eqn (10.7)

The initial equilibrium is determined by the intersection between Md (i, Y_1) and Ms at E_1 in Figure 10.3, with its equilibrium interest rate at 4%. At this point of equilibrium, the level of income is at Y_1. However, suppose the economy expanded by increasing RGDP from its current level of Y_1 to Y_2. Based on the previous explanation of shifting money demand, the increase in RGDP to Y_2 will shift the Md curve upward to the right, as shown by Md (i, Y_2) in

Figure 10.3. The change results in an equilibrium interest rate at 6%, given no change in the money supply.

10.5.2. Monetary Policy Implications of Money Market Equilibrium

Now suppose the Fed considers the rise in the equilibrium interest rate at 6% to be above the desirable rate. If the Fed wants to reduce this short-term interest rate from 6% back to its initial equilibrium at 4% or somewhere in between 6% and 4%, then the Fed can pursue an expansionary monetary policy by purchasing Treasury securities. The bank reserves and money supply will increase by shifting the Ms curve vertically to the right. This shifting is shown in Figure 10.3 where the new Ms curve intersects with the new Md curve at $E_{3,}$ with equilibrium interest rates settled at say 5.25%. Such changes in the equilibrium interest rate in the short run, influenced by an active monetary policy, can also influence the outcome of the goods market by changing components of the AD curve. This transmission mechanism of monetary policy is briefly explained in Section 10.5.3.

10.5.3. Transmission Process of Monetary Policy Actions from the Money Market to Goods Market

As shown earlier, an expansionary monetary policy undertaken by the Fed has reduced the equilibrium interest rate from 6% to 5.25%, illustrated in Figure 10.3. The transmission process of this monetary policy action is expected to increase investment and consumption in the goods market so that the AE or AD curve increases. Increase in AD thus increases output and employment in the economy. On the other hand, if the Fed wants to reduce AD in the goods market to slow down the economy for the purpose of reducing inflation or expected inflation, then the Fed can decrease bank reserves and money supply by selling Treasury securities or mortgage-backed securities. Selling of Treasury securities will shift the Ms curve to the left and the interest rate will increase. This increase in the interest rate is expected to decrease investment and consumption in the goods market. Therefore, AD will decline to lower RGDP, employment, and inflation. The expansionary monetary policy is usually undertaken by the Fed during a recession, and contractionary monetary policy action is undertaken during inflation or a booming economy. The complete flow of the transmission process under the expansionary and contractionary monetary policies of the Fed is shown in Figure 10.4.

Figure 10.4 Transmission Flow of Monetary Policy

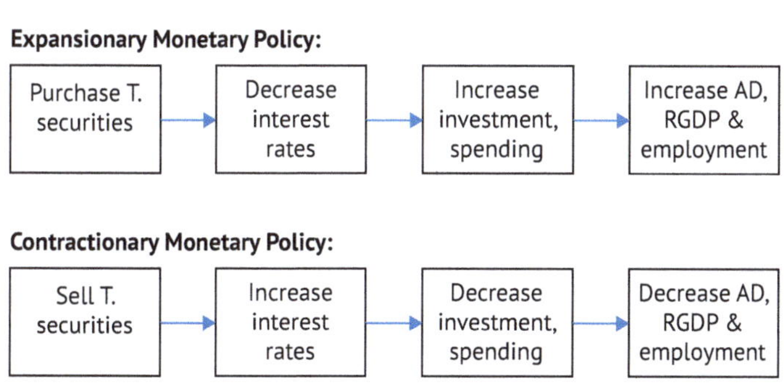

10.5.4. Monetary Policy and Determination of Equilibrium Interest Rates in the Long Run

In the previous section, applications of monetary policy actions were discussed to determine the short-term interest rate and its transmission to affect investment, spending, output, and employment in the goods market. In the long run, however, monetary policy actions are expected to remain neutral in changing the interest rate. This phenomenon is called money neutrality in the long run. Figure 10.5 is similar to the illustration shown in Figure 10.3.

In Figure 10.5, the initial equilibrium is shown at E_1 at the intersection between money supply (Ms) and Md (i, Y_1), with the equilibrium interest rate at 6%. Now suppose the Fed wanted to decrease the interest rate by buying Treasury securities from bond investors. As a result, the bank reserves and money supply would increase, shifting the Ms curve to the right at Ms'. Given the same Md curve at Md (i, Y_1), the new short-run equilibrium interest would be at E_2 at 4%. The decrease in the interest rate from 6% to 4% would increase RGDP in the goods market through the transmission mechanism shown in Figure 10.3. An increase in RGDP would increase the price level by shifting the AD curve to the right in the goods market (not shown). This increase in price level requires more money for the use of individuals and business entities, shifting the Md function from Md (i, Y_1) to Md (i, Y_2), as shown in Figure 10.5. This rightward shift of Md would intersect with the new Ms curve at the equilibrium point E_3, where the interest rate has increased to its initial level of 6%. The equilibrium point E_3 is thus the long-run equilibrium interest rate at its initial level before an expansionary monetary policy was undertaken.

Figure 10.5 Money Market Equilibrium in the Long Run

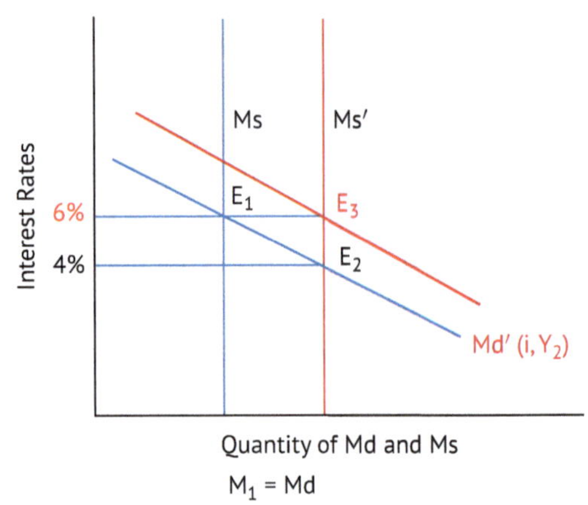

Chapter Summary

Section 10.1 introduced the money supply process and measures of money supply aggregates. Money has three functions: *medium of exchange, unit of account, and store of value.* The money supply aggregates categorized and estimated by the Fed are mainly two types: M_1 and M_2.

M1 = Currency (C) + Checking account deposits,

where C is the currency held by the households and business institutions outside the bank deposits.

M2 = M1 + Savings deposits + CDs less than $100,000 denomination + Money market accounts.

Section 10.2. introduced the structure of the Fed, the central bank of the United States, as the top monetary policy-making institution. The Fed is also the government agency that issues legal tender and thus controls the money supply aggregates M_1 and M_2. This section also explained all other key functions of the Fed and its governing process of controlling the money supply to combat inflation and recession.

Section 10.3.1. introduced the structure of bank reserve in the banking system and its connection with the Fed's balance sheet in operating and managing assets and liabilities.

Section 10.3.2. discussed the details of the Fed's monetary policy tools and how it uses the tools to control money supply in conducting day-to-day monetary policy operations through lending creation in the banking system.

Section 10.3.2. used the monetary tool of reserve requirement to explain the step-by-step process of money creation through lending and borrowing activities in the entire banking system of the economy. These steps were presented in Table 10.1 through Table 10.4. Students are encouraged to review them and practice by using the same process with different hypothetical deposits in the banking system.

Section 10.3.3. explained money supply creation by using the Fed's discount rate and federal funds rate and the relative effectiveness of the two.

Section 10.3.4. explained the real-world example of the Fed's creation of money, and it's control of money supply aggregates by using OMO. The step-by-step process of conducting OMO was presented in Table 10.4 with numerical examples.

Sections 10.3.5. to 10.3.7. introduced the details of the Fed's use of the federal funds rate as the short-term interest rate target in controlling money supply in the economy. These subsections provided details of the effectiveness of the federal funds rate operation by the Fed as one of the most effective monetary policy targets in recent decades. The example of the actual operating process of the federal funds rate market was illustrated in Figure 10.1.

Section 10.3.8. extended the explanation from previous sections of the Fed's monetary policy to emphasize the role of the Fed in using OMO in controlling the federal funds rate.

Section 10.4. introduced the Keynesian theory of money demand as a function of interest rate and income with equations (10.5) and (10.6):

Md = F (i, ...), ...Eqn (10.5)

Md = F (i, Y, ...). ....Eqn (10.6)

Section 10.5.1. introduced the equilibrium condition of the money market using equation (10.7) as Ms = Md, and the short-run money market equilibrium was illustrated in Figure 10.3.

Section 10.5.2. and Section 10.5.3 explained the monetary policy implications for the determination of the money market equilibrium to stabilize the interest rate fluctuations to control inflation and recession. The transmission process of changes in the equilibrium interest rate from the money market to the goods market is explained in detail in these subsections and illustrated in Figure 10.4.

Section 10.5.4. explained the long-run determination of the interest rate in the money market and its policy implications for the long-term stability of the interest rate and inflation. This process of long-run interest rate behavior is illustrated in Figure 10.5. Students may practice drawing diagrams similar to those in Figures 10.3, 10.4, and 10.5 and become familiar with the real-world monetary policy implications in fine-tuning the US economy.

Application Activities

Q1. Briefly describe the structure of the Fed in its operational authority in conducting monetary policy of the economy. Do you think the Fed operates its monetary policy with full independence without political pressure from the US Congress or the White House? Why or why not?

Q2. Briefly describe how the Fed creates bank reserves and more monetary transactions in the economy than the actual volume of currency issued by the Federal Reserve Banks. Assume that the reserve requirement by the Fed on bank deposits is one-tenth. Also, assume that the banks under consideration have zero excess reserve (ER) (all ER is lent out). With fixed currency in circulation, what specific monetary policy tool can the Fed use to increase checking account deposits to $1 billion?

Q3. Based on the information in Q2, if the households and business entities hold currency of $75 million, how much more would have to be added to bank reserves if the Fed still wanted to increase checking account deposits to $1 billion?

Q4. Distinguish between the federal funds rate and the discount rate. Why do you think changes to the discount rate are less effective than changes to the federal funds rate?

Q5. If the Fed makes a massive purchase of Treasury securities, how will this purchase affect the equilibrium interest rate in the federal funds market? Illustrate your explanation with a demand and supply diagram of the federal funds market.

Q6. Assume that the demand for lending by financial institutions increases significantly because of a booming economy and business activities. Also, assume that the Fed is not interested in intervening to support the increase in demand for lending by banks. What change do you expect to see in the direction of the short-term interest rate? Will it increase, decrease, or stay the same? Explain, briefly, with the help of a relevant diagram, the federal funds market.

Q7. Suppose there is a massive withdrawal of deposits by households and business entities (a run on a bank) caused by a rumor of the bank's financial insolvency. What would be the effect of this event on short-term interest rates? If the Fed wants to intervene to prevent this, what would be the appropriate action?

Q8. Draw a demand and supply curve of the money market and explain why the long-run interest rate is not affected by the Fed's action of changing interest rates in the short run.

Q9. While describing the concept of the Keynesian money demand function, critically analyze the factors that affect the money demand curve and how that shift affects the equilibrium interest rate. (You need to use the money supply curve as well in your analysis.)

Q10. Critically describe how the OMO (open market operations) of the Fed can be used to affect the following activities of macroeconomics:

10a. Federal funds rate

10b. Money market interest rate

10c. Inflation rate

10d. Consumption expenditure

10e. Investment expenditure

10f. AD

10g. Employment and output (RGDP)

Chapter 11

Budget Deficit, Public Debt, and Fiscal and Monetary Policy Implications

Learning Objectives

As they read the chapter, students will learn the following:

- Budget deficit and public debt under fiscal policy and its effect on output and employment in the short run and in the long run
- Fiscal and monetary policy debate in the context of price stability and full employment
- Monetary and fiscal policy debate: discretionary versus rules

In Chapter 9, the working mechanisms of fiscal policy and monetary policy were introduced. The AD-AS model structure of macroeconomics, developed by Keynes in the 1930s, is still a predominant part of understanding the economic policy implications in fine-tuning the economy from business-cycle fluctuations. In Chapter 10, the theories and applications of monetary policy under the Keynesian framework were explained further, along with their real-world applications in the context of the US economy. In this chapter, the importance of both fiscal policy and monetary policy actions are discussed in more detail to determine the short-run and long-run effects on key macroeconomic variables, such as RGDP growth, unemployment rate, inflation rate, and interest rate. Integration of both the short-run and long-run implications of fiscal and monetary policy actions is the key focus of this chapter. In the process of this integration, the analysis of the budget deficit and public debt and their short-run and long-run effects on interest rates, employment, and output are also discussed. At the outset, the structure of fiscal policy and its connection to budget surplus and deficit is introduced.

11.1. Fiscal Policy and Budget Deficit (and Surplus)

With the mandated responsibility of the US federal government to achieve and maintain full employment, the Keynesian aggregate expenditure (AE) model clearly indicates that during a recession, government spending tends to rise sharply with either no change in taxes or a decrease in taxes. This expansionary fiscal policy helps boost AE to combat a recession. However, it is also a process under which the budget deficit increases significantly because of declining tax revenue and simultaneous increases in government spending. The budget deficit or surplus equation is introduced here to provide a basic understanding of how the budget deficit or surplus can be estimated for the government's yearly budget activity.

Government budget deficit/Surplus = G – T, where G = Government expenditure and T = Tax revenue.
Now if G –T > 0, it is a case of budget deficit; G exceeds tax revenue.
If G – T < 0, then it generates a budget surplus; tax revenue exceeds government spending.
If G – T = 0, then it is a balanced budget; tax revenue is exactly equal to government spending.

In the context of the US economy, the size of the federal government is so large that the recent data from the CBO shows that the GDP contribution by the US government itself is close to 25% of the $19 trillion economy. The Employment Act of 1946 also mandates the government to achieve and maintain full employment by spending enough to make a quick recovery from business-cycle fluctuations caused by recession and inflation. Table 11.1 shows the actual budget deficit and surplus for the US economy since 2000.

The data in the table shows that during the last 18 years, the United States had a budget surplus only in 2000 and 2001, with an increasing deficit in every subsequent year up to 2018, with exception of 2014 and 2015. For example, the budget surpluses of $236.2 billion and $128.2 billion were generated in 2000 and 2001, respectively, followed by a deficit of $157.8 billion in 2002. The growth of the deficit continued to rise every year since then to reach its highest level of $1,412.7 billion in 2009, the second year of the economic recovery process after the Great Recession of 2008. In 2010 and 2011, the budget deficit remained high at $1,294.4 billion and $1,299.6 billion, respectively, with only a slight decline to $1,087 billion in 2012. However, as the economy started to show solid recovery toward full employment in subsequent years, the budget deficit started to decline significantly to $438.5 billion in 2015, with a slight increase to $584.7 billion in 2016 and $665.4 billion in 2017. But the budget deficit started rising again in 2018 to $785.2 billion, despite the continuing trend of the historically low unemployment rate. It is also worth noting that government spending and tax revenue have also increased steadily since 2000. For example, tax revenue increased from $2,025.2 billion in 2000 to $3,328.7 billion in 2018. On the other hand, government spending has increased from $1,789 billion to $4,107.8 billion during the same period. The accumulated public debt (the cumulative sum of yearly deficits) increased from $3,409.8 in 2000 to $15,751.2 billion in 2018.

Table 11.1: US Budget Deficit and Surplus, 2000–2018 (Data in Billions of $s)

Year Debt	Revenue	Expenditure	Budget Deficit (−)/Surplus (+)	Accumulated Public
2000	2,025.2	1,789.0	236.2	3,409.8
2001	1,991.1	1,862.8	128.2	3,319.6
2002	1,853.1	2,010.9	−157.8	3,540.4
2003	1,782.3	2,159.9	−377.6	3,913.4
2004	1,880.1	2,292.8	−412.7	4,295.5
2005	2,153.6	2,472.0	−318.3	4,592.2
2006	2,406.9	2,655.1	−248.2	4,829.0
2007	2,568.0	2,728.7	−160.7	5,035.1
2008	2,524.0	2,982.5	−458.6	5,803.1
2009	2,105.0	3,517.7	−1,412.7	7,544.7
2010	2,162.7	3,457.1	−1,294.4	9,018.9
2011	2,303.5	3,603.1	1,299.6	10,128.2
2012	2,450.0	3,536.9	−1,087.0	11,281.1
2013	2,775.1	3,454.6	−679.5	11,982.7
2014	3,021.5	3,506.1	−484.6	12,799.9
2015	3,249.9	3,688.4	−438.5	13,116.7
2016	3,268.0	3,852.6	−584.7	14,167.6
2017	3,316.2	3,981.6	−665.4	14,665.5
2018	3,328.7	4,107.8	−785.2	15,751.2

Source: Congressional Budget Office at https://www.cbo.gov/about/products/budget-economic-data#2

The growing budget deficit and its accumulated public debt shown in Table 11.1 have caused a great deal of concern for citizens, business firms, and political leaders. The political debate on this issue is one of the key sources of rising political bickering in the US Congress, dividing members down party lines between the Republicans and the Democrats. At issue in this never-ending debate is whether to reduce the budget deficit by shrinking government spending or increasing taxes. But the reality is that either of these two options poses a danger because they would reduce the AE and thus reduce output and job opportunities—a source of recession. With the use of the multiplier process, it is easy to figure out the negative consequence of reducing the budget deficit, which would reduce output and employment. Therefore, despite political bickering, neither of the two political parties can take the risk of throwing the economy into a severe recession by cutting down the budget deficit, called the sequester. But the real economic question is whether this skyrocketing budget deficit is too large or whether it is bad for the economy in both the short run and the long run. Another question may be whether this growing budget deficit and public debt will translate into higher taxes for future generations when it eventually needs to be paid off to the bondholders. To find clear and reasonable answers to these questions, it is important to analyze the pros and cons of increasing the budget deficit and public debt, as discussed in the next section of this chapter.

11.1.1. The Balanced Budget Approach and Its Limitations

Although there is a federal law on the books called the **Gramm-Rudman-Hollings Act of 1985**, passed by the US Congress to bring the rising budget deficit to a balanced budget by 1991,[1] it was never implemented successfully because of continuous business-cycle fluctuations that happened during that time, with the stock market crash in 1987 followed by an economic recession in 1989. In combating that recession, tax cuts and increased government spending actually increased the budget deficit during the early 1990s. The only way to bring the fiscal budget into a balanced state is to adopt a *"spend as you earn revenue" approach*. This automatic balanced budget stabilizer approach is extremely difficult and sometimes unrealistic when business-cycle fluctuations (recession and inflation) happen so frequently, as they do in a free market system like the US economy. Active fiscal policy measures to minimize the business-cycle fluctuations must compromise with the balanced budget principle of "spend as you earn revenue." As explained in the previous section, during a recession, the government must increase spending in the public sector and reduce taxes to boost the AE model = AD = C + I + G (ignoring the trade sector of export and import).

This AE equation implies that during a recession, AD or AE must be increased by spending more in the G component to compensate for the decline of the I component of AE (investment in the private sector). Tax has to be decreased also to boost the C component of AE. In addition, the government must provide unemployment insurance and medical support to people who lose their jobs. Because the transfer payments of government outlays (expenses) far exceed the declining tax revenue during a recession, the budget deficit continues to rise.

On the other hand, during an economic boom, the government budget condition may reverse the situation just described by creating a budget surplus. The budget data in Table 11.1 indicates that the surplus in 2000 and 2001 during the peak of the economic boom carried over from a 1996 massive capital investment in information technology and the internet revolution. This was the only time that the economy generated a balanced budget as it reached full employment or near full employment. But that type of coincidence is very rare. Therefore, balancing the budget may not be in the best interests of the fiscal policy makers. This discussion clearly indicates the nature of complexity in pursuing the balanced budget approach, because of its negative ramifications on output and employment. The debate on this matter has been growing in recent years amid the skyrocketing budget deficit and public debt. As part of the debate, a mix of fiscal and monetary policy is advised by some pundits in the field of economics. The next section discusses the approach of conducting monetary and fiscal policy simultaneously to reduce the budget deficit without triggering recession or inflation.

---

1 Regional Oral History Office, "1985 Balanced Budget and Emergency Deficit Control Act," Slaying the Dragon of Debt, http://bancroft.berkeley.edu/ROHO/projects/debt/1985grammrudmanhollings.html.

11.1.2. The Role of Fiscal and Monetary Policy in Reducing the Budget Deficit

With its limitations and negative consequences on employment and RGDP growth, the balanced budget approach has been avoided by fiscal policy makers (the US president's office and the US Congress) since the Great Recession of 2008. However, a careful mix of fiscal and monetary policy in opposite directions may have the potential to sustain a low inflation rate and a low unemployment rate while maintaining a positive RGDP growth rate. For example, if expansionary fiscal policy causes a higher budget deficit while increasing GDP growth and employment, the price level tends to increase as well. Because the price level or inflation rate and interest rates tend to move together, expansionary fiscal policy may also cause interest rates to rise. The way it happens is illustrated in Figure 11.1.

Figure 11.1 Fiscal Policy and Interest Rate Changes

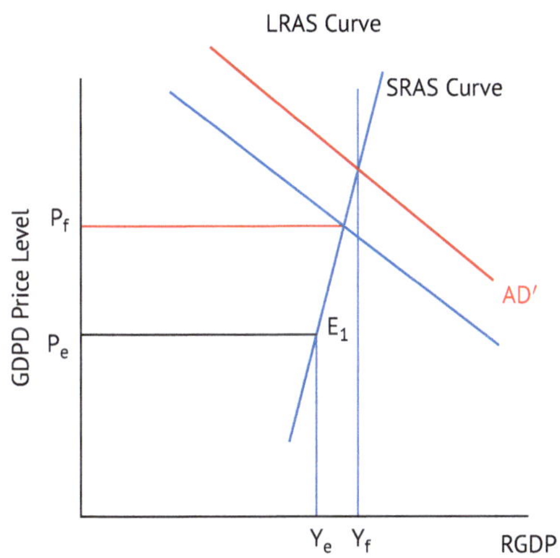

In Figure 11.1, the equilibrium point E_1 is a state of recession, where RGDP at Y_e is below the potential full employment RGDP shown as Y_f. With expansionary fiscal policy, increasing government expenditure and/or reducing taxes will shift the AD curve to the right to achieve full employment at the point of intersection ($E_{2)}$ between SRAS and AD'. The achievement of full employment would also increase the price level from P_e to P_f. The increase in the price level, along with an increase in RGDP and national income, would tend to increase the demand for money. As discussed in regard to the theories and applications of the money market in Chapter 10, an increase in RGDP shifts the demand curve to the right in the money market and thus increases the nominal interest rate with a given level of money supply (illustrated in Figure 10.3). This expansionary fiscal policy is expected to increase budget deficits, as explained in the previous section of this chapter.

On the other hand, if the fiscal and monetary policy actions try to complement each other during a recession by conducting expansionary policies on both sides for quick recovery, then it is possible for the AD = [C+ I + G + (EX − IM)] to move faster than just expansionary fiscal policy alone. Suppose this faster movement of AD is powered by combined expansionary fiscal and expansionary monetary policies. This complementary policy mix was actually performed during the recovery from the 2008 Great Recession. Then it is possible to boost the AD curve further to move beyond the equilibrium point (E_2 in Figure 11.2) to the right. The effects of a rightward shift of the AD curve on actual the RGDP and price level are illustrated in Figure 11.2.

Figure 11.2 indicates that the complementary policy mix shifted the AD curve further to the right, with the RGDP greater than full employment RGDP shown by Y_e' at the new equilibrium point of E_3 at an even higher price level of P_e'. This state of the economy is called an economic boom—overheating the production and demand side of the economy. This situation creates a tight labor market with a shortage of skilled labor, which strengthens the bargaining power of workers (both skilled and unskilled workers) to raise their wages. Also, private investors and corporations would have to hire less-skilled workers than they need because of the labor shortage. The hiring of unskilled labor causes a short-run adverse effect by decreasing labor productivity. This phenomenon of overemployment also causes a shortage of raw materials and capital, thereby raising the prices. The suppliers pass along this higher cost of labor and raw materials to consumers by raising the prices of final products. The process thus increases inflation and expected inflation. At this point, the government can pursue contractionary fiscal policy by raising taxes and/or reducing government expenditure to affect the changes in the G and T components of the AD function, causing it to shift leftward. This process of tight fiscal policy can serve to reduce the inflation rate and budget deficit at the same time without the fear of immediate recession.

Figure 11.2 Fiscal and Monetary Policy and Interest Rate Changes

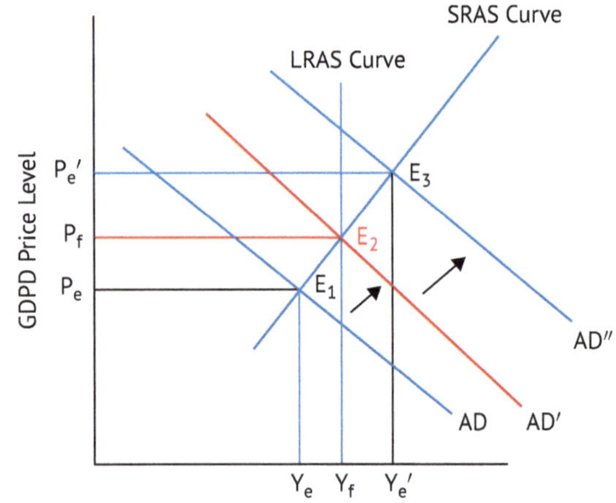

From the analyses made in Figures 11.1 and 11.2, it seems clear that the government's policy effort to reduce the budget deficit is much more complicated than the theoretical foundations of an alternative policy mix of fiscal and monetary policy. Because both monetary and fiscal policies may change the interest rates to affect the investment and consumption components of AE or AD, the net effect of this policy mix in reducing the budget deficit and inflation would depend on the size of the Keynesian multiplier (Tax multiplier = −MPC/MPS; Expenditure multiplier = 1/MPC). But it is also true that this multiplier does not consider changes in tax rates, changes in the price level, changes in export and import, and changes in interest rates as part of investment. If these changes were integrated into the multiplier equations for taxes and government spending, then the realistic multiplier would be much lower than the oversimplified multipliers I have explained here.

Nevertheless, a policy mix in opposite directions is expected to reduce the budget deficit, even with a lower-sized multiplier. For example, if an expansionary fiscal policy causes a rise in the budget deficit with lowering tax rates, then interest rates will increase. If the monetary policy authority (the Fed) doesn't like seeing a rise in interest rates, it can conduct expansionary fiscal policy actions by purchasing Treasury securities or mortgage-backed securities to increase the bank reserve and money supply. Increasing the money supply will thus decrease interest rates to fulfill the Fed's desire to keep interest rates low.

This policy mix is called **monetization of government deficit**. The real risk of monetizing the budget deficit is inflation. Therefore, the Fed usually avoids pursuing the monetization option to lower interest rates unless a combination of both policies is needed under a severe economic downturn. As a matter of fact, both fiscal and monetary policy expansion was undertaken during the Obama administration (2009–2016) to combat the Great Recession of 2008 successfully with no significant inflation.

Our discussion in this section clearly indicates that the budget deficit will continue to rise even with the policy mix (both monetary and fiscal policy expansion) because of the decline of tax revenue from job losses and an increase in transfer payments for unemployment insurance, Medicaid, and other related welfare benefits. The costs of Medicare and social security payments are also expected to rise significantly because millions of people in the workforce from the baby boomer generation (born between 1946 and 1964) started retiring in 2010. Putting all these government expenses together does add up to significant government outlays (structural deficit) as unavoidable expenses. As mentioned earlier, these unavoidable government payments and the cyclical fluctuation in the economy keep the structural budget deficit rising and thus accumulating more public debt as noted in Table 11.1.

11.2. The Effects of the Deficit and Public Debt in the Short Run and the Long Run

11.2.1. What Are the Short-Run Effects of the Deficit and Public Debt?

From discussions in Sections 11.1.1 and 11.1.2, it is clear that the increasing budget deficit and public debt actually do boost the economy by increasing AE and thus increasing output (RGDP) and employment in the short run. Also, financing the budget deficit and paying interest against accumulated public debt is easy through open market sales of short-term Treasury securities. The short-term securities issued by the US government are still extremely popular with bond investors and foreign governments because of high confidence in US economic stability, a history of zero defaults by the US government, political stability, and global domination of military defenses. This position makes it easy for the US government to borrow money at a very low interest rate (the yield of Treasury securities) to finance the budget deficit and debt. This easy financing method for the budget deficit has two positive effects: It increases GDP and employment, and it keeps inflation under control in the short run because selling Treasury securities indirectly reduces bank reserves and the money supply for the time being (unless monetary policy increases the money supply by other means). Therefore, the short-run effect of the budget deficit offers a positive economic outcome, except that it may increase interest rates, which would have a negative effect on private investment. However, given the high confidence of private business entities in future economic trends fueled by expansionary fiscal policy, net investment by the private sector is expected to increase as well.

11.2.2. What Are the Long-Run Effects of the Deficit and Public Debt?

In the long run, the economic and financial implications of the skyrocketing budget deficit and public debt of the US government is not so straightforward. Also, the long-run effect of the budget deficit and public debt is more focused on public debt, because the latter is accumulated over time with the continuous rise of debt while the former increases once each year. The real question is what will happen to the economy and financial health of the government and financial institutions in the long run?

First, the key question is, who bears the burden of this public debt? The burden of the debt actually falls on all Americans, meaning that every citizen owes the debt to the creditors. It is just like the individual burden of household debt on home mortgages, car loans, and other types of individual loans that are paid in installments with interest and principal and that may take years or decades to pay off. On the other hand, the creditors (the bondholders) are happy with the monthly interest payments from the US government. In other words, creditors are financial institutions and borrowers are the public (not individuals or households). Technically, we all owe the debt to ourselves. If we agree on that technical concept, then paying off that debt or reducing it in the long run can be seen from a very different perspective than in the short run, as discussed earlier. The next consideration is how to pay in the long run and what happens if the US government cannot pay or if it defaults.

11.2.3. How to Pay the Debt in the Long Run

There are two ways the government can pay the debt, or at least some of it, to reduce the rising trend: either impose higher taxes in the future and/or reduce government expenses (the sequester). The government is not pursuing either of these options at this point because it wants to keep the economy moving forward while it piles up more debt. As a matter of fact, the current government is doing just the opposite. Cutting more taxes for corporations and high-income groups and increasing spending. The 2017 Trump tax cut actually provides the lowest tax rate in history for corporations and wealthy households. Tax and budget experts said that the Trump tax cut and increased spending will increase the public debt by over $1 trillion in the next five years. Therefore, the government is not expected to choose either of the two options anytime in the near future, meaning the public debt will continue to accumulate.

11.2.4. What If the Debt Is Not Paid or the Government Defaults on Its Monthly Payment?

Whether the government is able to pay the debt in the future or not will depend on certain possibilities. One thing is sure, the US government can always impose higher taxes to pay some debts if it really has to. But this has not happened since the debt started to accumulate in the 1980s under the supply-side economic policy of the Reagan administration. However, there is confidence in the government's ability to pay by imposing higher taxes whenever needed. The question is, who would bear the burden of this tax hike, and when might it happen? No one actually knows for sure because the government is able to continue borrowing at a very low interest rate and paying the monthly payment with no immediate need to impose politically and economically damaging tax hikes.

11.2.5. What If the Government Defaults in the Future?

The possibility of defaulting on a debt payment is highly unlikely for four key reasons:

- The government has the power and ability to impose higher taxes, as discussed earlier.
- The government's ability to pay is highly likely to continue just as it has been, without default, over the last 40 years.
- Investment in US Treasury securities (the public debt) is considered a safe haven for investors with no default risk, no liquidity risk, and very low taxes on returns. That is the reason it has been so easy for the US Treasury to borrow money from investors at a very low yield.
- If the US government ever faces any difficulty selling Treasury securities to pay its debt installments, it can always sell a small fraction of its tens of trillions of dollars of assets, such as gold, silver, land, buildings, parks, airports, transportation industries, and financial assets.

Given this enormous asset portfolio, there is no risk of defaulting on the debt, even in the long run.

11.2.6. What Is the Worst-Case Scenario of Public Debt in the Long Run?

The answer to this question varies depending on who we ask. Politicians would say this would impose a huge tax burden on future generations, despite the fact they are the ones who are borrowing to finance the budget deficits they created. If you ask economists and financial experts, the answers would be very different. They would say that it depends on the state of the economy in the long run. If the economy keeps doing very well, no negative effect is expected. However, if the economy falls into frequent recession with no quick recovery, the government may have to sell massive Treasury securities. When there is an excessive sale of Treasury securities with a decline in confidence in the economy, the price of the Treasury securities will tend to fall, and thus interest rates will rise. Rising interest rates, along with a rising deficit and public debt, will cause inflation. The combination of these effects in macroeconomics will likely reduce private investment and consumption to shift the AD curve to the left significantly enough to outweigh the rightward shift AD from the increase in government expenditures. This phenomenon is called the **crowding out effect** of excessive budget deficit and public debt in the long run. The net result of the crowding out effect is expected to lower output and employment, causing a recession. Although a theoretical argument can be made that the crowding out effect is a possibility in the long run, the US economy so far has not faced this crisis. The reasons are mainly attributed to the four factors of confidence in the US Treasury explained in Section 11.2.5.

11.3. The Fiscal and Monetary Policy Debate in the Context of Price Stability and Full Employment

In previous sections, the role of a policy mix (fiscal and monetary) was discussed in detail for providing price stability and full employment. In this section, a philosophical debate about the pros and cons of active fiscal and monetary policy is discussed. This debate is centered on the context of conventional policy questions as to whether we should depend more on fiscal policy, monetary policy, or a combination of both. To address this ongoing question, it is important to look at the scope and limitation of these two policies in influencing macroeconomic fundamentals, such as recession, inflation, unemployment, and interest rates.

11.3.1. Relative Effectiveness of Fiscal Policy and Monetary Policy

The ongoing debate on the relative importance of conventional fiscal and monetary policy started back in the 1930s when the crisis of the Great Depression was addressed by Keynes with his revolutionary concept of fiscal and monetary policy prescriptions in dealing with the crisis. This debate emerged in full force again during the Great Recession of 2008, when an active policy prescription was needed to stop the rising unemployment and rapidly declining output. The big question of the debate was which of the two Keynesian policy prescriptions would be appropriate to bring about economic stability. As discussed in previous chapters, the relative effectiveness of these monetary and fiscal policies depends on time lags and the state of the economy.

As explained previously, fiscal policy actions are undertaken by the legislative and executive branches of the federal government. The US president and the lawmakers of the legislative branches are elected officials responsible for managing fiscal policy prescriptions. The conventional fiscal policy tools are tax policy and government spending. However, the democratic process is constrained from taking quick actions on fiscal policy measures because of three factors:

The time lag to realize the state of the economy while gathering data on key macroeconomic fundamentals, such as the unemployment rate, GDP growth rate, and inflation rate. It takes between three and six months to convince elected officials to take policy actions.

The time lag for the voting process in both the House and the Senate committees means that decisions to make changes to existing taxes and government spending can take longer. The difference of opinion among the party lines requires months of negotiation to come to an agreed-upon bill. This process takes another three to six months to reach final approval.

The time lag for getting the president's signature is another hurdle if the political bickering between the two parties (Republican and Democrat) is noncooperative. The whole process takes between six and nine months after the economic crisis starts.

Therefore, without immediate action by fiscal policy makers, the voting process and related debate on differences of opinion among legislative members in the US Congress potentially limits the effectiveness of fiscal policy. During the Great Recession of 2008, however, this process was quickly adopted by both parties because of the urgency of the crisis. The effectiveness of monetary policy, on the other hand, can be much faster and timely for the reasons outlined next.

The members of FOMC, the supreme decision-making body of the Fed, are not elected officials. When making policy decisions, they are not accountable to the legislative body or their respective constituents. Therefore, the Fed's decision on using conventional monetary policy tools, such as discount rates, interest rate targets, and OMO to change the money supply can be made very quickly. This quick decision-making process can have a more rapid effect than waiting months for fiscal policy actions to take effect. During the Great Recession of 2008, the Fed's FOMC acted quickly to lower the federal funds interest rate close to zero to achieve a faster economic recovery.

The simultaneous policy actions by both fiscal and monetary policy authorities during the Great Recession of 2008 helped the economy recover from the crisis. However, the recovery process was slow in the first few years because there were certain other factors that could not be controlled by the policy makers at the Fed or by the legislative branches of the government. Those factors are stated next:

Confidence of investors in the economic recovery process takes longer to rebound, especially in the aftermath of a severe recession. For example, during the 2008 Great Recession, the confidence of business entities, such as financial institutions, real estate investors, and Wall Street bankers, to reinvest in the economy was very low, despite the big push made by fiscal and monetary policy expansion. For example, despite the lowering of the federal funds rate to close to zero by then Fed chair Ben Bernanke, the real estate market in general was not rebounding. This phenomenon of loss of confidence in the economy is called a **liquidity trap**, originally dubbed by Keynes. The liquidity trap occurs when the loss of confidence by the private sectors causes reinvestment in business to cease, even when the interest rate is at its lowest possible level.

Unconventional monetary policy actions were initiated by the Fed in 2010 to mitigate the problem of the liquidity trap. While the economic recovery process was initiated by conventional fiscal and monetary policy expansions in 2008 and 2009, the Fed's FOMC, led by Ben Bernanke, adopted an extraordinary and unconventional approach that had never been tested before. In this approach, named quantitative easing (QE), the Fed started buying massive amounts of mortgage-backed securities from the depressed bond market caused by the housing crisis during the Great Recession of 2008. The Fed aggressively bought the bonds at a premium rate to boost the housing market and achieve a faster recovery. This extraordinary approach of QE occurred in three different phases dubbed as **QEI, QEII**, and **QEIII**, with a total purchase of over $1 trillion worth of mortgage-backed securities between 2010 and 2014. Under this approach, the Fed also continued buying back hundreds of billions of long-term US Treasury bonds to keep the short-term interest low. This approach was successful; the housing market rebounded, and the economy showed close to full employment by October 2014, when the Fed stopped the QE program to prevent potential inflation.

The shape of the AS curve is also important when considering the effectiveness of expansionary and contractionary fiscal and monetary policies in achieving economic stability. For example, with a relatively flat AS curve, expansionary fiscal and monetary policy actions would be able to increase the GDP growth rate and reduce the unemployment rate faster without much concern for a rise in the inflation rate. The same advantage would also be true for the ability of contractionary policies to control inflation without much concern for a deflationary effect on the economy. On the other hand, with a relatively steep AS curve, fiscal and monetary policy actions tend to increase or decrease GDP growth rate much more slowly than the corresponding increase or decrease of the inflation rate (the price level). Both of these possible scenarios are illustrated in Figures 11.3 and 11.4.

Figure 11.3 Flat AS Curve and Policy Effectiveness

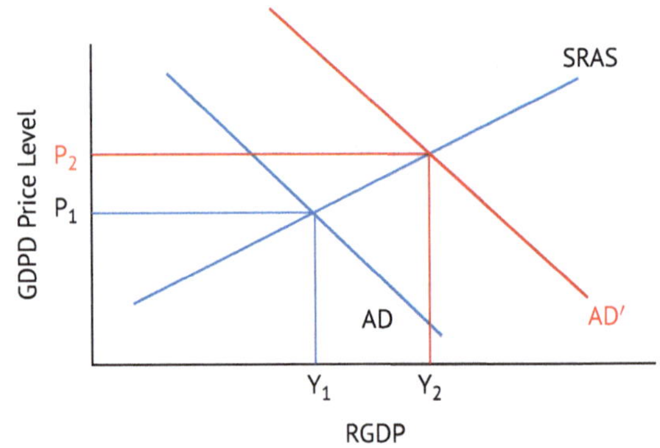

Figure 11.4 Steep AS Curve and Policy Effectiveness

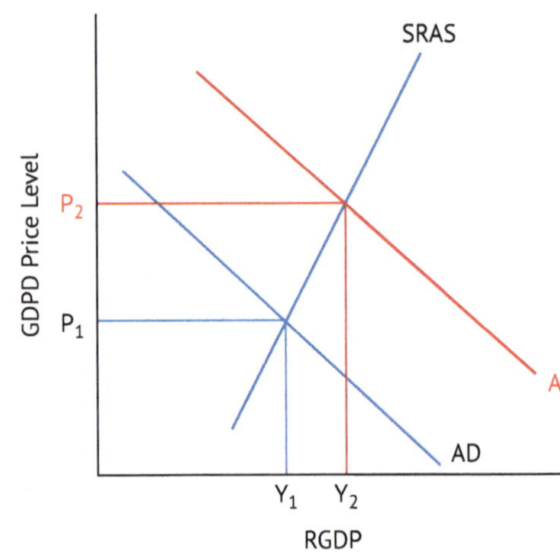

In Figure 11.3, given the flat AS curve, expansionary fiscal or monetary policy actions would shift the AD curve from AD to AD' to increase RGDP from Y_1 to $Y_{2,}$ with a very small increase in the price level from P_1 to P_2, as indicated on the vertical axis. By the same token, contractionary monetary or fiscal policy would do the same trick in reverse by lowering RGDP at a much higher rate than the corresponding decrease in the price level. On the other hand, a steeper AS curve, illustrated in Figure 11.4, shows relatively ineffective fiscal and monetary actions taken to stabilize the economy.

Figure 11.4, with its relatively steep AS curve, indicates that the increase in the price level is much higher than the corresponding increase in the RGDP induced by expansionary monetary or fiscal policy actions to shift the AD curve from AD to AD'. Reversing the policy with contractionary measures would show the same pattern of results. Therefore, Keynesian monetary policy actions may not necessarily be effective if the SRAS curve is steeper than normal circumstances. In that case, the conservative politicians and economists suggest adopting the supply-side economic policies that were first tried in the 1980s and again in 2003 and 2017. On the other hand, liberal politicians and Keynesian economists believe that during a recession, the SRAS curve is relatively flat for achieving economic recovery effectively without any concern for a rise in inflation. Although it is difficult for economists and other financial experts to measure the exact slope of the SRAS and LRAS because of the complicated structure of cost functions of individual firms and industries, it is commonly perceived from empirical studies that the shape of the AS curve is relatively flat in the short run, and it is relatively steeper in the long run. Since economic policies are focused on the short run to stabilize an economic crisis, arguments for active policies under a Keynesian framework seem to be stronger than supply-side arguments when pursuing expansionary or contractionary policy actions. Nevertheless, the debate on this matter continues because empirical studies have yet to figure out the deciding factor for policy effectiveness. The next section in this chapter focuses on the debate over discretionary policy versus the long-run rules of the automatic stabilization policy options for achieving economic stability.

11.4. The Monetary and Fiscal Policy Debate: Discretionary versus Rules

Given the complexity of the fiscal and monetary policy actions discussed in Section 11.3., the debate ultimately arrives at a discussion of whether active economic policy is necessary or if the economy would be better off without a discretionary policy at all. This debate has become stronger over time, with opinions not only from the economics profession but also from politicians. The ideological differences between the liberal and conservative wings of the two major political parties in the United States have made this debate even more controversial in recent decades. The conservative wing of the Republican party favors less policy intervention and the liberal wing of the democratic party supports active policy intervention to achieve faster economic recovery when the crisis caused by the cyclical fluctuations of the economy.

11.4.1. Economic Arguments against Discretionary Policies

Aside from political controversies, the economic arguments against discretionary monetary and fiscal policy are based on an inability to rely on data for accurate forecasts, a degree of uncertainty, and the time lags between recognizing an economic crisis and implementation of policies. As pointed out in previous sections discussing the relative effectiveness of fiscal and monetary policies, the complex nature of data availability and reliability makes it difficult to accurately forecast the effect of policy actions toward economic recovery and stability in the long run. Given those difficulties, the case against active policy measures emphasizes that discretionary policies tend to do more harm than good. Therefore, they recommend passive policy rules for long-run stability in price and employment without any direct intervention in fixing the short-run fluctuation.

11.4.2. Economic Arguments for Discretionary Policies

Keynesian economists argue that active and discretionary policies are necessary at a time of economic crisis because the market forces do not respond positively during a recession and inflation. For example, they argue the need for increasing government spending and reducing taxes during a recession to boost the AD faster for a quick recovery without a rise in expected inflation. During an unexpected state of inflation caused by an external shock, the discretionary fiscal policy of raising taxes and/or reducing government expenditure would do the trick by shifting the AD to the left to mitigate inflation. They also make this argument stronger in the sense that in the absence of policy intervention, market failure might take too long to correct itself. To avoid prolonged recession and/or inflation, discretionary fiscal and monetary policies help restore the price level and employment stability quickly without causing too much suffering to the people who lost jobs and businesses. The arguments for active and discretionary monetary policy are also based on the positive effects of lowering interest rates during a recession. Expansionary monetary policy during a recession increases the money supply and lowers the interest rates, which increases investment and consumption within a short period of time to restore full employment. During inflation, contractionary monetary policy is expected to do the opposite by causing a downward shift of the AD curve to achieve new equilibrium output at a lower price level.

11.4.3. Case Studies for Rules versus Discretionary Policies in the US Economy

The advocates of both sides of the policy options described in the previous section have made their cases by looking at evidence dating back to the 1950s. For example, the group supporting discretionary policies refers to the successful economic results of massive government intervention in the post–World War II era, especially the massive expansionary fiscal policies undertaken in the 1950s and 1960s. The fiscal expansion during those two decades after World War II brought unprecedented economic prosperity and a high standard of living for Americans. They also refer to the same results in tackling the recessions in the 1970s, 1980s, early 1990s, and the Great Recession of 2008, when a combination of active monetary and fiscal policies helped bring about a quick recovery from recessions. On the other hand, the critics against discretionary policies also make their points with evidence of policy failures in managing the hyperinflation in the early 1970s and the wrong interest rate policies undertaken by the Fed in 2004 that brought the economy into a severe recession in 2008.

The debate on this unsettled issue continues in an effort to determine what exactly is the best approach. Until that happens, it is apparent that fiscal policy makers on both sides of the aisle are following the discretionary approach to keep the economy moving forward. On the other hand, monetary policy makers (with their full independence in controlling the money supply and interest rates) use a mix of both discretionary approach and the rules option. For example, during the 2008 Great Recession, the Fed took an active and discretionary approach by lowering the federal funds rate close to zero, and they took the extraordinary and unconventional approach of QE, restoring full employment by taking an enormous risk. But since 2015, as the economy reached full employment, the Fed changed its course from a discretionary approach to a rule approach by targeting the inflation rate to keep it at 2% over the next few years. For more information on the Fed's policy strategy, students may visit the Fed's home page at.[2]

---

2 Visit https://www.federalreserve.gov/newsevents/testimony.htm to read the most recent testimony by the Fed Chair to the US Congress.

Chapter Summary

Section 11.1 introduced the issues with the continuing increase in the budget deficit and accumulated public debt for the US economy since the 1980s. The expansionary fiscal policy prescription under the Keynesian framework, which includes a reduction in taxes and an increase in government spending, has caused this chronic budget deficit and public debt accumulation for over four decades. Table 11.1 showed the yearly deficit and accumulated public debt from 2002 to 2018, which have increased from $157.8 billion of annual deficit to $785.2 billion. At the same time span, the accumulated public debt skyrocketed from $3,540.4 billion to $15,751.2 billion. The growing budget deficit and its accumulated public debt shown in Table 11.1 have caused a great deal of concern to citizens, business firms, and political leaders. The political debate on this issue is one of the key sources of rising political bickering in the US Congress, dividing members down party lines. At issue in this never-ending debate is whether to reduce the budget deficit by shrinking government spending or increasing taxes. But the reality is that either of these two options poses a danger because they would reduce the AE and thus reduce output and job opportunities, a source of recession.

Section 11.1.1 explained the pros and cons of reducing the budget deficit and public debt by undertaking tight fiscal policy spending and increasing taxes. This issue is an ongoing political and economic debate with no clear ending in the near future. The balanced budget approach doesn't seem to be a viable option at this state.

Section 11.1.2 introduced a possible scenario with the option of mixed fiscal and monetary policy actions to reduce the budget deficit and public debt while keeping sustained economic growth and employment. Two possible scenarios were presented in this section: discretionary fiscal policy action with changes in taxes and government expenditure; and, expansionary fiscal policy actions to change the interest rate by the Fed. The purpose of these complimentary policies by is to offset the rise in interest rate caused by expansionary fiscal policy. The analysis of these two alternative policy actions was explained and illustrated in Figure 11.1 and Figure 11.2.

Section 11.2.1 provided logical answers to the question regarding the short-run effects of the deficit and public debt. By the same token, Section 11.2.2 offered economic and political logic for identifying the long-run effects of public debt.

Section 11.2.3 discussed a possible way to pay the debt in the future and its effects on the economy followed by questions and answers concerning what would happen if the government failed to pay the debt and the effects in the short run and the long run. These issues were further presented in Sections 11.2.4 and 11. 2.5.

Section 11.2.6 discussed the worst-case scenario of the public debt in the long run and its likelihood. It is strongly recommended that students read this section carefully with its political and social implications for the future generation.

Section 11.3 critically explained the relative effectiveness of fiscal and monetary policy actions to bring full employment and price stability during business-cycle fluctuations. The discussion was made in reference to time lags involved in recognizing the economic crisis, the voting process by legislators, and the relative shape of the AS curve during policy actions.

Figures 11.3 and 11.4 illustrated the relative effectiveness of policy actions and the implications in relation to the detailed explanations made in this section.

Section 11.4 introduced the interesting debate on discretionary fiscal and monetary policy prescriptions under the Keynesian framework versus the policy rule under the neoclassical view. With that perspective, Section 11.4.1 discussed the argument against discretionary policy actions. Section 11.4.2 discussed the arguments in favor of active policy actions.

Section 11.4.3 provided case studies of rules versus discretionary fiscal policies from a historical perspective of the US economy and its prosperity since the end of World War II. This historical trend of US economic GDP growth, employment, and inflation clearly reflects the importance of understanding the role of economic policies in maintaining full employment and price stability both in the short run and the long run. From the practice questions in the "Application Activities" section for part of the homework assignment, students are expected to learn more about the important policy debate concerning the degree of government intervention in a cycle of economic downturn.

Application Activities

Q1. Define fiscal policy and its key objectives. What government agencies are responsible for making decisions on fiscal policy actions and implementations?

Q2. Critically and briefly describe the following fiscal policy tools and their relative effectiveness in controlling business-cycle fluctuations, such as a recession and/or inflation. How do they operate during a recession and inflation? Draw an AD-AS diagram of the macroeconomics model to illustrate your explanation.

- Government spending
- Tax policy

Q3. Define monetary policy and its key objectives. What government agency is responsible for making decisions on monetary policy actions and implementations?

Q4. Critically and briefly describe the following conventional monetary policy tools and policy targets, as well as their relative effectiveness in controlling business-cycle fluctuations, such as a recession and/or inflation. How do they operate during a recession and inflation? Draw an AD-AS diagram of the macroeconomics model to illustrate your explanation.

- Reserve requirements
- Discount rate
- OMO
- Federal funds rate (policy target)

Q5. Distinguish between the budget deficit and public debt with an example from actual data from the US government budget office discussed at the beginning of this chapter. Give at least three reasons why the budget deficit and public debt has been continually rising since 2001.

Q6. Give at least two reasons why the balanced budget approach for the US economy is not a realistic approach in the short-run, despite political advocacy to bring the budget back into balance.

Q7. Describe briefly the short-run and long-run effects of the rising budget deficit and public debt. What is the crowding out effect? Why has the US economy seldom been faced with the crowding out effect in recent decades despite the skyrocketing budget deficit and public debt?

Q8. Describe the role of a mix of fiscal and monetary policy actions in stabilizing inflation, unemployment, and RGDP growth.

Q9. List a few of the arguments made by business entities, politicians, and different groups in the economics profession for and against "discretionary" fiscal and monetary policy actions. How do they differ from the advocacy for adopting passive "rules" of economic policy? Give real-world examples in your answers in the context of the US economy.

Q10. On October 29, 2014, the members of the FOMC of the Federal Reserve Board voted to maintain the federal funds target within the same range of between 0.25% basis points to 0%, as it was set by the FOMC in August 2011. But in 2011, the economy was in severe recession and the purpose was to boost the economy by increasing liquidity in the banking system at this low rate when inflation was also very low. The specific action of the Fed trade was to purchase Treasury securities every day to increase the money supply and thus keep the interest rate (the federal funds rate) low to stimulate the economy.

But in the same month of October 2014, the economy showed a near full recovery and the stock market and financial institutions had been performing very well since 2011. On October 29, 2014, the FOMC also decided to end the asset purchase plans under QE III, under which the Fed had been buying mortgage-backed securities and long-term Treasury bonds since the recovery started in 2011. Following the Fed's decision to end the QE III of asset purchases and to keep the same federal funds rate target, the Dow Jones Industrial Average went down significantly and did not fully recover by the end of the trading day.

Question: What are the macroeconomic trends that prompted the FOMC to end the QE III but keep the federal funds rate at its historic low? You need to give reasons for both of these policy measures. Note: To study more background information on this question, please click on two url links I have added on the bottom in the footnote.[1]

Q11. One cornerstone of the Trump administration's economic policy for 2018 was tax cuts targeted toward high-income and high-net-worth households. Under his proposals, the marginal tax rate applied to capital gains taxes has been reduced, taxes on stock dividends have been eliminated, and marginal tax rates on wage and interest income (particularly

---

1 For more information, please visit the press release of the Federal Reserve Board at http://www.federalreserve.gov/newsevents/press/monetary/20141029a.htm.

Also, read some newswire analysis from CNN from the same day at http://money.cnn.com/2014/10/29/news/economy/federal-reserve-ends-qe-bond-buying/index.html?iid=HP_LN.

those applied to high-income brackets) have also been reduced. Please note that tax cuts by previous administrations under Bush and Obama were aimed at massive tax reductions, but they included tax breaks for the middle class and raised the tax rates for households earning more than $300,000 per year.

11a. What will be the short-run effects of tax cuts on interest rates and growth in RGDP given that the economy is in a state of full employment in 2018? Contrast the Keynesian and crowding out perspectives on this question.

11b. If question 11a were focused on the long-run effects of the proposed tax cuts, would the long-run effects of the proposed tax cuts represent a "supply-side" tax policy by the Trump administration? Why would an economist who believes that federal budget deficits create significant "crowding out" effects answer this question differently than most other economists? Explain.

Q12. In September 2019, the actual data on US unemployment showed a rate of 3.5%, the lowest rate since 1969. In this and previous chapters, we discussed the conditions under which the Fed takes expansionary and/or contractionary monetary policy actions to stabilize the price level and employment. Given the state of the present economy, is the Fed pursuing an expansionary, neutral, or contractionary monetary policy? Why?

Chapter 12

Comparative Analysis of Classical and Keynesian Monetary Theories and Their Policy Implications

Learning Objectives

As they read the chapter, students will learn the following:

- Classical quantity theory of money versus Keynesian monetary theory: empirical evidence and policy implications
- Monetarism versus Keynesianism in the debate over rules versus discretionary monetary policy for fine-tuning business-cycle fluctuations
- Debate on lags in monetary policy effectiveness in stabilizing the economy
- The role of monetary policy in controlling business-cycle fluctuations

In Chapters 10 and 11, the theories and applications of money demand and money supply were discussed from the point of view of a Keynesian model of money, interest, and employment. In this chapter, the monetary theory that existed prior to the Keynesian theory of money is introduced. This theory is called the classical quantity theory of money, which is more focused on measuring money supply and its implications for monetary policy. Keynesian monetary theory, on the other hand, focuses more on the demand side of the money market (the liquidity preference theory) to integrate the money supply with the money demand to determine the equilibrium interest rate in the money market.

12.1. Classical Quantity Theory of Money versus Keynesian Monetary Theory

In Chapter 10, the measures of the money supply, M_1 and M_2, as two alternative monetary aggregates, were discussed in detail. However, the classical view of monetary aggregates was not mentioned. The discussion was rather focused on how the Fed controls the money supply aggregates of either M_1 or M_2 to change the equilibrium interest rate and inflation for achieving economic stability by conducting OMO (open market operations) and/or changing the federal funds rates. But the classical approach of measuring the money supply and its interpretation for policy implications was based on the **"equation of exchange"** called the **classical quantity theory of money**. This theory and empirical evidence are explained in Sections 12.1.1 and 12.1.2, followed by the Keynesian approach to monetary theory and policy implications.

12.1.1. Classical Quantity Theory of Money

Originally developed by British economist John Stuart Mill (1806–1873), the classical monetary theory of money is stated in equation (12.1) by its commonly known name: **the equation of exchange**.

Classical quantity theory of money or the equation of exchange: MV = PY, ...Eqn (12.1)

where M is the aggregate money supply, V is the velocity of money, P is the aggregate price level in the goods market, and Y is the RGDP so that PY is the NGDP.

Velocity of money (V) is the average turnover rate from hand to hand in a fixed time period to purchase goods and services and other monetary transactions.

This equation of exchange (MV = PY) in equation (12.1) asserts that the NGDP (nominal GDP) is powered by the quantity of money in circulation multiplied by its velocity (V = the turnover rate of monetary transactions). However, it is not practical to count every transaction of money moving from hand to hand in the entire economy. An alternative but mathematically viable way to measure the realistic velocity is to divide the NGDP (PY) by monetary aggregates (M_1 or M_2), where money supply and NGDP are estimated real numbers. Therefore, the measurable velocity economists have come up with is stated in equation (12.2).

Velocity of Money: V = PY/M ....Eqn (12.2)

The money supply aggregates are measures in two categories, M_1 and M_2 (discussed in Chapter 10); based on the degree of liquidity, M_1 represents the most liquid assets (currency plus checking account deposits) and M_2 represents the least liquid (M_1 + Saving deposits + CDs + Money market accounts). Accordingly, the velocity of these two categories of the money supply can also be expressed as **$V_1 = PY/M_1$ and $V_2 = PY/M_2$**.

The classical approach to measuring the velocity of money is the relationship between the NGDP and the money supply to understand the role of monetary policy implications. This approach assumes that velocity is almost constant; thus, the velocity in equation 12.2 above implies that M_1 or M_2 are proportional to NGDP (PY). The advocates of this classical approach are called monetarists (the neoclassical view of monetary theories), led by Milton Friedman (1912–2006) in the 1960s at the University of Chicago. The monetarists went further by interpreting that the increase in the price level (P) is solely influenced by a money supply increase by the same proportion with no real impact on the RGDP (Y). The assumption made for this statement is that V and Y are constant or stable over time. For example, in the equation of exchange, if the money supply is increased by 10%, then the price level will also increase by 10% with no real change in velocity (V) or RGDP (Y). Monetarists also considered M_2 a more appropriate measure of the money supply for policy purposes because of its relative stability of velocity (V_2) in the long run as compared to the velocity of M_1 (V_1). The reason for considering M_2 as a relatively stable monetary aggregate is that M_2 is a broader measure of the money supply aggregates than M_1. However, in either case, the real-world data on velocity for both M_1 and M_2 do not seem to support the monetarist view of the constant velocity of the equation of exchange.

12.1.2. Empirical Evidence of the Velocity of Monetary Aggregates

Figures 12.1(a) and 12.1(b) for V_1 and V_2, respectively, show that velocity for both M_1 and M_2 has been modestly and continuously fluctuating from 1960 through 2018. The data also show that velocity declines with a high rate of volatility during recessions (shown in the shaded areas in both figures). For example, the values of V_2 show more fluctuation between the 1960s and the 1990s than the value of V_1 during the same period. In the late 1990s, the velocity of M_1 and M_2 actually moved in the opposite direction, with a declining V_1 rate and an increasing V_2 rate. On the other hand, during the 2008 recession, the values of both V_1 and V_2 showed a sharp rate of steady decline until 2018. Because of the long-term and steady volatility of velocity for both M_1 and M_2, the Fed's FOMC not only rejected the monetarist view of the stable velocity of money but also decided not to use a monetary target as part of its policy strategy. It uses interest rate targets instead, known as the short-term interest target of the Fed.

Figure 12.1(a) Data on the Velocity of M_1 (1960–2018)

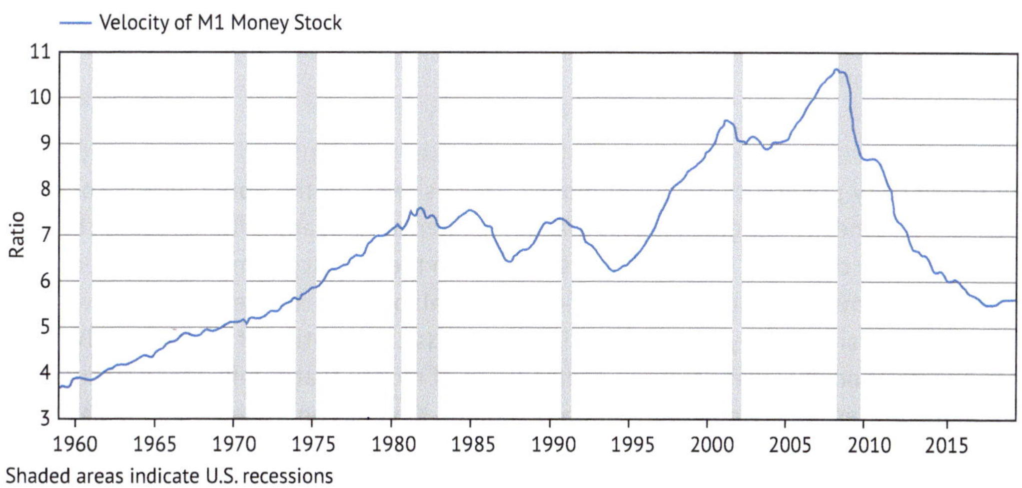

Source: Federal Reserve Bank of St. Louis, https://fred.stlouisfed.org/series/M2V

Figure 12.1(b) Data on the Velocity of M2 (1960–2018)

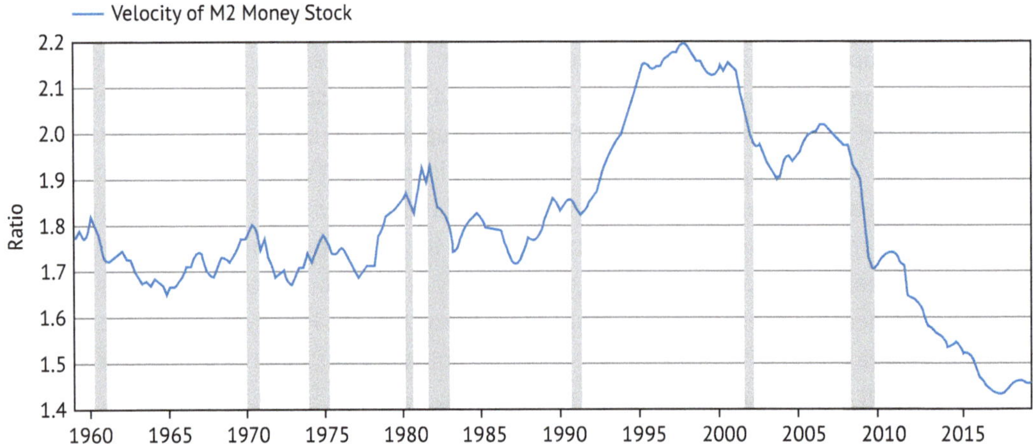

Shaded areas indicate U.S. recessions

Source: Federal Reserve Bank of St. Louis, https://fred.stlouisfed.org/series/M1V

The trend of volatility in the velocity of money recorded since 1960 also indicates that the Keynesian argument against the constant velocity assumption of the classical view was correct and consistent. The Keynesian view of fluctuating velocity was confirmed by recent data that showed higher rates of fluctuation in both V_1 and V_2 because of the massive expansion of noncash forms of transactions, such as credit cards and digital payments (e.g., Apple Pay, PayPal, Bitcoins). It is also important to notice that changes in interest rates do also change the velocity. This is because a rise in interest rates increases the opportunity cost of holding money as liquid. Therefore, increasing interest rates increases the velocity of money, and vice versa. The same logic applies during a rise in inflation; the higher the inflation, the higher the velocity, and vice versa. So the real-world data on velocity confirm Keynes's reasoning for his rejection of the classical assumption of constant velocity. Keynes also rejected the assumption of constant velocity in using the equation of exchange for policy purposes. He developed an alternative approach to monetary theory and practice, which is discussed in the next section.

12.1.3. Keynesian Arguments against the Classical Quantity Theory of Money

In his liquidity preference theory of money, Keynes rejected the notion of the constant velocity of money on the grounds that changes in interest rates and inflation cause changes in the velocity of money. The empirical evidence on the velocity of money between 1960 and 2018, shown in Figures 12.1(a) and 12.1(b), also supports the Keynesian view of velocity as a variable. Keynes also criticized the classical equation of exchange (MV = PY) for its lack of an explanation of the demand side of money that is influenced by changes in interest rates and income/output. For example, Keynes contended that the key variables that affect the quantity of demand for liquid money are absent in the equation of exchange. Because of the missing link between money demand as a function of interest rates and income and the money supply in the equation of exchange, Keynes considered the equation of exchange (MV = PY) to be more of an identity rather than an equation or complete theory. From the point of view of mathematical logic, it is obvious that to solve any theoretical equation, the number of variables must be equal to the number of equations. Because the equation of exchange MV = PY has four variables (as the data suggest they are all variables), four equations are needed to solve it rather than a single equation under the classical view. Therefore, the Keynesian monetary theory was developed as an alternative to the equation of exchange. Keynes explained the behavior of the money market and its link to the goods market as an alternative approach for monetary theory and practice for effective policy implications. The complete Keynesian money market model was discussed in Chapter 10. An extended explanation of the same money market model is provided in the next section.

12.1.4. Keynesian Complete Theory of Money, Interest rates, and Income

With his rejection of the classical equation of exchange, Keynes transformed the equation of exchange into two different equations: a **money demand function** and a **money supply function**.

Money demand = Md = f (i, Y) and ....Eqn (12.2)

Money supply = Ms = Fixed and solely controlled by the Fed,

where i is the interest rate, and Y is the income/RGDP. This equation and the money market equilibrium were discussed in Chapter 10.

The equilibrium condition in the market = Md (i, Y) = Ms. ....Eqn (12.3)

The equilibrium condition in equation (12.3) was a major improvement on the classical view of the money market and its link to the goods market. The Keynesian equation of the money market clearly explains how, at a given income level (Y), the equilibrium interest is determined by the intersection of Md and Ms, as already shown in Figure 10.3. From a policy perspective, this development of monetary theory and its application for achieving economic stability has been profoundly significant to post–World War II economic prosperity in the United States and the rest of the world. For example, the transmission process of the expansionary monetary policy under the Keynesian framework successfully links to the goods market for quick economic recovery from recession. This transmission process is a major and significant development for effective monetary policy measures during a recession. The reverse is also true when tight monetary policy action could be very effective in controlling inflation. Such transmission processes, explained previously in Figure 10.4, are displayed again in Figure 12.2 as a reminder of the discussion of monetary policy effectiveness in Chapter 10.

Figure 12.2 Transmission Flow of Monetary Policy

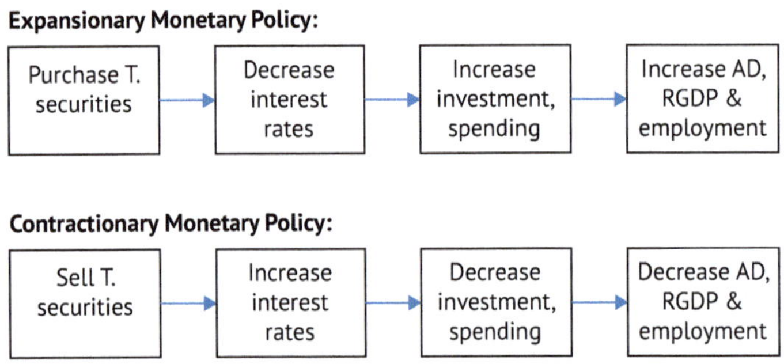

12.1.5. Monetary Policy in Action

The US economy has not only had steady and stable economic growth since 2010 but also currently shows the lowest unemployment rate since 1969: 3.5% in September 2019. This economic boom with a tight labor market has caused inflation to rise. To control this rising expected inflation, the Fed's FOMC raised its federal funds rate at a successive rate of 0.25% at least twice by mid-2018 and stayed neutral until its reversal of the interest rate increase on July 31, 2019, by decreasing the federal funds rate by 0.25%. The reversal of the Fed's policy was in response to an ongoing trade war between China and the United States and the potential effect of a recession in the near future. This discretionary monetary policy approach is based on a Keynesian policy recommendation to minimize business-cycle fluctuations. The effect of decreasing interest rates in the money market is shown in the first box of Figure 12.2 on the first line of the transmission process. This transmission starts with decreasing the federal funds rate to increase reserves and lending activities in the banks. It is expected that this will boost the rate of investment and consumption expenditure components of AD, causing it to shift rightward and thus reduce the fear of an expected recession. The only problem with this discretionary policy in a state of economic boom is the rise of expected inflation if the money supply increases far beyond the RGDP growth rate as a balanced growth of the money supply and output. The second line of the transmission process in Figure 12.2 shows the effect of contractionary monetary policy. This process starts with increasing the federal funds rate to reduce bank reserves and thus slowing the lending activities. This process is expected to increase overall interest rates, which would decrease consumption and investment expenditure. The decrease in investment and consumption as part of the components of AD would make a leftward shift of the AD curve. This leftward shift of AD would then reduce RGDP and employment. The purpose of conducting contractionary monetary policy is to combat the rise in expected inflation during an economic boom. However, the potential problem of this tight monetary policy action is the fear of a recession if the leftward shift of the AD reduces the level of the RGDO below the level of the full employment RGDP. This dilemma of choosing the right policy action is always a subject of a great deal of debate regarding the effectiveness of monetary policy actions. The next section will revisit this ongoing debate on the **"discretionary versus rule"** approach of monetary policy, which was introduced in Chapter 11.

12.2. Monetarism versus Keynesianism in the Debate on Rules versus Discretionary Monetary Policies in Fine-Tuning Business-Cycle Fluctuations

The discretionary monetary policy action taken by the Fed in the example in Section 12.1.5 is called a **Keynesian approach**. This discretionary policy approach has been pursued by all previous Fed chairs since 2004, when then Fed chair Alan Greenspan kept raising the federal funds rate to control the increasing inflation trend. But that was a reversal of his previous expansionary monetary policy to boost the housing market. He repeatedly increased the federal funds rate in subsequent years until the speculative housing bubble started to burst in early 2007. The housing market crash of 2007 eventually brought the economy into a severe recession, the worst financial crisis since the Great Depression of the 1930s. Many experts who are not fans of the discretionary approach blamed Greenspan for the Great Recession of 2008 because they contended that raising interest rates more than a dozen times in two years (2004–2006) to control inflation was not a rational decision without paying close attention to the eventual ramifications of the housing market crash in 2007. Many economists and financial experts still believe, including the author of this textbook, that focusing on raising interest rates only was mainly the cause of the housing market meltdown. What actually happened was the sudden increase of massive foreclosures of subprime mortgages because of the increase of monthly mortgage payments for low-income homeowners, mainly attributed to the Fed's raising interest rates.

The alternative approach to this discretionary monetary policy is called a **monetarist approach**. The conservative political wings of the United States and Europe favor the monetarist approach, which was pioneered by Friedman in the 1960s. The monetarists believe that the Fed should focus on a long-term stable money supply target rate instead of responding to short-run business-cycle fluctuations. In other words, the monetarists recommend that the FOMC should pursue a long-term goal of conducting OMO so that the money supply growth rate in the long run is consistent with a long-term, full-employment growth rate of RGDP. More specifically, the monetarists advocate for a **"3% money supply growth rate"** in the long run instead of a target on short-term interest rates, such as the federal funds rate target. The rationale for recommending a 3% money supply growth is to match the long-term full employment growth rate of the RGDP at 3% without causing inflation to accelerate. The argument for the 3% rule of monetarism is based on the notion that inflation is a monetary phenomenon; therefore, the money supply growth induces the power of consumer spending and investments. If the money supply growth rate exceeds the value of the RGDP growth rate, then the excessive money supply would cause demand for more goods and services than would be available in the market. This excessive demand for investment and goods and services would accelerate inflation. Therefore, the 3% rule would prevent a possible source of inflation caused by the discretionary policy of interest rate targets. The monetarists would also add that this 3% rule would help achieve automatic adjustment in the short-run fluctuations of the economy toward long-term stability. The key arguments for the monetarists' policy rule for long-run stability are as follows:

- A discretionary monetary policy (expansionary or contractionary) destabilizes the process of automatic adjustment.
- Because of the long-run stability of the velocity of money, discretionary monetary policy action causes the price level to fluctuate more sharply than the policy target on real output.

The way these two arguments work in the equation of exchange can be explained with equation (12.3), which is different from equation (12.1).

By taking the derivative Equation 12.1, we can see it as follows

Equation of Exchange: $MV = PY$ or $\Delta M/M + \Delta V/V = \Delta P/P + \Delta Y/Y$ ....Eqn (12.3)

Because monetarists assume that velocity is stable in the long run, $\Delta V/V$ would be zero.

Then equation (12.3) would become $\boxed{\Delta M/M = \Delta P/P + \Delta Y/Y}$ **......................Eqn (12.4)**

Now, with the 3% long-term growth rate of RGDP, equation (12.4) can be written as

$\Delta M/M = \Delta P/P + 3\%$. ....Eqn (12.5)

According to the monetarist view, if the long-term inflation target is set at 0%, then $\Delta P/P = 0$.

That implies that the Fed should follow the rule of maintaining a long-term growth rate of the money supply at 3% to keep the economy inflation-free. If the RGDP growth rate increases over 3%, then the Fed should also adjust its money supply growth rate accordingly. This conclusion by the monetarists is solely based on the assumption of a stable velocity of money. If that restrictive assumption is not true from real-world data, as seen in Figure 12.1, this argument fails to validate its claim.

12.2.1. Which of the Two Approaches Is Reliable for Policy Purposes?

There is no straightforward answer to this question. There is a degree of subjectivity in the debate between *discretion versus rules*, and the debate has been going on for decades. These two competing theories explain the effects of the money supply very differently, with monetarists contending that inflation is accelerated directly by changes in the money supply. On the other hand, Keynesian discretionary policy explains that money supply growth changes the interest rates first through changes in the money market before it transmits to the goods market, with very little effect on inflation. However, the discretionary approach of monetary policy has clearly dominated the monetary policy actions of the Fed since the 1990s and continues the same pattern in 2019. The current Fed chair Jay Powell, doesn't seem to depart from his predecessors Janet Yellen and Ben Bernanke in pursuing a discretionary approach of monetary policy actions. Nevertheless, this persistent practice of discretionary policy by the Fed did not seem to slow down the debate among political leaders and economists alike.

12.3. Debate on Lags in Monetary Policy Effectiveness in Stabilizing the Economy

Given the unsettled debate on the issue of a discretionary versus rule approach toward monetary policy, it is also important to recognize the reality that the discretionary monetary policy has no guarantee of achieving a quick turnaround of the economy from a recession or inflation. This is because of the difficulty in forecasting the time lag between actions taken by policies and their effect on economic variables. For example, suppose a discretionary monetary policy is undertaken during the recession to expand the AD by lowering interest rates. However, the time to get to the full employment level has taken much longer than the policy makers anticipated. Given this unanticipated longer time lag, inflation might kick in long before full employment is reached. This possible scenario can happen, and it is beyond the control of the Fed because prediction depends on many unforeseen circumstances that could arise after the actions are taken. The same is true during a state of economic boom when the Fed may try to reduce inflation by undertaking a tight monetary policy, which may take too long to maintain the stability of the economy with full employment. There are many questions regarding the exact time lag and level of uncertainty about the future, and there are no straightforward answers. This issue of time lag is so great that two renowned economists, Finn Kydland and Edward Prescott, were awarded the Nobel Prize in economics in 2004 for their contributions to "time inconsistency of economic policy," which focused on discretion versus rules. Therefore, sometimes policy makers adopt a mix of targets on variables with a great deal of flexibility to adjust to new information as it emerges.

For example, in the face of the 2018 economic boom, Fed chair Powell stuck to maintaining the inflation target at 2% by gradually increasing the federal funds rate by only 0.25% at each interval as the FOMC watched the inflation trend very closely. While sticking to this interest rate target, the Fed chair was a part of the discretionary approach. On July 31, 2019, the FOMC surprised Wall Street and the economics community by reversing its 2018 policy by reducing the federal funds rate by 0.25%. This unexpected complete reversal was justified as a response to growing uncertainty in the US-China tension on trade relations and the real estate boom in the first half of 2019. The speculation of a possible recession has actually put tremendous pressure on the FOMC from the political and business sectors to reverse its course despite the historically low level of unemployment and the modest growth rate of the RGDP and inflation. The only possible consequence of this reversal could be triggering the inflation rate in the current state of a booming economy. This discretionary monetary policy approach is clearly an example of understanding the complexity and difficulty in forecasting the future course of direction as a guiding principle in undertaking effective monetary policy, whether it is a monetary rule or a policy discretion. Despite the controversy regarding which approach is the best, there is a general consensus that during severe business-cycle fluctuations, such as the Great Recession of 2008, the choice of discretionary policy has been found stronger than the rule option.

12.4. The Role of Monetary Policy in Controlling Business-Cycle Fluctuations

In conclusion, it is important to emphasize the role of the central bank of the United States in achieving monetary policy goals for economic stability. The Fed's tasks are multidimensional: it must use appropriate monetary policy tools under different business-cycle fluctuations; it must forecast the targeted variables; it must understand the state of the economy in a timely manner; it must recognize the cause of the cyclical trends in the variables. The alternative courses of monetary policy action and the choice of appropriate policy tools also pose a challenge for policy makers in achieving their objectives. As mentioned in the previous section, the policy reversal undertaken by the Fed on July 31, 2019, is a good example of discretionary measures. Because money and interest rate changes are significant variables that affect the course of activities in financial institutions, being in charge of these two powerful components of the money market makes the Fed one of the most powerful economic policy and money management institutions not only for the US economy but also for the entire global financial market. For example, the investment decisions made by Wall Street agents respond immediately to any changes to interest rate policy by the Fed. The next chapter focuses on the theories of inflation and unemployment trade-off and the empirical evidence and policy implications in both the short run and the long run.

Chapter Summary

Section 12.1 introduced the classical quantity theory of money and the Keynesian monetary theories and their policy implications in conducting monetary policy actions during cyclical downturns of the economy. The comparison between the classical quantity theory of money, called the equation of exchange, and the Keynesian money demand equation is explained with equation (12.1) (equation of exchange), and equations (12.2) and (12.3) (Keynesian money market theory). The main focus of comparison between these two competing theories was centered on the assumption of the velocity of money as $V = PY/M$, which was assumed to be constant under classical theory. But Keynesian theory rejected that assumption and contended that velocity is a variable influenced by changes in interest rates and inflation rates. The empirical evidence shown in Figures 12.1(a) and 12.1(b) seems to support the Keynesian view of velocity as a variable. The importance of policy implications for this comparison between these two theories was discussed in this section. The empirical evidence of policy effectiveness was also discussed in detail in Section 12.1.1.

Sections 12.1.2 and 12.1.3 presented the details of Keynesian monetary theories of money demand and money supply to determine money market equilibrium and the policy implications for combatting recession and inflation. The transmission mechanism of monetary policy action from the money market to the goods market was also explained and illustrated in Figure 12.2. Section 12.1.3 summarized the discretionary policy actions under the Keynesian framework from the historical perspectives of the US monetary policy actions.

Section 12.2 explained the details of the ongoing policy debate on "discretionary versus rule" as monetary policy alternatives by using equations of quantity theory and the Keynesian monetary model. This phenomenon was further analyzed with the help of equations (12.3), (12.4), and (12.5), developed by the classical versus Keynesian monetary theories. Students may use these three important equations to compare and contrast these two philosophical views on policy options (rules versus discretion) in the context of US monetary policy actions.

Section 12.2.1 provided some insights by responding to a question about which of the two policy options (rules versus discretion) is considered reliable with recent examples of discretionary policy practice by the Fed.

Section 12.3 discussed some issues with the time lags in carrying out the effective discretionary policy of the Fed in the context of recent business-cycle fluctuations. The policy dilemma of the Fed in taking policy action in a timely manner and the related challenges were also highlighted in this section. An example of discretionary policy action being undertaken by the Fed on July 31, 2019, was also explained as a complete reversal of policy from tightening the money supply to loosening the money supply in an effort to cope with expected uncertainty fueled by the trade war between China and the United States.

Section 12.4 delivered concluding remarks on the importance of monetary policy in fine-tuning business-cycle fluctuations and further emphasized the role of the Fed in stabilizing the economy and the financial markets as one of the most powerful policy institutions in the world.

Application Activities

Q1. Writing appropriate equations, distinguish between the classical quantity theory of money and the Keynesian monetary theories. Give examples, along with their conceptual differences, as well as policy implications.

Q2. Distinguish between the theoretical arguments for a discretionary versus a rule approach in the Fed's monetary policy actions. What are the key assumptions that the monetarists have made in advocating for a rule approach to monetary policy? If those assumptions are not valid, does it make the rule approach ineffective? Why or why not? Briefly explain.

Q3. Suppose the Fed is maintaining a growth rate of the money supply M_2 at 8% per year for a three-year period. If the long-term RGDP growth rate is assumed to be at 3%, what would you expect to see happen to the average rate of inflation in terms of a monetarist explanation?

Q4. Explain why the velocity of either M_1 or M_2 is expected to rise during a rising interest rate trend and why it is expected to fall during a declining interest rate trend?

Q5. Why do neither monetarists nor Keynesians suggest maintaining a constant federal funds rate target? What potential consequences do they anticipate if a constant target were to be maintained?

Q6. Why does excessive money supply, usually called printing money, accelerate inflation? Give an example.

Chapter 13

Inflation and Unemployment Trade-Off—the Phillips Curve

Learning Objectives

As they read the chapter, students will learn the following:

- The relationship between inflation and unemployment under the Phillips curve theory
- Phillips curve in the short run and the long run with real-world evidence
- Policy implications for the Phillips curve in the short run versus the long run

In Chapters 11 and 12, the theories of fiscal and monetary policy effectiveness and their implications for bringing price stability and full employment were discussed. The two common policy objectives of both fiscal and monetary policy are price stability and full employment. In the same chapters, the focus was also on the complementary mix of fiscal and monetary policy measures undertaken during severe recessions in the past and as recently as the Great Recession of 2008. During the Great Recession of 2008, a combined effort of expansionary fiscal and monetary policy was pursued for a quick economic recovery. With a very low inflation rate during 2008 through 2010 (between 0.1% and 1.5%) and a very high unemployment rate of over 9% during the same time period, policy makers at the Fed, as well as the president and the US Congress, pursued aggressive expansionary policies to achieve full employment. This chapter discusses the merits of the theory of inflation-unemployment trade-off developed by Phillips in the 1960s. In economics literature, this theory is called the Phillips curve. The discussion will focus on both short-run and long-run perspectives of the Phillips curve and its economic policy implications in the context of the US economy.

13.1. The Relationship between Inflation and Unemployment under the Phillips Curve Theory

As a result of the lowest interest rate policy in history and a massive increase in government spending and the reduction of taxes for both businesses and individuals, the great recession ended in late 2009. On the other hand, inflation also remained low until 2011 when the inflation rate jumped up to 3% followed by a decline to 2.1% in 2012. During the subsequent years, however, while the economic recovery continued at a modest pace with the aggressive demand-side policies of the Keynesian framework, the inflation rate remained low at between 2.1% and 2.12% through 2018. Despite a very low unemployment rate of 3.7% in August 2019 (the lowest rate since 1969), the inflation rate stayed low at 2%. This 2% inflation rate was also targeted by the Fed to keep the inflation rate under control in the face of this economic boom. The stability of the price level and full employment during the post-recovery of the Great Recession was very unusual in the sense that a rising inflation rate is usually expected when the actual unemployment rate falls below the natural rate of unemployment (unemployment rate at full employment—called NAIRU). This theory of the Phillips curve mentioned in the introduction of this chapter is an inverse relationship between inflation and unemployment or known as the inflation-unemployment trade-off. This theory was based on statistical data of wage and price increases for the United Kingdom from 1861 to 1957. The graphical representation of the Phillips curve in Figure 13.3 illustrates the inflation-unemployment trade-off, as it was derived from original time series data of wage and price explained by Phillips for the economy of the United Kingdom. Before going into the details of the Phillips curve, it is important to provide the key sources of inflation from changes in AD and AS functions in macroeconomics.

13.1.1. Sources of Inflation: AD Shift and AS Shift

In the previous two chapters, students learned that both monetary and fiscal policy under a Keynesian framework focused mainly on the AD side of the AD-AS model of macroeconomics. That means both expansionary fiscal and monetary policy measures tend to shift the AD curve to the right. This rightward shift increases output and employment and thus reduces unemployment during a recession. The opposite happens when policy makers adopt contractionary policies (either fiscal or monetary) during inflation or an economic boom. Such discretionary policy measures, with their expected multiplier effects, move the equilibrium price level and the RGDP level in opposite directions given the unchanged position of the SRAS curve. The relative magnitude of this trade-off between inflation and unemployment would obviously depend on the steepness of the AD and AS curves. For example, if the AS curve is relatively flat, then the shifting of AD by expansionary policy in either direction is expected to have a greater change in RGDP compared to a corresponding change in prices. In that case, the trade-off would be in favor of output and price stability without fear of inflation or deflation. On the other hand, with a steeper AS curve, the rate of increase or decrease in the price level would be much greater than the change in output. In this case, the trade-off is at the expense of higher inflation. These sources of inflation and unemployment are due to demand-side inflation. This analysis is illustrated in Figure 13.1.

Figure 13.1 Steepness of the AS Curve and Demand-Side Inflation

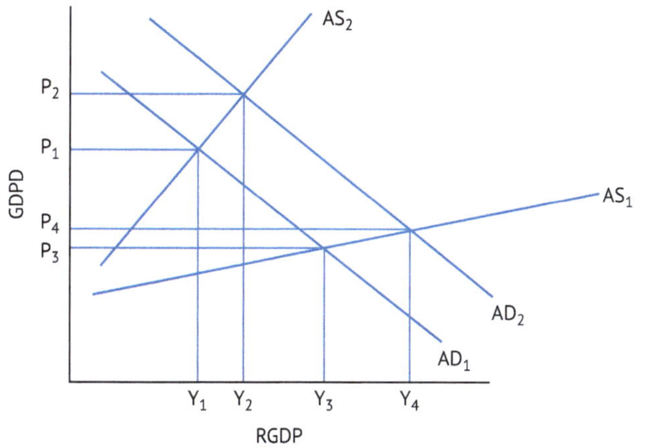

Figure 13.2 Supply-Side Inflation and Stagflation

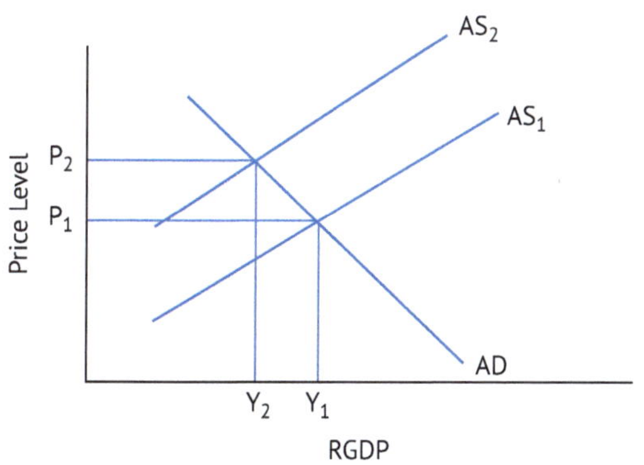

In the figure, the flatter AS curve, AS_1, shows that a shift of the AD curve from AD_1 to AD_2 gives a greater increase of output from Y_3 to Y_4 relative to a corresponding price level increase from P_3 to P_4. On the other hand, the opposite can be seen from the steeper AS_2 by the same demand shift, where the change in the price level from P_1 to P_2 is greater than the corresponding increase in output from Y_1 to Y_2. Therefore, the relative magnitude of the trade-off between inflation and output/unemployment would depend on the steepness of the AS curve. This phenomenon is called demand-side inflation.

The other source of inflation can sometimes be seen from the AS shock when the AS curve shifts leftward, causing not only inflation but also unemployment, which is called stagflation. This is known as supply-side inflation or cost-push inflation, as illustrated in Figure 13.2.

Figure 13.2 indicates that the negative supply shock by a leftward shift of AS from AS_1 to AS_2 not only lowered output from Y_1 to Y_2 but also increased the price level from P_1 to P_2, a simultaneous occurrence of inflation and unemployment—a state of stagflation. This situation happened in the US economy only once in the 1970s. It was caused by OPEC's embargo on oil production—also called the oil shock. Since oil is the major source of energy and raw materials of production and transportation, the oil embargo of the 1970s caused worldwide hyperinflation by shifting the AS curve to the left. Again, the steepness of the AS curve (not shown in the figure) would also determine the relative magnitude of changes in the output and the price level because of the supply shock.

On the other hand, a positive supply shock, such as a rapid increase in productivity because of advancements in technology and education, discovery of vast natural resources, and low cost of production, would shift the AS curve to the right, say from AS_2 to AS_1 in Figure 13.2. Under this scenario, the price level would decrease, and the output level would increase. This phenomenon happened in the US economy in the late 1990s because of the internet revolution and massive investment in information technology. Actually, both

AD and AS have shifted positively to the right with the historic economic boom in the US economy at the end of the twentieth century. Therefore, it can be said for fact that the inflation and unemployment trade-off explained by the Phillips curve may not necessarily be the case when AS shock (positive or negative) exists, as seen in the 1970s and 1990s. The next section describes the original theory of the Phillips curve and its statistical evidence since the 1960s.

13.1.2. The Phillips Curve and the Inflation-Unemployment Trade-Off

As mentioned at the beginning of this chapter, the Phillips curve concept was originally based on statistical data on wage increases and unemployment rates collected from the economy of the United Kingdom for more than almost 100 years (1861–1957; Baumol and Blinder, 2015, p. 338). It is important to note that the inverse relationship between inflation and unemployment, as illustrated in Figure 13.3, was not the curve Phillips developed in the early 1960s. Phillips's original explanation of the inflation-unemployment trade-off was actually based on the relationship between an increase in wages and unemployment data. Because the wage rate increases in a tight labor market during an economic boom, the employers do pass along the increasing cost of labor by raising the prices of final goods and services sold in the market. The opposite happens during the state of a recession when the bargaining power of labor to get higher wages weakens. The Phillips curve in its present form of inflation-unemployment trade-off was derived later from the original Phillips curve, as an increase in prices during a tight labor market is attributed to the increasing trend of wages. Therefore, the derived Phillips curve from the original inverse relationship between wage-price and unemployment rate for the United Kingdom during that period, as explained by Phillips, is illustrated in Figure 13.3.

Figure 13.3 The Phillips Curve and the Inflation-Unemployment Trade-Off

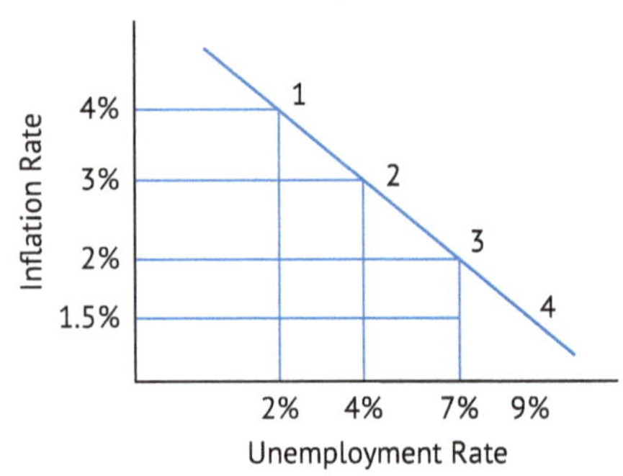

Figure 13.3 shows four different combinations of hypothetical rates of inflation and unemployment moving in opposite directions because the data indicate an inverse relationship between the inflation rate and the unemployment rate. Although this is a hypothetical graph, it is a close approximation to the actual wage-price and unemployment data used by Phillips for the UK economy. From Figures 13.1 and 13.2, it can be expected that the Phillips curve drawn in Figure 13.3 is a possible case during a state of recession and inflation when the AD curve goes beyond the full employment level of output along the vertical line of the LRAS curve. In other words, the movement of the AD curve to the right of the LRAS causes inflation and movement to the left of the LRAS curve causes a recession. However, at the point of intersection between the SRAS curve and the AD curve along the LRAS curve, there is a state of full employment with no recession or inflation—a situation called the natural rate of unemployment or NAIRU.

13.2. Phillips Curve in the Short Run and the Long Run with Real-World Evidence

13.2.1. Short-Run Phillips Curve

To understand the difference between short-run and long-run Phillips curves, assume that the NAIRU (the unemployment rate at full employment) is at 4% in Figure 13.3. The corresponding inflation rate is at 3% at equilibrium point 2. At the 2% unemployment rate, the inflation rate rises to 4% because a tight labor market under an economic boom raises the wages for labor and the related cost of producing goods and services—a state of higher inflation and an unemployment rate lower than the natural rate of unemployment (NAIRU). On the other hand, at an unemployment rate above 4%, say actual rates of 7% or 9%, inflation rates fell to 2% or 1.5%, respectively. This inverse relationship is only possible in the short-run fluctuation in the economy illustrated by the short-run Phillips curve in Figure 13.3. This is due to a shift in the AD curve to either the right or to the left of the full employment equilibrium. The scenario of the inverse relationship of the short-run Phillips curve was not seen, however, during the 1970s (because of stagflation) and 1990s (because of the rise in labor productivity and thus rightward shift of the AS curve). In the 1970s, the economy faced a state of stagflation caused by negative supply shock shifting the AS curve to the left. In the 1990s, the economy experienced a positive shock in both AD and AS, shifting AD and AS to the right and keeping inflation stable with a high growth rate of RGDP and jobs (as explained by Figures 13.1 and 13.2, respectively). Similar patterns of positive shock of the AS curve have been seen in the current decade (the 2010s) because of an increase in labor productivity and the stable price of oil in the US market. However, because of constant business-cycle fluctuations in the economy, the unique situations of the 1970s (negative supply shock), 1990s, and 2010s (positive supply shocks) are not expected to remain most of the time. In the short run, the economy fluctuates frequently to either direction from its full employment level; rather than changes in the AS curve, it is the AD curve that shifts. Therefore, the short-run Phillips curve explained in Figure 13.3 does not necessarily stay in the same place either in the short run or in the long run. Therefore, the trade-off between inflation and unemployment may not be a sure thing in the long run because of the vertical shape of the LRAS curve in the goods market.[1] In other words, many monetarists like Friedman argued that the long-run Phillips curve is actually vertical. Friedman's comparison of the short-run and the long-run Phillips curves and their policy implications are explained in Section 13.2.2.

13.2.2. Long-Run Phillips Curve

As explained previously, the vertical LRAS curve indicates the level of full employment output (RGDP) with no inflation or recession because the actual unemployment rate along the vertical LRAS curve is at a natural rate of unemployment (NAIRU). The connection between

---

1 R. Glenn Hubbard & Anthony Patrick O'Brien. (2017). *Macroeconomics*, 6th Edition, 2017 Page. 606, Chapter 17, Pasrson Publishing; Friedman, M (1968). The role of monetary policy, *American Economic Review*, vol. 58, no.1, March, 1968, p.1–17.

this vertical LRAS curve and the long-run Phillips curve is illustrated in Figure 13.4 followed by analytical discussion.

Figure 13.4 Long-Run, Employment-Output Phillips Curve

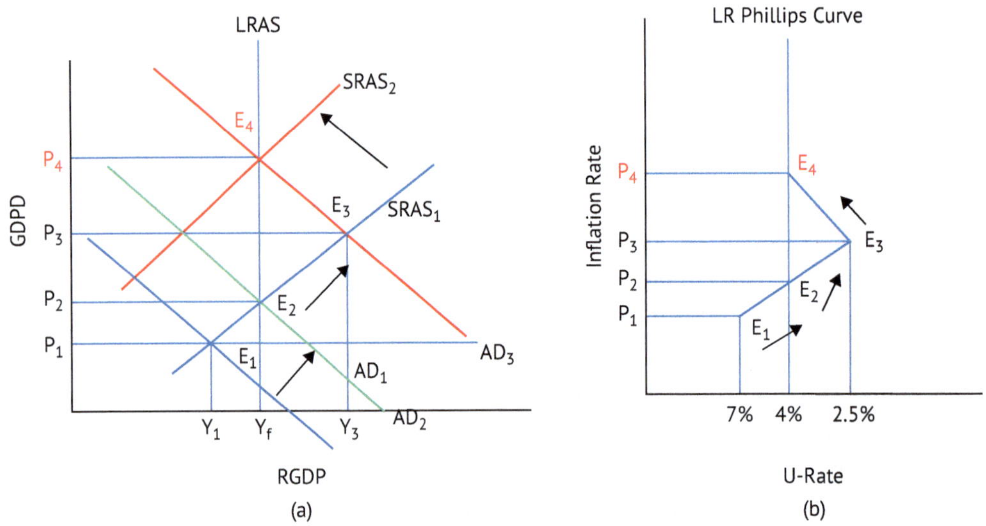

Figure 13.4(a) with its vertical LRAS curve indicates the adjustment process in the long run from the short-run fluctuation of the economy. The short-run, business-cycle fluctuations are shown by a leftward or rightward shift of the AD curve along the SRAS curve, with equilibrium combinations of the RGDP and price level at E_1, E_2, E_3, and E_4. Points E_2 and E_4 are the combinations of the RGDP and price level equilibrium in the long-run, full-employment output at Y_f. On the other hand, equilibrium point E_1 is in a state of recession, and point E_3 is in a state of inflation. The movement from E_1 to E_2 is the movement from recession to full employment. The price level at P_2 is not inflationary, despite $P_2 > P_1$. This recovery process from recession to full employment by increasing the price level from P_1 to P_2 is shown in Figure 13.4(b) on the right-hand side. In panel (b), the decrease in the unemployment rate from 7% to 4% is because of an increase in the output level. In this case, the price level (from P1 to P2) is considered to be NAIRU (unemployment rate at full employment).

If the economy continued rising by shifting the AD curve further to the right, as shown in panel (a), say reaching to equilibrium at E_3 with the RGDP at Y_3, then the price level would increase to P_3. This scenario is called a state of inflation. This state of an economic boom would reduce the unemployment rate below its NAIRU level of 4% in panel (b). Suppose the actual unemployment rate has fallen from 4% to 2.5%. This fall of the unemployment rate from its NAIRU level of 4% would increase labor wages and thus cause a rise in inflation. This rise in inflation is caused by an increase in the costs of labor and other related raw materials in the long run. This adjustment process would shift the SRAS curve to the left until the economy gets back to the LRAS curve at the equilibrium point E_4. Since E_4 is on the vertical LRAS curve intersecting with the new AD_3 and $SRAS_2$ curves, the new equilibrium price at P_4

is normal and not considered inflationary. It is not considered inflationary because this price is the price level adjusted in the long run with the decrease in output and income from Y_3 to Y_f. Although $P_4 > P_3$, P_4 is not inflationary and the economy went back to full employment level with no unemployment-inflation trade-off.

The corresponding long-run Phillips curve is derived from Figure 13.4 (a) as a vertical Phillips curve from the long-run adjustment of inflation and unemployment, and it is illustrated in the Figure 13.4 (b) with its price at P_2 and P_4 at the natural rate of unemployment of 4% (the NAIRU). The reader should not be confused about the unemployment rate showing a backward direction on the horizontal axis of Figure 13.4 (b). It only indicates the higher percentage of unemployment with lower inflation during a recession at E_1 and a lower rate of unemployment with higher inflation at E_3 just to keep the consistency of the inflation-unemployment trade-off in the SR. The path of the inflation adjustment from the short run to the long run is shown by the arrows moving from E_1 to E_2 to E_3 and back to the LRAS curve at E_4. This derived long-run Phillips curve is thus a vertical curve indicating no trade-off between inflation and unemployment. Most of the economists (monetarists and Keynesians alike) have concluded that there is no inflation-unemployment trade-off in the long run because of the vertical shape of the Phillips curve in the long run. This is because the long-run expectations of inflation rates and wage rates are equal to the actual changes in these two key variables in the labor market adjustment. The mathematical derivation of expected inflation and its adjustment with an increase in wages in the short run and long run are beyond the scope of this book.

13.3. Policy Implications for the Phillips Curve in the Short Run versus the Long Run

The previous sections of this chapter discussed the theoretical foundations of the Phillips curve and its empirical evidence in both the short run and the long run. The real usefulness of an in-depth understanding of this concept and its nature lies in the demand-side macroeconomic policy debate. From the earlier discussion, students should understand the importance of the foundation of the Phillips curve for its policy implications for achieving full employment and price stability in the face of frequent business-cycle fluctuations. The inflation-unemployment trade-off in the short run presents a fundamental challenge to policy makers and politicians: Should they pursue expansionary fiscal and monetary policy measures during a recession and contractionary policy measures during inflation, or should they leave the economy to correct itself? In this ongoing debate, the different shapes of the Phillips curve in the short run and the long run provide a clear guideline. This guideline is based on the downward-sloping Phillips curve in the short run and its connection to the demand-side policy of Keynesian economics. Since the demand-side policy is a short-run response to business-cycle fluctuations, given the downward-sloping Phillips curve in the short run, an expansionary policy during a recession cannot possibly achieve simultaneous low recession and low inflation. In other words, it may be very difficult to achieve full employment without accelerating inflation in the short run unless the SRAS curve is relatively flat. But identifying the actual shape of the SRAS curve is a difficult task in the first place. The same issue presents a challenge when policy makers try to reduce inflation during an economic boom. But the issue of this trade-off depends on the effectiveness of both fiscal and monetary policy actions taken in the short run. Given the complexity of the shape of the AD and AS curves, policy makers have been risking this possible trade-off in the short run by pursuing active policy actions instead of relying on self-correcting mechanisms. The two key reasons for taking this risk are outlined next:

The government has its own obligation to execute aggressive policies when the state of the economy (recession or inflation) warrants it.

The basic foundation of the theory of SRAS curves indicates that the lower part of the AS curve is relatively flat, and the upper part of the same curve is relatively steep.

Therefore, when the economy is in a recession with equilibrium on the lower part of the SRAS curve, equilibrium sits on the flatter part of the AS curve. As a result, expansionary monetary and fiscal policy actions can be effective by shifting the AD to the right to reduce the unemployment rate (GDP would rise faster than prices would increase) without much increase in inflation (shown in Figure 13.1). By the same token, during an economic boom, contractionary policies can shift the AD curve to the left from the steeper part of the AS curve to reduce the inflation rate at a faster rate than decreasing the rates of output and employment. The bottom line is, policy makers have the ability to select a target level of inflation and/or unemployment to manipulate the demand-side components to reach their target in the short run. Policy makers can also opt to do nothing in the short run and let the economy correct itself in the long run. Although it may be possible for the economy to correct itself in the long run, uncertainty about the length of time it may take and the severity of the lingering problem may cause policy makers to take action for a quick recovery. Since they pursue this active policy in the short run, the long-run mechanism has its own adjustment process to bring the economy back to its full employment level. The monetarist argument on the vertical shape of the Phillips curve in the long run has certainly influenced the decision-making process of policy makers. The policy makers at the Fed weigh in on this monetarist view by closely monitoring trends of inflation and the targeted interest rate while pursuing discretionary monetary policy actions in the short run. Nevertheless, in its effort to maintain price stability and full employment, the role of the Fed has never been more significant than in this new century. This important policy role vested in the hands of the FOMC members and the Fed chair undoubtedly makes them the most powerful money managers not only for the national economy but also on a global scale. The role of the Fed in the global economy and foreign exchange market is discussed in more detail in the next two chapters.

Chapter Summary

Section 13.1 introduced the theory of inflation-unemployment trade-off known as the Phillips curve after A. W. Phillips, who originally developed this theory based on his empirical study on time series data analysis between wage and price relationships for the UK economy from 1861 to 1957.

Section 13.1.1 explained the theoretical background of sources of inflation as demand-side inflation and supply-side inflation. Figures 13.1 and 13.2 illustrated these two sources of inflation graphically. These two diagrams also demonstrated the rate of inflation increase, which depends on the relative steepness of the AS curve. With the relatively flatter AS curve, the rate of inflation rises much slower than the rate of RGDP growth as the economy expands by shifting the AD curve to the right. On the other hand, with the relatively steeper AS curve, the inflation rate increases much faster than the RGDP growth rate as the AD shifts outward to the right during economic expansion. This section also explained why the inflation and unemployment trade-off developed by Phillips is not necessarily the case in situations when AD and AS curves shifts to the right simultaneously by lowering the price level and increasing output and employment. We have seen this situation in the periods of economic boom in the late 1990s and the entire 2010s. Another situation concerning the leftward shift of the AS curve, called a supply shock, may also defy the theory of inflation-unemployment trade-off—an economic cycle called stagflation. This event happened in the US economy in the 1970s as a result of an oil embargo by OPEC.

Section 13.1.2 explained the original theory of the Phillips curve in reference to Phillips's empirical study of the wage-price relationship for the UK economy. This inflation-unemployment trade-off is illustrated in a hypothetical diagram in Figure 13.3 as a close approximation to the original Phillips curve published in 1958.

Section 13.2.1 introduced the theoretical foundation of the short-run Phillips curve with a detailed analysis in reference to Figures 13.1, 13.2, and 13.3.

Section 13.2.2 introduced the theories of the Phillips curve in the long run, explained with an illustration in Figure 13.4. In Figure 13.4, the long-run Phillips curve is derived from the long-run adjustment process in the AD-AS model of the goods market under the Keynesian framework. Students may practice this derivation by drawing similar diagrams as part of their learning practice.

Section 13.3 provided the policy implications of the Phillips curve in both the short run and the long run with concluding remarks on the context of the recent economic policy actions undertaken by policy makers for the price and employment stability of the US economy.

Application Activities

Q1. Briefly describe the theory of the Phillips curve and its origin of development as a theory of inflation-unemployment trade-off.

Q2. In terms of the effectiveness of expansionary or contractionary fiscal or monetary policy actions, how serious is the Phillips curve when the SRAS curve is relatively flat? Draw a hypothetical figure to illustrate your explanation.

Q3. When the SRAS curve is relatively steep, how is the Phillips curve different from what you described in your answer to Q2? Draw a hypothetical figure to illustrate your explanation and to compare with the figure in Q2.

Q4. Draw a hypothetical diagram of the AD-AS model of macroeconomics and explain in your own words the sources of accelerating inflation. Provide historical evidence as an example.

Q5. Critically, but briefly, explain why the Phillips curve failed to explain the inflation and unemployment data for the US economy in the 1970s, late 1990s, and late 2010s. Were these situations identical or different? Give examples.

Q6. Collect the inflation and unemployment data for the 1960s and 1980s to indicate whether the Phillips curve fits the data during these time periods. Why or why not?

Q7. With the help of a hypothetical diagram of the AD-AS model of macroeconomics, explain in your own words the arguments monetarist made that the inflation-unemployment trade-off does not exist in the long run. Give an example using real data as evidence to support their view.

Q8. Briefly explain the importance of understanding the conceptual framework of the short-run and long-run Phillips curves for economic policy implications in the US economy.

Q9. Is the Fed's current monetary policy contractionary or inflationary? Briefly explain your answer. Is this policy in line with the short-run Phillips curve or with the long-run Phillips curve? Why?

Chapter 14

International Trade and Macroeconomics

Learning Objectives

As they read the chapter, students will learn the following:

- The theories of international trade and its rationale for economic growth and employment under the Keynesian macroeconomics model
- The Bretton Woods Agreement of 1945 (the historic abolition of the gold standard) and the start of the fixed exchange rate regime for promoting international trade and globalization
- The fixed exchange rate regime versus the floating (flexible) exchange rate regime to determine the exchange rate equilibrium
- Exchange rate fluctuation and its effect on economic growth and employment
- Purchasing power parity and interest rate parity in determining foreign exchange rates in the long run and the short run

International Trade and the Open-Economy Macroeconomics Model: Theory and Practice

The previous 13 chapters of this textbook have focused on various theories and applications of the goods market and money market models in the context of a closed economy—mostly concentrated on the US domestic economy. Although no country in the new economy of the twenty-first century can operate efficiently without opening the economy to foreign trade, discussion was mainly limited within the framework of the domestic economy to understand how the domestic economy works and the importance of policy actions for economic stability. Moving beyond that framework, this chapter and the next chapter extend the closed macroeconomics models to integrate economic theories of trade and the foreign exchange market. Although the structure of the US economy is predominantly domestic (AD = C + I + G), its contribution to foreign trade is very significant because of its size and its influence on global finance since the end of World War II. To begin this discussion, the first section of this chapter explains the basic foundation of international trade and its importance to faster economic growth and development for not only the US economy but all nations.

14.1. The Theories of International Trade and Its Rationale for Economic Growth and Employment under the Keynesian Macroeconomics Model

14.1.1. What Is International Trade?

International trade is the flow of goods and services among different nations, with nations specializing in goods and services and creating surpluses of production for trade. This specialization and division of labor to produce certain goods and services helps a country to produce those goods and services at a lower cost than other nations. This specialization generates a surplus after the nation meets its domestic needs, and the surplus is then exported to other nations in exchange for importing other goods that cannot be produced domestically at a lower cost. The opposite is true for importing from other nations. This system of free flow of goods and services among nations is the international trade that increases production and consumption for all trading partners, leading to economic prosperity and development. History suggests that before becoming involved in international trade, countries stayed very poor or in a state of low income with a low standard of living. Since the end of World War II in 1945, almost every country in the world has joined international trade and commerce with the common goal of achieving economic prosperity. The economic statistics also indicate that rapid globalization through trade has indeed contributed to significant economic growth and improved the well-being of every nation on Earth since 1945.

14.1.2. The Case for Trade

No country in the world is self-sufficient in all the resources needed to satisfy its consumers' demands; most nations are interdependent and engage in specialization and international trade for goods and services. The differences in climate, skill of labor force, education and technology, agriculture production, labor availability, and factor endowments are the key reasons for engaging in international trade. For example, the United States has two border countries, Mexico to the south and Canada to the north, as its largest trading partners. These three countries have different natural resources, labor force skill levels, human capital, and technology. Despite the differences and similarities in some areas of economic goods and human capital and labor, the free trade among these three countries under the North American Free Trade Agreement of 1992 has had a significant effect on economic prosperity and development for all three nations in North America. Similar benefits can be seen from US-China trade relations established in 1978—this was a turning point for China, transforming it from a low level of income and production to one of the fastest-growing economies in the world. Free trade is always a win-win situation, regardless of the difference in the economic size of the countries involved. To explain the mechanism for this win-win case, the next section introduces the theory of comparative advantage.

14.1.3. The Theory of Comparative Advantage versus Absolute Advantage and Benefits of Trade

The theories of **comparative advantage** and **absolute advantage** of production between different goods and services are based on the concept of opportunity cost. The opportunity cost is what a firm or producer has to give up for producing other products or services with a lower cost of production. The key assumption for this concept is that the firm has to use the same combination of factors of production (resources), capital, and labor for example, with fixed production technology. Given the concept of opportunity cost, economic agents in a country can specialize in producing goods and services with lower opportunity costs instead of producing other goods and services with higher opportunity costs. The difference in opportunity cost of production is called the comparative advantage of producing one type of good or service compared to another type of good or service. The specialization of goods and services makes producers more efficient, reducing costs and thus raising the productivity of labor and capital. Specialization captures the comparative advantage of engaging in international trade, allowing countries to gain from higher production and consumption for producers and consumers for all countries. Table 14.1 illustrates a hypothetical example of comparative advantage and opportunity cost of producing iPhones and iPads.

Table 14.1: Comparative Advantage and Opportunity Cost

	iPhone	iPad	iPhone	iPad
Country	**Units per labor hour**	**Units per labor hour**	**Opportunity cost**	**Opportunity cost**
China	18	9	9/18 = 0.5 iPad	18/9 = 2 iPhone
United States	4	8	8/4 = 2 iPad	4/8 = 0.5 iPhone

The table provides a hypothetical example of the concept of opportunity costs of production of iPhones and iPads for both China and the United States given that the same technology is used in both countries. The hypothetical data of production indicates that China can produce both the iPhone and iPad more efficiently (in terms of units per labor hour) than the United States. Therefore, China has an absolute advantage in producing both the iPhone and iPad compared to the United States. China can produce 18 units of the iPhone versus the 4 units that the United States can produce in the same time period. China can produce nine iPads versus 8 units produced in the United States per labor hour. This position of relative efficiency in production between China and the United States shows an absolute advantage for China in producing both the iPhone and iPad.

Given the differences in production units per labor hour for both products in China and the United States, opportunity cost estimates for both countries are shown in the last two columns for producing both the iPhone and iPad. The opportunity cost to China for producing additional units of the iPad would be 18/9 = 2 units of the iPhone and that for producing additional units of the iPhone would be 9/18 = 0.5 units of the iPad. On the other hand, the opportunity cost of US production would be 4/8 = 0.5 units of the iPhone and 8/4 = 2 units of the iPad. This comparison between the opportunity cost of producing additional units of iPhones versus iPads in China and the United States shows that the United States has lower opportunity cost when producing the iPad. Therefore, the United States has a comparative advantage in producing the iPad over the iPhone.

By the same token, China has lower opportunity costs for producing iPhones than iPads: 0.5 for one unit of the iPad compared to the opportunity cost of 2 units of iPhones for producing one additional iPad. Therefore, China has the comparative advantage in producing the iPhone over the iPad. The theory of comparative advantage clearly indicates that, given the difference in comparative advantage of producing the iPhone and the iPad, both China and the United States can benefit from engaging in trade and specializing in the production of iPhones in China and iPads in the United States, despite the fact that China has the absolute advantage in producing both the iPhone and iPad. These two nations would gain from trade with a higher level of production and a higher level of consumption when compared to producing iPhones and iPads domestically. The gain from specialization after trade is higher for both countries. The estimates of the comparison of gains from trade are illustrated in Table 14.2.

Table 14.2: Gains from Trade under Comparative Advantage

	Before Trade		Production Change after Trade		Consumption Change after Trade		Net Gain in Consumption
Country	**iPhone**	**iPad**	**iPhone**	**iPad**	**iPhone**	**iPad**	
China	27,000	4,500	36,000	0	30,000	4,500	3,000 iPhones
United States	6,000	4,000	0	16,000	6,000	11,500	7,500 iPads

Assume that both China and the United States have a maximum of 2,000 hours of labor to devote to the production of iPhones, iPads, or a combination of both. Given the hypothetical production units per labor shown in Table 14.1, the total domestic production possibilities without trade are shown in Table 14.2. The allocation of hours includes 1,500 hours to produce iPhones and the remaining 500 hours for the production of iPads. Given this allocation of labor hours and the hourly production units per hour from Table 14.1, the domestic production and consumption for China is 27,000 units of iPhones and 4,500 units of iPads; for the United States, it is 6,000 units of iPhones and 4,000 units of iPads.

Now suppose both countries make a free trade agreement to exchange iPhones and iPads by specialization based on their comparative advantage of production (shown in Table 14.1). After specialization, the production changes for both countries are shown in Table 14.2, with 36,000 units of iPhones and zero units of iPads by China and 16,000 units of iPads and zero units of iPhones by the United States. If China exports 6,000 units of iPhones to the United States in exchange for 4,500 units of iPads imported from the United States, then consumption for both countries is shown in the consumption gain column in Table 14.2. The change in consumption that has taken place after trade indicates that China has 30,000 units of iPhones and 4,500 units of iPads, with a net gain in consumption of 3,000 units of iPhones compared to domestic production and consumption before trade. For the United States, the net gain in consumption is 7,500 units of iPads compared to domestic production and consumption before trade. This simple analysis of gain from trade through specialization by both China and the United States clearly suggests that the efficiency of production has improved based on the theory of comparative advantage. This improved efficiency generates a net gain in consumption for the trading countries, even if one country has an absolute advantage. These consumption bundles for both countries are showing net gain because China maintains its same consumption of the iPad it had to produce domestically before trade. China also increased its net gain of 3,000 units of iPhones compared to the situation before trade. Similarly, the United States increased its production of iPads by four times what it is used to produce before trade. By exporting 4,500 units of iPads as surplus in exchange for importing 6,000 units of iPhones, the United States increased its consumption bundle as well.

Figure 14.1 illustrates the simple production possibility curves before and after trade and their corresponding consumption levels drawn from the hypothetical data of Tables 14.1 and 14.2. These diagrams are useful for readers to visualize the case for trade and its gain for countries with both absolute and comparative advantage of production.

Figure 14.1 Production Possibility Curves and Gains from Trade

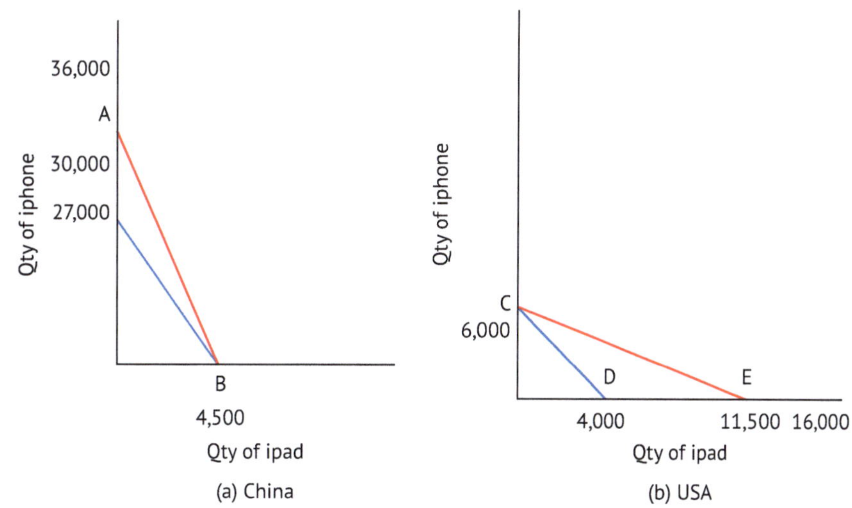

Students may notice that China has the production possibility curve before the trade with the United States by the line connecting the points between 2,700 and 4,500. China's consumption and production bundles for the iPhone and iPad are 2,700 and 4,500, respectively, without trade shown in panel (a). For the United States, the production and consumption bundles for iPhone and iPad before trade are, respectively, 6,000 and 4,000, connecting the line between points C and D shown in panel (b). Table 14.2 and Figure 14.1 indicate that China has absolute advantage in the production of both the iPhone and iPad, and the United States has comparative advantage in producing the iPad only. After free trade takes place, China will specialize by producing 36,000 units of the iPhone and no production of the iPad. On the other hand, the United States can specialize in the production of 16,000 units of the iPad and no production of the iPhone. With this specialization, China is able to increase its consumption of iPhones by 3,000 units with a surplus of 6,000 units to export to the United States. The United States is also able to increase consumption of iPads by 6,500 units and export the surplus production of 4,500 units to China. The consumption lines for China and the United States are depicted by the lines AB and CE, respectively, as marked in red. These two consumption lines are outside the production lines before trade. Therefore, both countries are better off opening trade with each other by increasing production and consumption, even with the absolute advantage for China in producing both the iPhone and iPad.

The case for free trade has been very strong and sustainable in most of the real-world case studies found in numerous research. It is important to keep that in mind that to have a net gain in consumption, the countries involved in trade do not necessarily have to have complete specialization. Partial specialization may also be beneficial in gaining consumption and production. If the exports of quantities are less than the amounts shown in the earlier table for both countries, then net gain can still be achieved in most of the trade relations. This two-country model of trade for comparative advantage between China and the United States can also be generalized for multilateral trade and commerce, with the same results of benefits from trade. As long as comparative advantage exists for trading partners, export and import transactions under free trade are always a win-win. However, for national security and geopolitical reasons, not all goods and services are traded internationally. Protectionism and unfavorable trade practices cause some governments to impose trade restrictions. Retaliation by the countries the trade restrictions are imposed on has several effects on export and import volumes, jobs, and distribution of income. The most common trade restrictions are tariffs and quotas imposed by trade agencies through political decisions. For example, President Trump imposed massive tariffs in 2018 on hundreds of Chinese products and services imported to the United States. The arguments for this tariff are unfair trade practices by China that negatively affect competing domestic industries and the increasing trade deficit with China. The net effects on the American economy of Trump's tariffs and the retaliatory actions by the Chinese government are not straightforward. The analysis of those effects using economic models is beyond the scope of this book. Students taking upper-level international trade classes will learn the theoretical and real-world applications of tariffs and quotas in global trade. For this book, the integration of foreign trade with the closed-economy macroeconomics model is discussed in the next section.

14.1.4. Keynesian Macroeconomics Model with Foreign Trade

Adding the foreign trade sector of the economy, the aggregate demand of the Keynesian macroeconomics model is expressed in equation (14.1).

$$Y = AD = C + I + G + (EX - IM), \quad \text{..........................Eqn (14.1)}$$

where EX is export and IM is import. Along with the first three components of this complete open economy macroeconomics model, equation (14.1) has four components of AD.

Students may recall from previous chapters the connection between private savings (S = Yd − C), where Yd = Y − T (= disposable income) and S = investment (I) and government deficit/surplus by government spending minus taxes (G − T). Equation (14.1) can be rewritten as the equilibrium condition of GDP:

$$Y = C + I + G + (EX - IM) = C + S + T \quad \text{..........................Eqn (14.2)}$$

From equation (14.2), the foreign sector can be expressed as equation (14.3):

$$EX - IM = (S - I) - (G - T). \quad \text{..........................Eqn (14.3)}$$

Equation (14.3) is the foundation for balancing payments in international trade even when trade (exports minus imports of goods and services) is not balanced. Although equation (14.3) implies that reducing the budget deficit should reduce the trade deficit as well, it may not happen all the time because of unexpected changes in savings and investment. With low savings, the government deficit may also go up because of engaging in more government spending. In the 2000s and 2010s, it was noticed that an increased government budget deficit actually increased the trade deficit simultaneously because of the increase in the price level of domestic goods and demand for the US$ to invest in US assets. Since the volume of exports is determined by changes in the exchange rate of the US$ value with respect to other currencies and changes in domestic income, the rise in the exchange rate and increase in income for US consumers would increase import and decrease export. This is because a higher exchange rate lowers the quantity of export, and vice versa, and higher domestic income increases the demand for imports leading to a trade deficit. The US economy has been experiencing not only a chronic budget deficit in recent years but also suffers from a chronic trade deficit. The accounting principle of US trade balance and the balance of payment for 2017 data are displayed in Table 14.3.

Table 14.3 indicates that the account trade balance for the US economy with the rest of the world was almost half a trillion dollars in 2018 (−490,978 million of US$). With the adjustment of financial transfers and payments and liabilities (ignoring the capital transfer), the balance of payments after adjusting for statistical discrepancies must be equal to zero. The next section in this chapter is an introduction to the sources of exchange rate determination in the foreign exchange market. Changes in the exchange rate affect the volume of exports for every country involved in international trade. Exchange rate fluctuation is a source of changes in export and import.

Table 14.3: Balance of Trade and Balance of Payment for the United States, 2018

Current Account Items	In Millions of $	Indicates That the Trade
Export of Goods and Services and Income Receipt	3,735,684	
Export of Goods and Services	2,501,310	
Export of Goods	1,674,330	
Export of Services	826,980	
Income Receipts, Primary and Secondary	1,234,374	
		Balance of Current Account=
Imports of Goods and Services and Payments	**4,226,662**	**3,735,684 – 4,226,662 = –490,978**
Import of Goods and Services	3,128,989	
Import of Goods	2,561,667	
Import of Services	567,322	
Income Payments, Primary and Secondary	1,097,673	
Capital Account Items		
Capital Transfer Receipts and Credits	**3,247**	
Capital Transfer Payments and Debits	**12**	**Balance in Capital A/C = 3,235**
Financial Account Items		
Net Acquisition of Financial Assets Except Derivatives	**310,827**	
Net Incurrence of Liabilities Except Derivatives	**735,583**	**Balance on Financial A/C = 424,756**
Net Financial Derivatives	**–20,721**	
Statistical Discrepancies	**42,266**	**= –445,477 – (–487,743) = 42,266**
Balance of Payments	**0**	

Source: US Bureau of Economic Analysis, International Services Tables at https://apps.bea.gov/international/bp_web/tb_download_type_modern.cfm?list=1&RowID=1.

14.2. The Bretton Woods Agreement of 1945 and the Fixed Exchange Rate Regime for Promoting International Trade and Globalization

14.2.1. Gold Standard Versus the Bretton Woods System of Fixed Exchange Rate

The Bretton Woods system of fixed exchange rate determination was a major step forward in bringing a new order to the international trade and monetary system after the collapse of the gold standard during World War II. The historic **Bretton Woods Agreement** took place in 1945 at the Mount Washington Hotel in Bretton Woods, New Hampshire, United States, where the leaders of the major industrialized nations gathered to find an alternative financial system to replace the collapsed gold standard. This historic event was pioneered by Keynes, the then economic adviser to the UK government. All countries that signed the Bretton Woods Agreement replaced the gold standard with the US$ as the pegged currency. This new **fixed exchange rate system,** later dubbed the Bretton Woods System, in fact abolished the gold standard. Under the gold standard, the currency exchange rate was determined by the market value of gold and thus controlled the money supply aggregates. The Great Britain pound was the monopoly currency against the gold reserve in controlling the international monetary system. After the abolition of the gold standard by the Bretton Woods Agreement, the US$ became the pegged currency against the gold reserve by the US and the rest of the world. The balance of payment deficit shown in Table 14.3 used to be financed by selling gold or buying gold from those countries with a balance of surplus. This gold standard was also responsible for interest rate fluctuations and thus destabilized the economy by reducing output and employment. The other problem was the scarcity of gold in the world market; the gold rush movement drove gold prices higher and higher at the expense of higher unemployment and recession worldwide.

14.2.2. The Fixed Exchange Rate System

As mentioned earlier, the Bretton Woods Agreement created a new world order of international trade and monetary policy under which all nations under the accord would peg the US$ as a reserve currency to fix their own exchange rates instead of gold reserves. On the other hand, the United States would buy and sell gold at a fixed rate to maintain the gold price and control its supply of currency based on its gold reserve. The Bretton Woods system was welcomed by almost all nations in the free world in the postwar era that brought monetary policy and fiscal policy institutions as standard economic institutions for successful economic growth and prosperity for decades to come. The Bretton Woods system worked very well for all participating countries in increasing their economic growth, jobs, and education. The system also gave enormous power and economic stability to the United States by enabling the country to reach world superpower status in economics, finance, and national defense. The way the fixed exchange rate system under the Bretton Woods Agreement works is illustrated in Figure 14.2.

Figure 14.2 Fixed Exchange Rate System

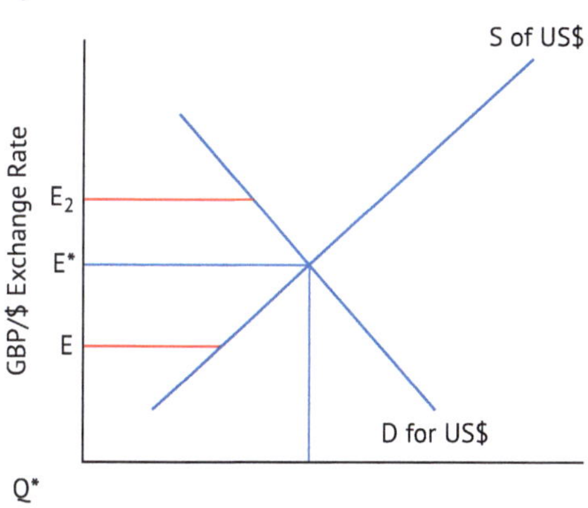

With the quantity of the US$ demanded and supplied in Figure 14.2, the exchange rate equilibrium for a typical foreign exchange market would be at E* to clear the D and S forces with the quantity of currency at Q*. However, under the fixed exchange system of the Bretton Woods Agreement, an individual country can manipulate its currency exchange rate via decree of the central bank by devaluing the currency exchange rate from an equilibrium rate of E*, say at E_1, to boost the country's exports and reduce imports and thus improve the balance of trade deficit. On the other hand, revaluation of its currency by fixing at E_2 reduces exports and increases imports. The downside of the fixed exchange rate system was explained by many experts as being that too much currency manipulation has caused unexpectedly high inflation (by too much devaluation) or deflation (by revaluation), thus destabilizing the domestic economy. In addition, undervaluation of currency under the fixed exchange rate regime has also caused unfavorable terms of trade for many countries, including the US trade balance. The practice of currency speculation and expected hyperinflation can also destabilize the economy under the fixed exchange rate system. For these reasons, and despite the glorious decades of success in using the fixed exchange rate system after World War II, the official status of the Bretton Woods system collapsed during the 1970s because of the outbreak of global hyperinflation caused by the OPEC oil embargo.

14.3. Fixed versus Floating Exchange Rate System

The negative AS shock happened in the 1970s because of OPEC cutting their production of petroleum. The oil embargo made the EU countries abandon the use of the Bretton Woods system in an effort to stop the increasing hyperinflation caused by the oil supply shock. They adopted the floating exchange rate system as an alternative by letting the demand and supply forces determine their exchange rates. The exchange rate determination under the floating exchange rate system would be like the exchange rate at E* in Figure 14.2. When the D or S curve shifts under the influence of external factors, the equilibrium exchange rate will change accordingly and thus affects the balance of payment position and inflation rate. The Federal Reserve Bank of the United States also stopped buying more gold to maintain a stable exchange rate of the US$ during that time. Although the Bretton Woods system is officially absent in international trade, the majority of nations in the world still use the Bretton Woods system by fixing their currency exchange rates against the US$ to improve their balance of trade positions. The details of the fixed versus floating exchange rate regimes and their impact on exports and imports with their policy implications are discussed in Chapter 15. At this point, it is important to emphasize the importance of both the fixed exchange rate and the floating exchange rate systems, which are being practiced in today's global markets (as mentioned earlier, the majority of nations still use the fixed exchange rate system). For example, most of the Asian countries, except a few developed countries, such as Japan, still follow the fixed exchange rate by frequent decree from their central bank authorities. African countries and Latin American countries also use the fixed exchange rate system. Despite being the second-largest economy in the world, China still intervenes in its fixed-rate system and thus manipulates the effect on its balance for exports and imports.

In the context of the exchange rate for the US$, floating exchange rate behavior has shown a significant degree of volatility since the 1970s, with an average rate of steady increase in recent decades. Figure 14.3 illustrates the degree of volatility of the US$ exchange rate as a composite index, with 100 in 1973 up to August 2018. The trend in the graph indicates lower exchange rates during recessionary periods of business-cycle fluctuations when the exchange rate for the US$ tends to decline. But during an economic boom, the exchange rate tends to rise as investors from foreign countries desire to invest during positive economic growth in the United States. This trend is consistent with the positive correlation between economic growth and exchange rate. For example, during recent years, the exchange rate continued to rise amid faster economic growth and low unemployment in the US economy. On the other hand, during the recession of 2007–2008, exchange rates continued to decline as investors invested elsewhere. It is also worth noting that during the early second half of 2018, the exchange rates indicated a state of flat rate, meaning a state of very little fluctuation against other major currencies. This could be attributed to the Trump administration's trade war with China with its imposition of tariffs on Chinese exports to the United States. The next section of this chapter discusses the effect of the volatility of the exchange rate on macroeconomic variables.

Figure 14.3 US$ Exchange Rate Index

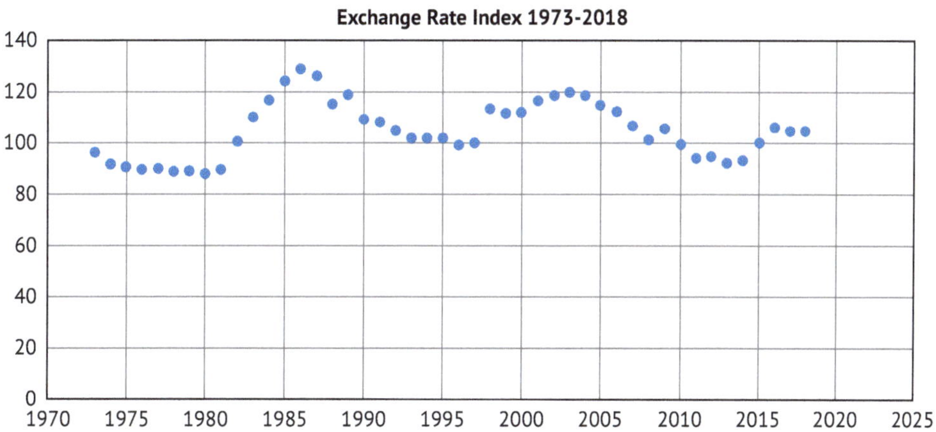

Source: Estimated from Federal Reserve Exchange Rate Index relative to major currency https://www.federalreserve.gov/releases/h10/weights/default.htm

14.4. Exchange Rate Fluctuation and Its Effect on Economic Growth and Employment

Exchange rate fluctuation under the floating exchange rate is the key driving force in capital mobility and changes in balance trade positions in the global economy. The floating exchange market is predominantly influenced by market demand and supply. There are several factors in both domestic and international currency markets that constantly make the demand and supply shift around. Those changes happen around the clock, even after regular business hours, because international banking continues through electronic transactions. The floating exchange rate is determined on a daily basis in the same way as any other financial assets, such as bond market and stock market pricing, are determined. For example, the NASDAQ composite index—the stock market index for technology growth companies—is a primarily dealer-operated mechanism that completely relies on demand and supply behavior. The buying and selling of NASDAQ stocks are operated through computerized programming that changes every second because of the constant changes in demand given the fixed supply of total shares outstanding. When the demand shifts upward, the NASDAQ price index goes up, and vice versa. The changes in the floating exchange rate market happen exactly like the NASDAQ price index determination. The working mechanism of the exchange rate determination under the floating exchange system is illustrated in Figure 14.4.

Figure 14.4 Exchange Rate Determination under the Floating Exchange Rate System

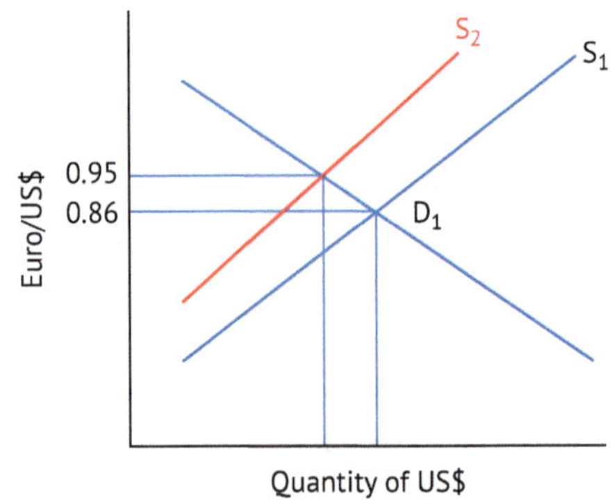

Figure 14.3 is an example of real-world demand and supply interactions in the currency exchange market with the exchange rate unit of euros per dollar as the price of the US$ to purchase or sell against the euro. The initial equilibrium exchange rate of 0.86 euro (the actual market rate as of October 1, 2018) per 1 US$ means that if a trader is interested in buying or selling the US$ against the euro, then the exchange of 0.86 euro per US$ would be the price of euros per dollar. Two major forces change this exchange rate equilibrium in foreign exchange markets:

- **Flow of goods and services as exports and imports, plus travel abroad**
- **Capital outflow and inflow by investors in the global assets market**

Exports of US goods and services to EU countries creates demand for the US$ by the buyers of US goods in Europe, thus demand for the US$ would shift right. On the other hand, US buyers importing European goods and services creates demand for the US$ to pay for the imports.

If investors abroad want to invest in US assets, they will need to buy the US$ against their own currencies, say the euro in this example. This new demand for the US$ would shift the demand curve to the right. At the same time, some investors will sell euro-based assets, causing an economic downturn in EU nations. As a result, the supply of the US$ would shift to the left. Combining these two opposite forces would drive the equilibrium exchange rate of euros per dollar from its current rate of 0.86 euro/US$ to 0.95 euro/US$. The floating exchange market always balances excess demand for currency by simultaneously decreasing or increasing the currency supply. The trade surplus or trade deficit of one country against another country does the same to make the balance of payment equal to zero, as shown in Table 14.3, for the case of the US trade deficit with the rest of the world. In other words, if the US trade deficit creates an excess supply of the US$ and shifts the S to the right, then the exchange rate will fall. However, if foreigners increase their investments in US stocks, bonds, and real estate, the demand for the US$ will increase, bringing the exchange rate upward. In recent years, foreign investors have been showing a keen interest in investing their assets (from China, Japan, South Korea, EU countries, Australia, and Canada) in US portfolio assets. This continuous capital inflow has shifted the D curve for the US$ to the right, thus reflecting a steady increase in the US$ against major currencies (explained in Figure 14.1).

Changes in the currency exchange rate can have both positive and negative effects on the balance of trade and balance of payment position. For example, the rising exchange rate of the US$ lowers the volume of exports and raises the volume of imports, increasing the trade deficit. It makes consumers better able to purchase foreign goods more cheaply, but exporters are adversely affected by selling fewer exports as sales fall because of higher exchange rates. The other effects of persistently increasing the US$ exchange rates against other currencies would be cheaper travel abroad for Americans. Foreign exporters are also beneficiaries of the strong value of the US$ by selling more exports to US importers and consumers. This effect of exchange rate changes on the balance of trade and thus the balance of payment is very common in the automobile; jewelry and cosmetics; beauty and fashion; clothing; machinery, equipment, and parts; oil and energy; aircraft and arms industries; and hardware and software industries. From a macroeconomic perspective, an increase in the exchange rate for the US$ decreases export volume and increases import volume, therefore reducing the AD. It may also have a negative effect on the RGDP and employment unless it is more than compensated for by increases in other components of AD, especially increases in direct foreign investment. More details of these effects on the economy are discussed in Chapter 15.

14.5. Purchasing Power Parity and Interest Rate Parity in Determining Foreign Exchange Rates in the Long Run and the Short Run

Exchange rate determination in the foreign exchange market is made by the following methods: purchasing power parity (PPP) and interest rate parity (IRP). The PPP method is also the method for exchange rate determination in the long run. And the IRP method is used for exchange rate determination in the short run. The exchange rate determination discussed in previous sections of this chapter is an example of a short-run determination of the exchange rate. Both the Bretton Woods system of fixed exchange rate and the floating exchange rate system of demand and supply behavior are examples of short-run determination. However, the concepts of IRP and PPP, with their model structure and applications, are much more advanced than the simple demand and supply models discussed in previous sections. In this section, the process of exchange rate determination under PPP and IRP methods will provide a better understanding of the real-world applications of exchange rate behavior and the source of changes that affect the economy. The analysis of these two methods will also provide students with a better outlook on policy implications for exchange rate stability and the connection with the global monetary system and balance of payments. The discussion in this section is limited to introducing the conceptual framework of PPP and IRP. The details of the applications and their policy implications are discussed in Chapter 15.

14.5.1. PPP and the Long-Run Exchange Rate

PPP is a method of calculating the exchange rate by comparing the price index for a bundle of traded goods and services between two countries. The measurable equation for estimating the PPP exchange rate is

$$\mathbf{PPP = P^*/P^d}, \quad \text{......................} \mathbf{Eqn\ (14.4)}$$

where P^* is the price index of a bundle of traded goods in a foreign country and P^d is the price index of a bundle of traded goods in the domestic economy.

Because the price index of bundled goods and services does not change frequently, the use of the PPP method to determine the value of a country's goods and services relative to another country's goods and services doesn't change every day. The information on the relative price index is usually published once in a year, so there is a time lag for updating the price index. Determination of the exchange rate under PPP is based on existing published data. Therefore, the exchange rates available or estimated under PPP are the trend for long-run exchange rate data. The PPP method is widely used by the International Monetary Fund (created by the Bretton Woods Agreement), OECD, United Nations, World Bank, the Central Intelligence Agency, and many other international organizations and economic research firms to estimate economic data, such as GDP, GDP per capita, GDP growth rate, income distribution, standard of living, poverty, and other economic indicators and budgetary expenses. The PPP method is important to the process of valuation of these economic data by converting the values from local currencies into the US$ for real comparison.

PPP is also used to compare the actual exchange rate in the current market with its effect on trade flows. The actual exchange rate is determined by the market demand and supply interaction discussed earlier. Because the actual exchange rate does not necessarily have to be exactly equal to PPP, deviation of the actual exchange rate from PPP has its effect on changes in the flow of goods and services between the countries. For example, in a country like China, where the actual exchange rate is perceived to be less than PPP, exported goods and services made in China are much cheaper in the US market. As a result, China generates a trade surplus at the expense of the US trade deficit, because the US$ exchange rate is above the PPP. Many economists and business entities involved in international trade use the McDonald's Big Mac index as a proxy for the PPP method in figuring out whether the actual exchange rate or official fixed exchange rate is less than PPP. Although the Big Mac is not a tradable item, it is considered an identical product allowing for a relative price ratio between countries. For example, if the average price of a Big Mac in major cities in China is 24 renminbi and in US cities it is sold for $3, then PPP would be calculated as follows:

PPP = P for Big Mac in China/P for Big Mac in US = 24/3 = 8 renminbi per US$

If the actual exchange rate by demand and supply in the currency market is 7 renminbi per US$, then Chinese currency is believed to be undervalued, creating a trade surplus. Under the fixed exchange rate system (which China uses currently), if the central bank of China (the People's Bank of China) fixes its exchange rate lower than 7, say 6 renminbi per US$, then China can generate even more trade surplus at the expense of more trade deficit for the US economy. This is one of the key factors that caused ongoing trade conflicts between China and the United States, prompting a trade war and Trump's $200 billion tariffs in 2018 on Chinese products imported to the US market. More details about the PPP exchange rate determination and its effects on trade are discussed in the next chapter.

14.5.2. IRP and Exchange Rate Determination

The short-run exchange rate determination discussed earlier in the models of demand and supply interaction is actually based on the IRP method. Under this method, the domestic interest rate in the short run is equal to the foreign country's short-run interest rate minus the expected currency exchange rate (depreciation or appreciation). This condition is an important indicator in the determination of capital inflow and outflow between nations. The equation for IRP is

$$\mathbf{IRP = i^d_t = i^*_t - (E_{t+1} - E_t)/ E_t,} \text{ ....}\mathbf{Eqn\ (14.5)}$$

where i^d_t is the domestic interest rate in time t, i^*_t is the foreign country interest rate, E_{t+1} is the expected currency exchange rate one year from now, and E_t is the current exchange rate.

The equation indicates that interest rate differences and expected exchange rates affect investors' decisions as to whether to invest in domestic assets or foreign assets. As long as the interest rate is higher in the foreign country and the expected exchange rate is favorable when foreign investment and return are transferred back to the home country, capital outflow will take place, and vice versa (capital inflow otherwise). If this capital outflow and inflow continues in the long run, then the interest rate difference may disappear. However, the capital inflow and outflow may still continue depending on the future expected exchange rate. But if $E_{t+1} = E_t$, then $i^d_t = i^*_t$, and there will be no capital inflow or outflow. The IRP condition assists in understanding the sources of shifting demand and supply of the foreign exchange market and their effect on exchange rate fluctuation in the long run. More details of this fluctuation of the exchange rate are discussed in Chapter 15.

Chapter Summary

Section 14.1 introduced the concept of international trade with economic arguments for global trade. The theories of comparative advantage and absolute advantage based on relative opportunity cost of production were explained to make the case for international trade. Specific examples for comparative advantage and absolute advantage are given to indicate gains from trade for both China and the United States. Tables 14.1 and 14.2 illustrated the examples of gains from free trade for both countries.

Section 14.1.4 introduced the foreign trade sector, adding to the Keynesian macroeconomics model. Equations (14.1), (14.2), and (14.3) illustrated the complete Keynesian model of macroeconomics by incorporating the export and import sectors of the economy. Table 14.3 provided the actual export and import data for the US trade position in 2018 with the rest of the world, including its trade balance and balance of payment position. The actual data in Table 14.3 shows a trade deficit of almost half a trillion dollars in 2018 for the US foreign trade sector. It is mainly attributed to the high value of the US$ exchange rate and high cost of production of US exports as compared to its trading partners in the rest of the world.

Section 14.2 introduced the economics of the exchange rate system with a bit of history of the abolishing of the gold standard and replacing it with the Bretton Woods system of fixed exchange rate regime in 1945. The effect of the fixed exchange rate system on global trade is explained in this section and illustrated in Figure 14.1.

Section 14.3 discussed the economics of foreign trade under flexible exchange rates as an alternative to the Bretton Woods system of fixed exchange rate. This section also explained why the Bretton Woods system collapsed in the 1970s, although a majority of nations still use the fixed exchange rate system to their trade advantage, including China. Figure 14.2 illustrated the actual data on exchange rate fluctuation from the floating exchange rate regime since 1973.

Section 14.4 explained the effect of the fluctuation of the floating exchange rate system on economic growth and employment over the decades since the 1970s. Figure 14.3 illustrated this process with its trade policy implications in the context of rapid globalization in this century.

Section 14.5 introduced the theoretical foundation of exchange rate determination in both the long run and short run. The long-run process of exchange rate determination is called the PPP method. The short-run exchange rate determination is called the IRP method.

Section 14.5.1 explained the exchange rate determination in detail under the PPP method with equation (14.4) and provided specific examples with policy implications for affecting the trade balance.

Section 14.5.2 explained the exchange rate determination with equation (14.5), along with real-world examples and policy implications. Students may practice the applications of these basic equations for exchange rate determination under both PPP and IRP methods in regard to their effect on the balance of trade fluctuations for US foreign trade.

Application Activities

Q1. Provide a few reasons for engaging in international trade (the case for trade) in a new economy in this new century.

Q2. What are the theories of comparative advantage and absolute advantage? Give examples.

Q3. Using the theories of comparative advantage and absolute advantage, along with the data in the following table, numerically show the opportunity costs of producing one good versus another good for both countries.

Country	Output per Labor Hour	
	Good X	Good Y
Country A	15	9
Country B	3	6

Q4. Based on the opportunity costs estimated in Q3, estimate the gains after trade. Hint: you need to assume a maximum number of labor hours dedicated to specialization and use the same hours for both countries. Also, use the labor hours to estimate domestic production and consumption before trade, followed by estimating production and consumption after trade.

Q5. Using AD = C + I + G + (EX − IM), indicate the relationship between the budget deficit and trade deficit. Why might an increase in the budget deficit also increase the trade deficit for the US economy?

Q6. Distinguish between the gold standard and the Bretton Woods system in determining the currency exchange rate.

Q7. List the pros and cons of the Bretton Woods system. Why did it collapse in the 1970s?

Q8. Distinguish between the fixed exchange rate system (the Bretton Woods system) and the floating exchange rate system. Provide examples and diagrams.

Q9. Why is the US$ exchange rate volatile but still high and steadily increasing against other major currencies? List the effects of the increasing US$ exchange rate on AD and other economic variables for the US economy.

Q10. What is PPP and how does it differ from IRP? Give real-world examples for each of these two methods of exchange rate determination.

Chapter 15

Foreign Exchange Market and Globalization

Learning Objectives

As they read the chapter, students will learn the following:

- The foreign exchange market and open-economy macroeconomics model for globalization, with policy implications and case studies
- The working mechanism of foreign exchange markets with examples
- The effect of changes in currency value on trade balance and economic growth and employment
- Trade deficit and budget deficit and their policy implications
- Balance of trade versus balance of payment and policy implications

15.1. Working Mechanism of the Foreign Exchange Rate with Examples

This section of the chapter is an extension of the concept of foreign exchange rate determination already discussed in Chapter 14 with AD components AD = C + I + G + (EX − IM). In Chapter 14, the theories of the floating exchange rate and fixed exchange rate, along with their applications, were also discussed. The current chapter analyzes the effect of the exchange rate on the volume of exports and imports in the context of the US economy.

15.1.1. Exchange Rate Fluctuation and Effect on Export and Import

The theoretical foundation in the previous chapter taught students that changes in the exchange rate affect the quantity of exports and imports and thus affect the balance of trade. From that conceptual framework, it is also noticed that a rise in the relative prices of US goods and services was attributed to the rising trend of the US$ exchange rate against major currencies during the economic boom of 2015–2019 (see Figure 14.5). For example, suppose the US$ exchange rate increased by 20% against the Japanese yen. The effect of this appreciation would reduce exports of US goods to Japan and increase imports from Japan to the United States. With the ceteris paribus assumption (other things staying the same), the AD = C + I + G + (EX − IM), net export will decline and thus AD will decline by shifting to the left. The exchange rate on net export is shown in Table 15.1 with a hypothetical example of automobile exports and imports between Japan and the United States.

Table 15.1: Exchange Rate Effect on Export and Import of Automobiles

Yen/US$	US$ Price of Japanese Car	Yen Price of American Car
100/1	3,000,000/100 = US$30,000	40,000 * 100 = Yen 4,000,000
120/1	3,000,000/120 = US$25,000	40,000 * 120 = Yen 4,800,000

Assume that an automobile manufactured in the US is $40,000 before taxes and the same manufactured automobile in Japan is 3,000,000 yen before taxes. To keep the rate of return the same for both Japanese and US auto manufacturers, assuming a 20% increase in the US$ exchange rate, the price of a Japanese car in US$s would fall from 30,000 to 25,000, and the price of an American car in Japanese yen would increase from 4,000,000 to 4,800,000. The changes in relative prices indicate that Japanese cars are cheaper for consumers in both Japan and the United States compared to American cars. Therefore, the demand for Japanese cars will increase and demand for American cars will decrease. As a result, the export of the United States will decrease, and import will increase, causing an increase in the US trade deficit. The opposite effect will be seen on net exports for Japan. In other words, the US$ appreciation would have a negative effect on the US trade balance. This example indicates the rising trend of the US trade deficit in recent years mainly attributed to a steady increase of the US$ exchange rate against major currencies. The next section explains the possible sources of the steady increase in the US$ exchange rate in recent years. The changes in the exchange rate are influenced by central bank intervention and/or changes in factors outside policy intervention. The example that follows is based on external factors other than policy intervention by the central bank.

15.1.2. Sources of Change in Exchange Rates in a Floating Exchange Rate Regime

Because exchange rate fluctuations are due to shifts in demand and supply under the floating exchange rate regime, this section will focus on which factors actually shift the D and S curves in the currency market. In other words, when events make a country's financial assets attractive for investment, there will be more capital inflow from foreign investors. In addition, the overall positive health of the economy and expected stability in economics, society, and political institutions will also attract foreign investment. The high quality of goods and services produced at a lower cost also attracts foreign buyers, causing an increase in exchange rates. This has been very positive for the US economy for decades, with some exceptions during the severe recession of 2007–2008. The following list provides some reasons why the demand and supply of the currency market for the US$ tends to shift in the direction of a higher exchange rate equilibrium.

- Increase in productivity in the domestic economy
- Higher rate of return in investing financial assets, such as bonds and stocks
- Legal security of foreign investment and return on investment
- Tax incentives on return on direct foreign investment
- Increase in the RGDP growth rate and high quality of goods and services produced
- Lower inflation rate and effective monetary policy and fiscal policy
- Lower default rate and liquidity risk of investment in government bonds
- Stable interest rate

Figure 15.1 Demand and Supply Shifts of the US$ against the Yen

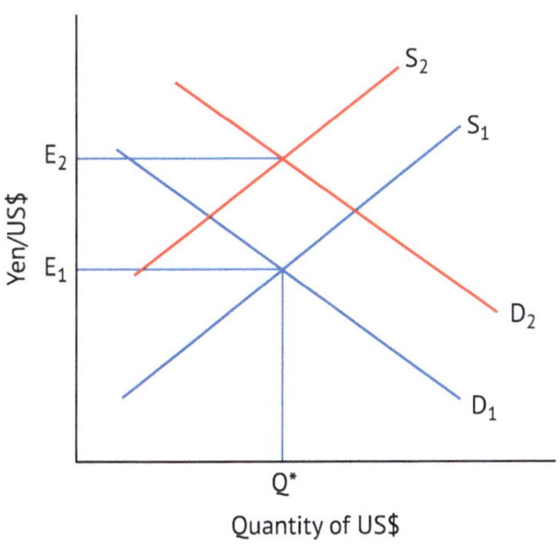

Based on these factors, the demand and supply shifts of the US$ are illustrated in Figure 15.1.

The Figure15.1 clearly indicates how external factors other than the exchange rate itself may shift the D and S curves in opposite directions by creating excess demand for currency and thus raising the exchange rate. The economic boom in the US economy from 2015 to 2018 caused its exchange rate to increase continuously, as shown in Figure 15.1.

15.2. The Effect of Changes in Currency Value on Trade Balance and Economic Growth and Employment

Given a clear understanding from the previous section regarding the sources of changes in the exchange rate and their effects on export and import, this section is focused on the connection between changes in the exchange rate and their effect on macroeconomic models. In this analysis, it is important to use the net export equation previously introduced in Chapter 14:

$$EX - IM = (S - I) - (G - T). \quad \text{.........................} \quad \text{Eqn (15.1)}$$

Based on the equation, it is clear that the trade deficit can come from two sources of the AD equation of macroeconomics. The negative value of the left-hand side of equation (15.1), with imports being greater than exports, can occur from a budget deficit and/or from saving less than investment. As explained in the previous chapter, an increase in the budget deficit raises the price and interest rate. There are two outcomes: domestic goods become more expensive, and the exchange rate rises as foreign investors make capital inflow to invest in financial assets. These two outcomes increase imports and decrease exports, thus increasing the trade deficit.

The other source of a trade deficit is low savings, resulting in more borrowing for investment in capital and financial assets and government spending. This event also increases interest rates and the price level, causing a trade deficit. This phenomenon is exactly what has been observed in the US economy in recent decades, except during the Great Recession of 2008. But why is the US economy still showing strong growth and employment despite the chronic twin deficits? The reason is very simple: US monetary and fiscal policy actions seem to be very effective in controlling interest rates, price, and inflation. Therefore, the US government and financial institutions are able to borrow at a very low rate with a high rate of return on investment. The other part of the puzzle comes from the positive effect on the AS side of macroeconomics when the US$ appreciates. For example, appreciation of the US$ may make US exports of goods and services more expensive by shifting the AD curve to the left. But at the same time, US$ appreciation makes it cheaper to import parts for use in domestic production and services. The cheaper imported parts lower the cost of production and thus shift the AS curve to the right. These opposite forces of AD and AS shifts have kept the price level lower for the United States in recent years. Figure 15.2 illustrates this process of economic growth and inflation reflected in the US economy.

Figure 15.2 Exchange Rate Change and AD-AS Model

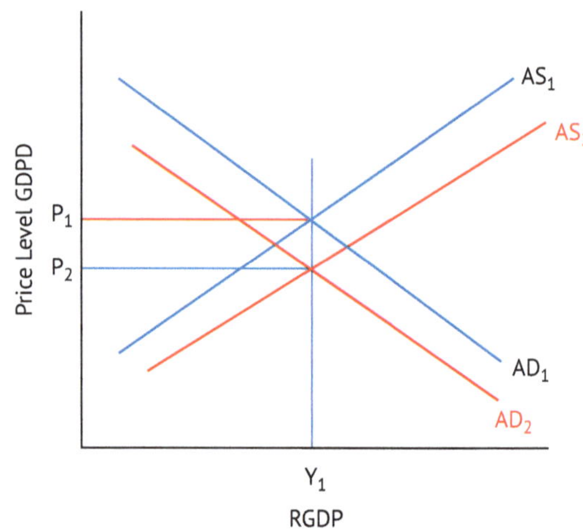

In Figure 15.2, an increase in the exchange rate for the US$ shifted the AD curve to the left (assuming other things stay the same). However, the AS curve shifted to the right instead because of a decrease in the cost of importing parts and inputs of production as a positive effect on the AS side of the macroeconomics model. Although the relative magnitude of the shifts of the AD and AS curves in opposite directions is shown as almost the same, in reality, they are unlikely to offset each other. The difference in the relative magnitude of the shift will determine the net effect in the appropriate direction of the equilibrium RGDP and price level. Information on actual data to fit this model would give the net result, but given the relatively smaller contribution (about 16%) of foreign trade to the total GDP for the United States, the relative magnitude and its effects on employment and output may not be so significant. So Figure 15.2 is a close approximation to the actual effect of a rising exchange rate in the US economy. However, it is reasonable to expect that the actual data might shift the AD to the left at a higher rate than the rightward shift of the AS curve, or vice versa. The next two sections will discuss the policy implications for the twin deficits (budget deficit and trade deficit) in the context of the US economy.

15.3. Trade Deficit and Budget Deficit and Their Policy Implications

Conducting effective monetary and fiscal policy in the face of the increasing trade deficit and budget deficit, the twin deficits, is not so straightforward because of the trade-off between interest rate stability and foreign exchange rate stability. The complexity of policy effectiveness while reducing the twin deficits makes economic policy a bit challenging, especially in a world of floating exchange rates. The analysis of this challenging task is discussed here for both fiscal policy and monetary policy implications for the US economy.

15.3.1. Monetary Policy Effectiveness under Twin Deficits

As discussed in the previous section, monetary policy makers face a dilemma regarding whether they should leave the AD-AS model alone or intervene. If they intervene, what are the possible effects? In examining the policy implications of the Fed in this situation, it is commonly perceived that the Fed's primary target is to control inflation when there is a state of economic boom, such as that witnessed in 2018. On the other hand, if the economy is in a state of recession, like in 2007 and 2008, then the Fed's priority is to target the interest rate to keep it at a very low level. During 2018, the higher rising exchange rate prompted the Fed to adopt a tighter monetary policy to target the inflation rate and keep it at 2%. This tight monetary policy action is reflected in the Fed's repeated attempts to increase the federal funds rate slowly to keep AD at a low level or shifting to the left to keep an economic soft landing from overheating. This action by the Fed seems consistent with the notion that the Fed actually left the exchange rate alone to allow it to keep rising by allowing foreign capital inflow into the US economy. This capital inflow is expected to maintain price stability through the decline of AD to the left. It can be observed from Figure 15.2 that shifting the AD to the left has two positive outcomes, in addition to maintaining a low inflation rate. One is to keep wages low from upward pressure in a tight labor market; the other is to keep the expected inflation rate low for stability in investments and consumption expenditures. These two additional benefits of leaving the exchange rate alone may provide full employment stability. However, this policy neutrality of the Fed is not always ideal or straightforward because expectations about the future exchange rate, confidence level of foreign investors and, crises in the budget deficit process in the legislative and executive branches of the government may complicate the policy dilemma. The risk of falling back into a state of recession is another source of policy dilemma if the Fed leaves the rising exchange rate and higher interest rate target together for too long. The choice of a fiscal and monetary policy mix is an alternative way to address this dilemma and is discussed in the next section. This phenomenon of continuous dilemma clearly reflects the Fed's change in its interest rate policy from a tightening monetary policy approach to a loosening monetary policy on July 31, 2019, when its reduced the federal fund rate by 0.25% in response to heightened uncertainty caused by the US-China trade war and speculation of a recession in the near future.

15.3.2. Fiscal Policy Effectiveness under Twin Deficits and the Case for Policy Mix

In previous sections, from the discussion of the application of exchange rate theories, we have learned that interest rate changes in the domestic economy and exchange rates in the global market are interrelated. The interrelationship between interest rates and exchange rates also has significant effects on inflation, unemployment, and RGDP growth rate, including the effect on net export. For example, rising domestic interest rates cause the value of the US$ to appreciate, reduce exports, and increase imports, thereby increasing the trade deficit. On the other hand, a decline in the interest rate causes the opposite effect. It is also observed that monetary policy makers face a dilemma in deciding whether to control the exchange rate by manipulating the D and S of the currency market or to target the domestic interest rate.

Fiscal policy makers have the same issues when faced with controlling a recession or inflation by changing government spending and taxes. For example, during a recession, an expansionary fiscal policy increases government spending and/or reduces taxes to boost the AD to increase the RGDP and employment. This expansionary fiscal policy increases the price level and domestic interest rate. With an increase in the interest rate, capital inflow takes place with the increase of foreign direct investment into the US economy. This capital inflow will increase the exchange rate of the US$ and thus increase the trade deficit. This is why an increase in the budget deficit has increased the trade deficit for the US economy in recent decades. But the good news is that the possible crowding out effect (as discussed previously in the government budget deficit section in Chapter 11, Section 11.2.6.) has not yet happened in the US economy. The reason is very straightforward: the mix of discretionary fiscal and monetary policy was very effective in maintaining the interest rate and inflation rate at a reasonable target for achieving employment and output stability. A mix of tight monetary policy in response to expansionary fiscal policy seems to be working to maintain economic stability with low inflation and a low unemployment rate, despite the rising exchange rate in recent years. Figure 15.2 could be given as an example of this balancing act of the fiscal and monetary policy mix.

15.4. Balance of Trade versus Balance of Payment and Policy Implications

The last section of this final chapter of the textbook is focused on a brief conclusion about the relationship between the balance of trade and balance of payment accounting for international trade. To understand this important part of foreign trade, it is helpful to recall the balance of payment illustrated in Table 14.3. The same table is reproduced in Table 15.2. The balance of payments is the balance of the trade of goods and services plus the financial transactions between the United States and the rest of the world. Table 15.2 has two major sections: the **current account balance** and the **financial account balance (plus capital transfer)**. The current account balance consists of exports and imports of goods and services plus net income received from other business transactions in both the private and government sectors. The current account deficit is basically the net export component of the AD equation (EX – IM). The current account balance in Table 15.2 shows how large the current account deficit is ($490,978 million). This chronic trade deficit for the United States, along with the chronic budget deficit has been going on for decades without any short-run solutions. As discussed earlier, the interesting part about the twin deficits is the absence of possible crowding out.

Table 15.2: Balance of Trade and Balance of Payment for the United States, 2018

Current Account Items	In Millions of $	Indicates That the Trade
Export of Goods and Services and Income Receipt	**3,735,684**	
Export of Goods and Services	2,501,310	
Export of Goods	1,674,330	
Export of Services	826,980	
Income Receipts, Primary and Secondary	1,234,374	
		Balance of Current Account=
Imports of Goods and Services and Payments	**4,226,662**	**3,735,684 – 4,226,662 = –490,978**
Import of Goods and Services	3,128,989	
Import of Goods	2,561,667	
Import of Services	567,322	
Income Payments, Primary and Secondary	1,097,673	
Capital Account Items		
Capital Transfer Receipts and Credits	**3,247**	
Capital Transfer Payments and Debits	**12**	**Balance in Capital A/C = 3,235**
Financial Account Items		
Net Acquisition of Financial Assets Except Derivatives	**310,827**	
Net Incurrence of Liabilities Except Derivatives	**735,583**	**Balance on Financial A/C = 424,756**
Net Financial Derivatives	**–20,721**	
Statistical Discrepancies	**42,266**	**= –445,477 – (–487,743) = 42,266**
Balance of Payments	**0**	

Source: US Bureau of Economic Analysis, International Services Tables at https://apps.bea.gov/international/bp_web/tb_download_type_modern.cfm?list=1&RowID=1.

Another interesting part of this trade deficit can be found in the financial account and capital account items in Table 15.2. Given the current account deficit of $90,978 million in 2018, the financial account balance shows a surplus of $424,756 million. Leaving the capital transfer aside (just ignoring it), the net balance of the payment deficit is showing only $42,266 (after adjusting net financial derivatives) as statistical discrepancies to bring the balance of payment to zero—it will be always equal to zero. Where does this financial account balance surplus come from? It is the reserve of foreign currency from foreign investors invested in US assets in exchange for US currency. This magical source of current account surplus helps pay for the current account deficit. In a world of floating exchange rates, this is an easy fix without much concern for causing a crowding out effect from a rising trade deficit. However, in a fixed exchange regime, this imbalance of current accounts is difficult to balance, if not impossible.

On a final note, an analysis of theoretical foundations and their applications in global trade establishes the undeniable fact that the market forces of demand and supply, with the theory of comparative advantage, are very powerful in allowing free trade, faster economic growth, and economic prosperity for every nation, regardless of size or available resources. Tariffs and quotas are imposed by political interest groups at their own peril. The obvious retaliation from the countries upon which the trade restrictions are imposed ends up in a lose-lose outcome. No country wins through trade restrictions. The ultimate results of trade restrictions are actually higher prices paid by consumers and lower production and lower employment for the people of both countries. Free trade with careful protection of national defense and sustainable economic policy is the best option. The application of the theory of comparative advantage is always a powerful tool to promote free trade as a win-win strategy.

Chapter Summary

Section 15.1.1 explained the effect of exchange rate fluctuations on the volume of exports and imports in reference to the US$ exchange rate against the Japanese yen. Table 15.2 provided a numerical example of the exchange rate fluctuation of the US$ against the yen to show the effects on automobile trade between the two countries. This hypothetical example helped students learn how the changes in exchange rate change the balance of trade and the balance of payment position for US foreign trade.

Section 15.1.2 provided various factors that cause the exchange rate fluctuation in the foreign exchange market under the flexible exchange rate regime. Figure 15.1 illustrated the determination of changes in the equilibrium exchange rate for the US$ against the Japanese yen. Students may practice similar scenarios against other currencies by using the same demand and supply model shown in Figure 15.1.

Section 15.2 extended the effect of exchange rate fluctuation on the trade balance, economic growth, and employment. The trade balance equation (15.1) = (EX − IM) = (S − I) − (G − T), derived from the complete AD-AS model of macroeconomics, explained in detail how the trade deficit and budget deficit have occurred simultaneously in the United States for decades. The connection between the trade deficit and budget deficit was further explained in the context of the AD-AS model and illustrated in Figure 15.2.

Section 15.3.1 provided the economic policy implication of the twin deficits of foreign trade and the government budget discussed in **Section 15.2.** This section critically analyzed monetary policy effectiveness in coping up with the chronic twin deficits (trade deficit and budget deficit) in the US economy. Likewise, Section 15.3.2 explained fiscal policy effectiveness in reducing the twin deficits with critical overview and policy recommendations.

Section 15.4 provided the policy implications for both the balance of trade and balance of payment situation in the US economy. For this purpose, the actual data for the US foreign trade balance position for 2018 was illustrated in Table 15.2. Students should read and review the data in Table 15.2 to understand the connection between the current account and capital account to distinguish between the balance of trade and balance of payment. The export and import data and capital transfer shown in Table 15.2 also indicated the volume of the trade deficit for the US in 2018. Students should also read critically about the real economic effect of the twin deficits of the government budget and foreign trade.

Application Activities

Q1. Suppose that the exchange for euro/US$ starts at 1:1, and the exchange rate for the US$ increases by 20%. Now suppose the wholesale price of an automobile made in the United States is $40,000 and a similar automobile made in Germany is 45,000 euro. If the producers were to maintain the same profit rate after the exchange rate has changed, create a table showing the price changes for the US-made car in terms of euros and the German-made car in terms of the US$. How does this price change affect the values of exports and imports of cars between Germany and the United States?

Q2. Suppose the chief financial officer (CFO) of an American corporation with surplus cash flow had $100 million to invest last July 15, and the corporation did not believe it would need to use those funds to retool or expand production capacity for one year. Suppose further that the interest rate on a one-year CD deposit in US banks was 0.5%, while the rate on a one-year CD deposit in England (denominated in British pounds) was 2%. Suppose further that the exchange rate at that time was $1.68 per British pound.

2a. Suppose that a year later, the exchange rate is $1.55 per British pound. What rate of return did the CFO earn on the investment in the British CD? (Note: a specific numeric answer is required for full credit.)

2b. What must the CFO have expected about the value of the British pound in US$s to believe that investment in British CDs would be more profitable than investment in US CDs?

Q3. As explained in the chapter, in recent years, the exchange rate of the US$ has been steadily increasing against major currencies. If for some reason foreign investors expected that this increase was temporary and that the US$ would fall relative to the composite currency index in coming months, what would be the effect on prices of US Treasury securities (investment by foreigners in US government assets)? Explain.

Q4. Explain why US-based exporting companies prefer a weak US$ in currency markets.

Q5. Suppose a Chinese company buys a one-year TB with a face value of $10,000 today for $9,500. If the value of the dollar declined from 8 renminbi (yuan) to 7 renminbi during the year, what rate of return will the Chinese company earn on its investment?

Q6. In a state of economic boom, why does the Fed take a neutral position on the rising trend of the US$ exchange rate? Explain. On the other hand, if the exchange rate starts to decline in the wake of the increasing tariffs on Chinese imports to the United States imposed by the Trump administration, what policy action should the Fed take?

Q7. Draw a supply-demand diagram of the foreign exchange market for the dollar (valued in euros/$). Show the effects of the following events on the exchange rate. Explain your reasoning.

7a. The release of data showing stronger than expected RGDP growth in Germany

7b. An increase in the federal funds rate by the Fed

7c. An announcement that US trade deficits for the last quarter were much larger than previously expected

7d. A larger than expected increase in hourly wage rates in the United States

Q8. Why does the balance of payment always balance even when the balance of trade may not be in balance? How has the US government paid for its chronic trade deficit of over $400 billion per year for so many years? Does this trade deficit matter in the long run?

Q9. How can monetary policy actions reduce the trade deficit? How might the increase in the budget deficit from expansionary fiscal policy increase the trade deficit?

Q10. From the learning curve in this chapter and the previous chapter (Chapters 14 and 15), briefly list the winners and losers of the $200 billion worth of tariffs imposed by the Trump administration on the import of Chinese goods and services to the US market.

Index

About the Author

Nurul Samiul Aman was born in Patuakhali District, a southern part of Bangladesh, and received his BA with honors in economics from Dhaka University, Bangladesh, and master's in economics and MBA in finance from Northeastern University, Boston, USA. He also received his PhD from Capella University in Minneapolis, Minnesota, USA, with a concentration in information economics with applications in information technology and organizational management.

As a financial economist, Aman has been effectively teaching in Boston area colleges since 1988 in various courses in economics and business. He is currently a Senior Lecturer at the University of Massachusetts Boston (UMB) in Boston, Massachusetts, USA. He has been teaching at UMB since 2001, including the following courses: Principles of Micro and Macroeconomics, Micro and Macroeconomics Theories and Applications, Economic Development, Money and Financial Institution, and Comparative Economic Systems. He also taught at graduate-level applied economics courses at Northeastern University, including Sustainable Economic Development, Economics of E-Commerce, Economics of Human Capital, and Financial Management. Since 2006, Aman has served as a member of the editorial board of the *Asian Journal of Inclusive Education*, a peer-reviewed journal for inclusive education and development. He also teaches overseas as a visiting professor at different universities in China. As an international speaker, Dr. Aman is also affiliated with Allied Academies of Food and Nutrition Science and travels in North America, Europe, and Asia delivering keynote speeches on food sustainability and poverty elimination in developing nations. He also organizes and hosts the annual International Conference on Sustainable Development Goals at Harvard University in collaboration with the International Sustainable Development Institute (www.ISDIWorld.com) and the government of Bangladesh. In the 1990s and early 2000s, Aman worked as a business analyst and business control manager of information technology departments at PictureTel Corporation (now PolyCom), Rational Software, and IBM in Lexington, Massachusetts, USA.

9 781516 540914

Printed by Libri Plureos GmbH in Hamburg,
Germany